SCARING MYSELF AGAIN

SCARING MYSELF AGAIN
Far-flung Adventures of a TV Journalist

Allen Abel

HarperCollins*PublishersLtd*

First Edition

Canadian Cataloguing in Publication Data

Abel, Allen J., 1950-
  Scaring myself again

ISBN 0-00-215786-1

1. Abel, Allen J., 1950- . 2. Foreign correspondents — Canada — Biography. I. Title.

PN4913.A2A3 1992   070.4'332'092   C92-093932-5

92 93 94 95 96 97 98 99 ❖ RRD 10 9 8 7 6 5 4 3 2 1

This book was written on a typewriter given to me as a bar mitzvah present by Fay Bershad, my mother's sister. In 1979, Fay's only child, David, drowned while swimming in the Gulf of Mexico. He was twenty-three. Six months later, consumed by her loss, Fay took her own life. Each day, as I began to type, I thought of her.

PROLOGUE
Romania

A bright red, brand-new minivan blunders through the fog of a Transylvanian midnight. Five men are in the vehicle; the oldest—that's me—is thirty-nine. The headlights prowl the road ahead for the taillights of an escort, but the mist hides them, then reveals them, then encloses the lights again.

Four of the men in the red van are foreigners and the fifth, in heavy khaki woolens and a soup-bowl helmet, is a Romanian military officer who gives his name as Captain Mirça. He carries a ponderous, wooden-stock rifle that might have served a British private at the relief of Mafeking. It is December 26, 1989. In these desperate hours of the Romanian Revolution, Captain Mirça is half of our protective shield against harm. The other half is a series of strips of thick white "gaffer" tape on the windows and rear of the mini-van that spell out TV TV TV TV.

I am in the left-rear seat of the new red van and the other three men are my colleagues. One is a producer from the Canadian Broadcasting Corporation with whom I have worked and traveled many times before. The other two are a British camera and sound team we met, for the first time, at the Frankfurt airport yesterday morning. They are with us largely because they were the only free-lancers we could find who were willing to work over Christmas.

The vehicle ahead of us in a three-part convoy is an armored personnel carrier chockablock with Romanian recruits. We've just spent part of the evening with them in a hotel in a small town called Nadlac, near the Hungarian border, watching television in the public lounge. What we watched—it delayed our departure—was the trial, condemnation and execution of President Nicolae Ceauşescu and his insufferable wife.

Behind us, piloted by a young Hungarian student and his girlfriend, who has been serving as our translator, is an off-white Lada sedan on hire from Budget Rent-A-Car in Budapest, paid for with my personal Master-Card. The back seat of the Lada—and our entire van—is crammed with television lights, sound equipment, batteries, blank tape cassettes, personal luggage and eight sloshing cans of gasoline. In the trunk of the Lada, I have collected twelve loaves of bread, twenty-four containers of fruit yogurt, six enormous Hungarian salamis, some oranges and a few jars of jam. Both my Lada and the minivan, which is billed to the producer's Visa card, were rented to us on the specific condition—we signed our names to it—that the vehicles would not, under any circumstances, be driven into revolutionary Romania.

We have come through the city of Arad—deserted, silent, ghostly in the fog—and our destination is Timişoara, where, barely a week ago, demonstrations opposing the arrest of a valiant local priest who had dared to speak against the Ceauşescu tyranny erupted into violent revolt. At first, the army had obeyed their supreme commander, the *soi-disant* Danube of Thought. But then the army—men like the English-speaking Captain Mirça, and the kids in the APC—had turned. The contest now had become a murderous fire fight between the people's militia and the remnants of the dictatorship's Securitate assassins.

In the minivan, Captain Mirça is discoursing unconcernedly on life under the Ceauşescu's cultish rule. At one point, we actually turn on the "sun gun" (a small portable spotlight) and interview him as we motor along. (I suspect the producer hopes that the brightness will attract sniper fire.) I am dissolving in petrified anxiety when Captain Mirça inquires whether, among my food cache, I might happen to have a banana. He'd like to bring one to his daughter. She has never seen one, growing up in Romania.

Half an hour later, we are slowly making our way along the medieval alleys of central Timişoara with the rumbling personnel carrier in front of us and the underpowered Lada to the rear. The caravan halts in a narrow, one-way lane that leads, at its far end about fifty yards ahead, into a large open square.

"Wait here," Captain Mirça says. He grabs his blunderbuss, taps his helmet, opens the door and disappears.

Just as he vanishes, gunfire begins to ricochet through the fog above the van. Now it gets more frequent, louder—heavier weapons are being brought around. The armored personnel carrier starts up, turns left into the plaza, and is gone.

"Turn out the headlights!" the cameraman, who is in the back seat with me, commands in a loud stage whisper. In his haste to comply, the producer, who is driving, flips on the windshield wipers instead.

The gunfire escalates until it sounds like the celebratory bursts of firecrackers the Chinese use when they get married or open a restaurant.

"Why don't you do a commentary?" the sound man suggests. I emerge from my resting position on the floor of the van—nicely cradled by the cans of gasoline—and begin to speak.

"It's been going on for about five minutes now," I say, in a golf announcer's breathy voice. "Mostly small-arms fire, some artillery...here comes Captain Mirça now...he's waving to us.... No! It's not him!"

It is, actually, a young man in civilian clothes who is waving a sleek black pistol. He is frantically motioning for us to back up, but the way is blocked by the Lada, which has decided to experience an attack of gasline freeze-up, or some such disease, and won't start.

But when I scream at it, it does. The Hungarian student backs down the alley, we follow, and seconds later we have dashed into the darkened lobby of an abandoned hotel and have dived for cover on the hard marble floor.

"Abel, you surprised me," the producer says, a few minutes later, when the gun battle has ended and the lobby is revealed, when the lights are turned on, to be full of friendly Romanian soldiers. "I never thought you'd turn out to be the coolest, calmest one of all."

For the first eleven years of my journalistic career, an occupation for which I had absolutely no academic preparation, I covered professional, amateur and intercollegiate sports for newspapers in Upstate New York and Toronto. My training for this profession, it turned out, had been my years at Madison Square Garden, shouting "Hey ref, you suck!" at hockey officials I would later come to know as gentlemen and friends.

In the seventh year of my term as "featured" sports columnist of the *Globe and Mail*, I walked one day into the locker room of the Toronto Blue Jays, wherein I was greeted by a utility infielder named Mickey Klutts who was chanting, "Here come the scum."

That was enough.

From sports, I went to China for the *Globe*, to a venerable and prestigious bureau that I degraded with tales of penis transplants, disco-mania and miracle cures for hemorrhoids. ("There are one billion Chinese and 460 million of them have piles. When Chairman Mao said, 'China has stood up,' half the population knew why.")

Barbara Bush says that her husband moped around, confused and depressed, for six months after his term in China ended. That makes two of us. For me, at the end of the half year of muddled re-entry and culture shock, there was a change of life, an offer—actually, I begged them for it—to move to a television program called "The Journal" at the CBC, a long-established and highly regarded part of Canada's view of national and world affairs.

When I am asked why I switched from print to television, without demonstrable talent, I explain that it was part of a prisoner exchange, as when Natan Scharansky walked across a bridge between the two Berlins in trade for a Russian spy. In my case, the United States got Peter Jennings, and the CBC got me. This is why, for the past six years, I have spent long nights in the company of total strangers, bumbling down a host of foreign highways in vans marked, with gaffer tape, TV TV TV TV. The roads have led to Romania, to the Amazon, to Mexico and Panama and Germany and Russia, and to this book. It is an account of one such journey by a frightened and fascinated correspondent to a part of the world, and a part of himself, he never had visited before.

15 APRIL
Toronto–London–
Vienna–Tehran

I am in row 13 of the mammoth plane, picking my lip till it bleeds. We haven't taken off yet. I have my feet propped up on the bulkhead, my shoes off, my silly red knapsack stuffed under the seat. I have a blindfold in the pocket of my shirt.

This is Air Canada flight 856, overnight to Heathrow with connections to a trough of human misery, a valley in West Asia where a million strangers, maybe more, lie hungry and freezing tonight, while I pull on my elastic airline giveaway sockettes and watch the other passengers come aboard. An attendant hands me a purse of toiletries, a menu and a *carte des vins*.

Television documentaries are made on "shoots," and these are the opening seconds of what I know will be a grim and mournful one. Our assignment—there are five of us on the plane from the nightly current-affairs program of the CBC's English network—is to get somehow to the jagged border of Iraq and Iran and send back images of dead and dying men, mothers and young.

The certainty of the equation is well-known to us, and need not be expressed in words: were there not children perishing on a hillside halfway around the world, all five of us would be home with our wives this rainy evening, not embarking on this sad escapade. We are not doctors, caregivers, aid workers or peacekeepers; our immunity is not diplomatic, but professional. We will succeed on this long, expensive mission only if our presentation of the suffering we fly to touches hearts back home, while leaving our own hearts intact.

None of us is new at this. Contained in our collective experience are the famines of Africa, the bombing of Baghdad, the rape of the rain forests, the bloody expulsion of dictators from Panama City to Bucharest, the murdered hope of Tian'anmen Square. And now the Kurds, this awful spring, fleeing their homes in panicked haste across the beautiful mountains.

I've known for only two days that I'd be going on the Kurdistan trip. On Saturday afternoon, I got home from a shoot in Oklahoma, a profile of the pitcher Ferguson Jenkins, the first Canadian in the baseball Hall of Fame. It was a typical jaunt: Toronto–Windsor–Detroit–St. Louis–Oklahoma City–Chicago–Toronto, all in four days. When I walked in the condo door, Linda said, "Don't unpack. The office called. You're going to do the Kurds."

The story was hardly new even then. The Kurds already had been perishing miserably on the evening news for more than three weeks. We saw stragglers walking toward camera with tiny bundles: the infant dead. Makeshift camps sprawled across the rugged cliffs. It rained, and snowed.

Our network already had a news crew on the scene in eastern Turkey. They'd filed capably, in terrible conditions, with sympathy for the grieving migrants and no more than a tasteful amount of shrouded corpses. But, after a week of this, reporter and producer declared that they'd done enough. The Kurds were being moved into tents and were getting food and water. The death rate was falling. The story was over.

Then one of our senior producers heard on the BBC that even more Kurds were heading not north to Turkey but eastward, toward the Islamic Republic of Iran. More important, they were falling dead along the latter route at the rate of a thousand a day. This is what was explained to me when I phoned the senior producer on my return from Oklahoma.

"A thousand dead a day," the senior producer said.

It was my turn for a big foreign shoot. Our show owns a dozen documentary reporters. Four of my reportorial colleagues had been sent overseas during the war, to Israel, Qatar, Saudi Arabia and Iraq itself. Holding a United States passport, being of Jewish descent, I'd been passed over. I got to do "Home Front U.S.A." instead.

For six weeks, I had dragged around the "Journal" office in saturnine dejection, threatening to quit and nearly doing it, intensely envious of anyone who had been to the front. (Or even the rear.) On the Oklahoma shoot, relegated to the sports beat again, I pissed and moaned.

The chat with the senior editor shut me up, called my bluff, but good. The office was working on visas for Iran. We would leave Monday night on flight 856. I started to pack.

It was obvious that this shoot would require the full Third World ensemble: packaged food, malaria and dysentery tablets, camping gear, water purification gadgets, disposable syringes, insect repellent, cortisone creams, layers of winter clothing, hiking boots, gloves, extra passport-sized photographs and the rugged brown leather jacket, purchased in the Grand Covered Bazaar in Istanbul, that under certain lighting conditions almost makes me look like a foreign correspondent.

On the Sunday, while I busied myself with details, Linda went off to a charity fashion show. We met later at a friend's house for pizza and some silliness with the friend's two small children, shutting out the gathering clouds.

At three o'clock on Monday morning, I woke up, sweating, my stomach screaming, and an excruciating boil swelling in the folds of my left ear. I knew Linda was awake as well, though both of us were silent, the impending farewell pressing down an unspeakable sadness, a ghost hovering above our tidy bedroom. It hadn't been this bad in a long time.

"They can't make me go," I whispered, hoping she couldn't hear me. "I don't want to go. I don't want to go. I don't want to go."

It was the echo of a night eight years earlier, shortly after I traded the gullible banalities of sportswriting for the manly world of foreign reportage. We were on our way to China, passing, as Toronto *Globe and Mail* correspondents habitually had, through India on the outward journey. This was supposed to be a languid tour, a first inhalation of the scents of the mystic East. Then, in Sri Lanka, the Sinhalese started hauling innocent Tamils out of their houses and burning them alive in the road. The *Globe* called us at the Taj Hotel in Bombay and told me to get down to Colombo to sift the blackened bones.

I couldn't move. Nauseated, terrified, I hid under a thin, crisp bedsheet, groaning: "They can't make me go. I don't want to go. I'm just a sportswriter. I can't do this. I can't go. They can't make me go."

"You're going," Linda said, packing my bag. And she went, too.

In Colombo, on this first venture into the grim depths of human hate, I managed to pick at some pasta in the coffee shop of the hotel and to go out, when curfew restrictions permitted, to interview the shattered, wailing survivors of these first few days of the Sri Lankan civil war. I even found a small boy with a bandaged arm who told me, "My country is not paradise any more"—the kind of quote any reporter would kill for.

Eight years later, I thought I had conquered this unbecoming aversion to immersing myself in newsworthy horrors. Certainly, I'd done enough of it, two years across Asia for the newspaper and then all over the tortured planet on behalf of the CBC. But this shoot was different. The pictures from Kurdistan had got to me. Walking to the office on Monday morning, I wished I'd get hit by a truck.

At work, honored by having been chosen from the ranks for this important assignment, I tried to talk the senior editors out of actually having to go do it. I told them that the indomitable Cable News Network already was broadcasting live—using portable satellite transmission equipment the CBC cannot afford to acquire—from the very crest of the Iran-Iraq cordillera. We were still eight thousand miles and seventy-five thousand dollars short of their camera location and it would be at least a week before we could hope to get any pictures on the air. This futile expostulation was interrupted by a call from the Iranian Embassy in Ottawa informing us that our visas were ready.

At noon, I was given six thousand and seventy-five dollars in U.S. cash, an airline ticket with a return from Tehran booked for May 7, a few farewell hugs and handshakes and a one o'clock appointment with the CBC nurse for the requisite inoculations. Baring my right flank for the needle, I recollected that twice in the past year, I'd been given one of these gamma globulin antihepatitis preventatives, only to have both shoots—one to India, one to the U.S.S.R.—canceled mere hours before takeoff.

"Maybe they'll pull this one down, too," I told the nurse, wishing out loud. Then I went downstairs to a convenience store and loaded up on granola bars, bran crackers, peanut butter, President's Choice chunk white tuna in spring water, trail mix, pitted prunes and an assortment of flavors of a dried, pressed, leathery confection known as Fruit Roll-Ups that has become something of my trademark on the road: Abel's always got food.

I walked home to the condominium in a downpour, still hoping for a minor crosswalk accident, or perhaps to slip and wrench my ankle, as I once did on the rain-wettened steps of the Copacabana night club when I was a postman in New York City between college semesters. It was my last serious injury. Since then, I have been indestructible, but that kind of luck's gotta change.

At home, I made yet another big display of "Oh, darling, I don't want to go." It was nearly four. Friends arrived with their infant son, a prearranged supper visit I thought it best not to cancel, thinking that maybe the presence of others in the apartment would make departure time less maudlin and me less morose.

It didn't. I counted down the minutes—forty, thirty, fifteen, reading them off like war bulletins—checked CNN one last time to see if all the Kurds had packed up and gone home, and then Linda and I walked slowly down the hallway and kissed goodbye and I took the elevator to Iran.

Five of us are going: reporter, producer, camera operator, sound recordist and videotape editor. The cast of characters is not the same for every shoot, but neither have we been mixed and matched at random from the "Journal" stable. Each of us has traveled several times with every other individual on the crew, but never has the particular quintet gone anywhere in unison, not even to lunch.

We are to meet at Pearson International about two hours in advance of departure in order to check in our fantastic amount of gear. According to my watch, which I bought in Miami for one dollar, I arrive forty minutes early. As my father always says, "Nobody waits for the Abels." I sit alone on a baggage trolley, savoring the last moments of solitude before the forced camaraderie of the long shoot begins.

The producer, who is next to reach the airport, has had an absolutely extraordinary year, even by the standards of our international ambulance chasing: East Germany, in the last hours before unification; Panama, on the anniversary of American invasion; then, Baghdad and the al-Rashid Hotel. In Panama, he contracted dengue fever, resulting in weeks of night sweats, headache and pain in the limbs so intolerable the disease is often called "break-bone."

In Baghdad, he got bombed.

His name is Brian Denike. The oldest of our team by nearly a decade, he is fifty-one, tall, slim, white haired and now sprouting an incipient beard that is coming in salt and pepper. Denike is a "Journal" original, a career CBC executive who, ten years ago, helped formulate the framework of our nightly mix of interviews and documentaries.

The producer's role, reduced to its basics, is to tell the cameraman what to shoot, the sound man what to record and the reporter what to say. Also, to arrange interviews, hire translators, drivers and locally plugged-in "fixers," to keep a catalog of what is on every tape that is shot, to dope out a logical structure for the story and to maintain at least a semblance of civil relations within the unit while we are on the road. In addition, nobody gets to eat until the producer says it's lunchtime. That's why I carry Fruit Roll-Ups.

Denike and I have been through quite a bit together, including Germany and the Panama anniversary. (He also was in Panama during the actual invasion at Christmas, 1989; at the same instant, I was cowering behind the gasoline cans in the red van at Timişoara.) We also worked together on a portrait of the hydrophobic Quebec wrestler Mad Dog Vachon after he was hit by a car and lost a leg, and a sojourn in the Canadian Arctic during which we found ourselves hurtling madly through a blizzard in a tempest-tossed Twin Otter that we were certain would crash, but didn't. Yet I've never been to his home, nor he to mine.

When he gets to the airport, I tell him that he's the perfect choice for a trip to the Middle East, since, with the scraggy new beard, he already looks like a hostage of the Hezbollah. This is a rather weak joke. If any one of the five of us winds up blindfolded in a basement, it's likely to be the American Jew who'll be sharing a double room with Terry Waite.

We're in the international check-in area at Terminal 2, just a couple of skinny guys with some suitcases, until Chris Davies the sound man wheels in and we become a different animal, a TV crew. Davies, a shorter, stockier man, beckons a porter towing a monument of luggage: metal cases, big shiny boxes, packing crates, a food hamper, a medical kit and a canvas duffel the size of a three-cushion sofa that is stuffed with sleeping bags, ground sheets and a tent. The civilians in the lounge stand back and stare. We are not on the London Show Tour.

Davies was in Baghdad with Denike when the first thunderbolts of Desert Storm were hurled through the January sky. I think he enjoyed it. The frantic sanctuary in the hotel basement, the escape along the Amman highway, passing mobile Scud launchers, war's fearful flashes lighting up the middle distance—these tales he relates with studied nonchalance and a first-rate, phony Australian accent.

He is an utterly charming guy whose company I have shared only once before, on a pilgrimage by bus with an assemblage of weirdos to the tomb of Elvis Presley. This involved three full days in a coach with thirty cigarette smokers, a scene in which our fellow travelers collapsed in unashamed tears at the humble gravesite, and a flight home from

Memphis on which the airline managed to lose the onion bag containing all our tapes.

The sound man is an endangered species. Technically, he may be superfluous; there is a microphone already attached to the camera and adequate sound can be gathered using this and auxiliary mikes wired right into the camera's hardware. Most news crews, stripped down for quick response, don't include an extra body who handles nothing but sound. It is obviously cheaper to reduce the roster. But a longer piece—some of our documentaries run more than sixty minutes, broadcast over two consecutive evenings—is simply better if someone on the team is dedicated solely to capturing the river roaring, the wind respiring, a mother's mourning cry.

Assured, at our show at least, a reprieve from extinction, Chris joins the check-in queue with a cheerful greeting of "G'day, Bruce, g'day, g'day, g'day." He manages this disposition despite being hunched over like a Queensland Quasimodo, owing to the forty-pound video recorder—the "deck" or "BVU"—that is slung over his shoulder. This is a professional version of the common household VCR, a crippling, technological tumor that poor Davies will have to manhandle up mountains, down valleys and into whatever charnel house or battleground this shoot requires us to visit.

Usually, a "Journal" crew is a four-person menagerie. (About half the reporters and a few of the documentary producers are women. None of the camera or sound operators is.) We go out in the field, take our pictures and bring the tapes back to be edited into a finished story back in Canada. But this time, we are bringing our own editor, and his accompanying megalith of packing cases, to Iran with us.

Michael Claydon, the editor, has not been on a foreign shoot since he helped cover the precipitous collapse of communism in Czechoslovakia in 1989. Though he is the only man on our crew who must say goodbye not only to a wife but to small children, he seems thoroughly energized by the assignment. He has been added because we may also be filing brief news items for "The National," the CBC's nightly newscast, stories that will have to be "cut" on location and fed directly to Toronto, using whatever satellite equipment we can arrange at the courtesy of an American or British network. Claydon, like Denike, is a *Journal* original, a veteran of rapid-deployment shoots: Libya during the U.S. bombing raid; to the tense standoff between Canadian soldiers and militant Indians last summer at Oka, Quebec.

We are waiting for our cameraman to fly in from his home in Ottawa. As it is still raining and somewhat foggy, I grasp at the hope that his connecting flight has been nixed, but this is vain. When Maurice Chabot does finally arrive, hauling still more aluminum lockers, round black tripod cases, heavy corrugated metal lighting kits and the forty-thousand-dollar Sony video camera, fondly nicknamed "Lucille," on which all our work depends, the die is cast.

Chabot is an absolute bear of a man hiding—I don't know from what—behind a hedgerow of russet beard and a rage of uncut hair. Yet his demeanor is gentle. He comes to me in the airport and says, in his thick French-Canadian voice, "I am so happy to see you. You are the one for this assignment. A woman in the office asked me who would be the journalist and I said it was Abel and she said, 'Oh, he has the heart for it.'"

I would like to kiss him, but this is not the place, and the boil in my ear hurts when I pucker.

The baggage total comes to thirty pieces, not counting Lucille and the BVU—these are much too fragile and valuable to check—and not including our personal briefcases and my Eddie Bauer knapsack, which holds Roll-Ups and trail mix, my nonreflective "TV" glasses, blindfold and travel socks, a notebook, pens, the six thousand and seventy-five dollars and a squinting portrait of Linda, taken by a street photographer two years ago in Otavalo, Ecuador, with the inscription: *"Aunque el tiempo y la distancia nos separa, tu recuredo quedar grabado para siempre en mi corazón."*

Although distance and time separate us, your memory will remain engraved forever on my heart.

This is the kind of sappy, sickened mood I am in as we board flight 856. I collapse into row 13, the pre-reserved port-side window seat. (That's why I took the gamma globulin in the right hip, knowing I'd spend the night leaning on my left, against the cabin wall.) Maurice is right behind me, jiggling my seat back, trying to lighten my burden, and his.

The big burly French Canadian is an oenophile, a gourmet, a gifted and sensitive cinematographer, and if even a tidbit of fish or shellfish touches his tongue, he will probably seize up and die. When we last were teamed, it was on isolated Fogo Island off the northeast coast of Newfoundland, an unhappy panoply of too few codfish and too many fishermen, of weatherbeaten families facing disaster and exodus after seven generations on the same rocky shore. Maurice's pictures made the piece a haunting treasure, and this from a man allergic to seafood.

We are scattered around the 747; in the weeks to come, we'll be together all the time. No sense rushing it. A businessman settles in beside me, stashes his attaché, burrows into the old gray *Globe*. The plane holds 256 people and is overbooked. (There was an announcement in the boarding lounge, offering five hundred dollars and a free flight tomorrow for anyone who'd volunteer to be bumped. Maurice held me back.)

A few travelers seem to recognize me, either from my infrequent television cameos or the six years during which my tiny photograph adorned the *Globe*'s sports pages more than a thousand times. One woman wonders if I'm headed over to cover the London Marathon. I tell here where I really am bound and she gasps and says, "Oh, Lord. Those poor people."

I explain to her—it strikes her as a revelation—that her awareness of this tragedy has come because someone already has been there, among the dying, to take the pictures, record the sound, produce the interviews, write the commentary, edit the tapes. This I never recognized before coming to work for the CBC that all the medium's apparently seamless images need be sought after, captured and culled by sensating men and women.

In row 13 of the mammoth plane, awaiting takeoff, I reach for a tissue to dab against the blood on my lower lip. Rain is streaming down the window. The engines roar and it's the only time I pray: "God bring me home safe to Linda."

Seven hours later, at dawn, we are in London, parading groggily along the moving sidewalks, then, in the transit area, waiting three inert hours and then flying on to Vienna, whence we will depart at dinner time for Persia and the benighted Kurds. At Vienna airport, we each have been accorded a few hours' sleep in "day rooms" at the Novotel—immaculate cubicles as austere as monks' cells. But Maurice and Chris seize the time to investigate a *bierstube* downtown, near Mozart's house.

This has them gliding, lightly oiled, into the departure lounge for the Tehran flight half an hour after our scheduled rendezvous, a miscalculation that has Denike and Claydon pacing the terminal in agitated consternation and me sitting wearily on a luggage cart, hoping we all miss the plane so I can go back to bed.

The Airbus is encouragingly jammed—it always assuages my trepidation at going to a new country to see lots of seemingly normal people heading there with me. The plane's video screens project a map of our progress, and the cities we overfly are a gazetteer of recent catastrophes: Yerevan, where thousands perished in the Armenian earthquake of 1988; Tblisi, where Soviet troops gassed civilians demonstrating for Georgian independence; Baku, where Azerbaijani mobs carried out dreadful anti-Armenian pogroms. When we enter Iranian air space, well after midnight, the purser announces that liquor service has terminated and the young, pretty woman in the seat next to me disappears into the business-class toilet and emerges in sackcloth and veil.

At one-thirty in the morning of April 17, we have wheels down, flaps up and are about to make our landing in Tehran when the plane bucks skyward, engines roaring, and banks into a wide, sweeping turn. The captain comes on the loudspeaker and between the noise and my fractured college German I think he's saying there's been a coup in Iran and we can't land.

I'm looking forward to going back to Austria for tea and strudel when he repeats the message in English and the problem is a cow—*eine Kuh*—on the runway. A few loops later, the obstructive ruminant is prodded to safety, or the abattoir, and we are able to touch down on a gentle spring evening in the realm of the ayatollahs.

We gain the hotel within ninety minutes, the thirty cases of gear stuffed in, and piled atop, a couple of station wagons careering through the deserted roundabouts of the slumbering capital. At check-in, rousing the clerks, I register for a safe-deposit box and Denike hands me twenty thousand U.S. dollars—a wad of fifties and hundreds as thick as my leg—to stash there for him.

"Now I'll have to try not to get you killed," Denike says cheerfully. "Or at least I'll remember to take the safety-box key from your body."

17 APRIL
Tehran

The chamber in which I awaken after six hours of unconsciousness—I feel like Marlin Perkins has shot me with a tranquilizer dart and I'm just coming around in a cage in the back of his truck—used to be room 1134 of the InterContinental Hotel Tehran, part of a worldwide chain of luxury hostelries. This is no more. It has been twelve years since the InterContinental was, in the words of one correspondent who covered the Islamic revolution from its spacious and ornamentally appointed public rooms, "shot up, invaded, raided, searched for illegal alcohol," then, in the spirit of antiimperialism, nationalized by the righteous new state and renamed Laleh—"the Tulip."

Yet, even at this remove, traces of the *ancien régime* remain. In the drawer of the night table next to my bed, in addition to a cloth-wrapped prayer stone made from the clay of holy Mecca—one places it on the floor and, in his devotions, touches his head to the small, round object—is a room-service breakfast menu, still bearing the insignia of the InterContinental, but with a thin blue line drawn through the box where a touring infidel once could check off his preference for "ham, bacon or sausage."

It's the telephone that rouses me a little before ten. Producer Denike, already up and working on getting us to the mountains and the dying Kurds, has made contact with the relevant authorities from the Ministry of Islamic Guidance, which has established an office in room 801 of the hotel. Media tours to the border region are being organized. Producer Denike has refused to join them.

I can see nothing out the window but a bedazzling haze that, when I put on my glasses, materializes into an unappealing cityscape of apartment buildings, small shops, magnificently snarled traffic jams and, right across the street, a giant, fading billboard that once, in the era of the modernizing Shah, promoted Pepsi-Cola as the pause that refreshes the subjects of the Peacock Throne. In a stiff breeze, the window slams and crashes on its broken hinges, the curtains rise and fall as if salaaming to some Persian potentate, and an amusing stench wafts in from the bathroom in varying concentrations, depending on the prevailing winds, to mingle with the aroma of the tub of peanut butter in my food bag that, somewhere during its 6,297-mile journey (according to official airline statistics), has sprung a dangerous leak.

But compared, say, to the guest house at Friendship Village, a collective farm near the Soviet border in Chinese Manchuria where the pillow on my rope-mattress bed was a burlap bag full of straw—and the toilet was a metal bucket above which was hung a sign that said, in English, Welcome See You—even the sadly faded star of the Tehran Tulip is sublime. I have left the bathroom light on all night in the hope of discouraging the activities of unspeakable vermin, but when I slowly open the door, none is evident, and there is plenty of hot water in the sink and cold water in the shower, though, unfortunately, not the other way around.

Eventually, a trickle of tepid brown liquid deigns to jump lazily from the shower head and I close the curtain behind me; it, too still bears the rust-spotted InterContinental imprimatur. Then, wreathed like some bleary-eyed genie in great billows of steam rising from the hot water tap at the sink, I slice my chin open in two or three places and begin to remember that I am hungry, jet-lagged, sore eared, nerved up and now indefinitely resident in a republic whose founding fathers preached death to Americans and Jews.

I am deep in this disconcerting reverie as I dress, but then, as I bend over to lace my shoes, my eyes are lanced by a marvelous sight—the snow-capped crest of the Elburz Mountains, shimmering through the smog. I hadn't noticed them before, looking down at the street and the Pepsi sign, but now, with me bent over like a penitent Muslim mullah—but facing to the north, directly away from Mecca—they fill the window, a majestic rise of ash-brown aridity rising first to a dusting, then thick glaciers, of vanilla white. So this is where the plane has dropped me. You walk to your office, someone hands you a ticket, you wake up on the far side of the world.

In the lobby, sitting at a small table with editor Claydon, eating slices of yellow "English" cake dotted with hard, dried blackcurrants, Denike explains that we are not going on today's press junket to see the Kurds, a decision that seems to disappoint Claydon, who would like something to edit, but that balms my anxiety considerably, as it indicates there is at least some likelihood that when this parley is over, I can go back to room 1134 and resume sleeping.

In fact, our majordomo explains, both can happen. There already is a CBC reporter in Iran—Hal Jones of Radio News. Jones has been to the mountaintop, has filed radio reports on the Kurdish exodus, and today he is to interview a junior minister of the Canadian federal cabinet who has beamed up by private jet to certify the misery and offer a certain amount of relief. The minister has some home-video footage of her brief visit to the Iraqi border zone. This is to be edited together with the ministerial interview. Jones will craft a script, the two-minute item will be transmitted by satellite to the television newsroom in Toronto, our responsibility to "The National" will be at least partially taken care of, and we can go off and try to make a documentary of our own.

Denike is convinced that such a project cannot be accomplished by joining a media tour under the thumb of Islamic Guidance, the government department responsible for not letting foreign news organizations go wherever they want. As "The Journal" has been trying to get into Iran for nine years, without success—and since I have no expectation that we are going to be permitted to zip around the country in a private jet, like cabinet ministers—I am inclined to go wherever they tell us to go. But Denike and I have carved out a good working relationship over the years, a division of labor that, basically, means he sets up the shooting schedule, I make suggestions that he rejects out of hand, I write the script and he throws in revisions that I unhesitatingly include.

A more ambitious journalist might balk at playing such a secondary role, but Denike's years of experience, coupled with my propensity for emitting mordant wisecracks at especially inopportune moments, makes it completely acceptable to me that he handle our dealings with the Iranian bureaucracy. Similarly, I have no problem with radio's Hal Jones preparing tonight's news report, even though I am the alleged television correspondent on the scene and have been in Iran for nearly seven hours. Whenever my face can be withheld from public exhibition, so much the better. And while some network auditor in Ottawa may decry this duplication of reportorial beefcake in the same story, to me the multiple branches of the CBC remain a fascination, reminding me of the motto of my high-school newspaper: Sleepless, the hundred-eyed Argus watches.

The minion in charge of the foreign press, Denike reports, is a mincing little fellow, impeccably groomed and clean-shaven, whose French-language skills much exceed his English and whose name is Lemi Hatam. As are all middle-level mandarins in such situations, Hatam is caught between his government's desire for attention—in this case, publicity for Iran's appeal for aid from its erstwhile Western enemies—and his own wish that everyone would simply give up and go home. Arrayed against him is a small but representative assemblage of First World journalism, about fifteen television crews and various print reporters and still photographers sent to cover a sidebar to the grievous situation in Turkey and the tentative move by some Kurds there to bury their dead, turn around and walk home.

As gatherings of the world's media go, the number of journalists, producers, technicians and editors at the Laleh this morning does not approach the voracious mob that occupied, say, the Bucharest InterContinental during the Romanian uprising of December, 1989, a seething school of piranhas that commandeered every bed in the hotel—with others sleeping on sofas in the lobby—and that included, unforgettably, at the instant my crew and I arrived after a sixteen-hour drive through sporadic sniper fire, a good-looking young man standing at the registration desk, screaming, "We've been eating your shit for seven days. I'm Arthur Kent of NBC News and we need two more rooms! Now!"

He got them. They were *our* rooms.

But here, the Tehran Tulip does not seem to be sagging under the weight of the fourth estate. With CNN "reporting live" from the Iran-Iraq border itself—as if it would be possible to "report dead"—and with several other teams already gone on today's government-managed escapade to the city of Ourmiyeh and the refugees trapped in the mountainous tri-corner of Iran, Iraq and Turkey, the hotel lobby is fairly deserted. No one is minding the small candy-and-tobacco kiosk, and the handicraft and carpet shops are devoid of customers, despite signs promising seventeen percent discounts to journalists. (How on earth did they arrive at that figure?) The only other media people I see at the moment are a pair of haggard Scandinavian photojournalists in dirty jeans and parkas, with rucksacks as big as houses, who look as if they have just walked here from Trondheim.

It is only when these two overburdened pack mules have passed me to sit at a distant table and devour English cakes that I notice a framed portrait hanging on the wall behind them. It is the Ayatollah Khomeini—to his followers, inviolable successor to the Shi'ite caliphate, a messianic herald or, perhaps, the millennial Twelfth Imam himself. A strip of black crepe has been tacked to the frame; the holy man has been dead for twenty-two months and thirteen days. On the rear wall of the lobby, in large letters made from the careful placement of dozens of small wooden tiles, is the motto, no aid to my digestion, DOWN WITH U.S.A.

Four days out of Oklahoma City, after forty-eight hours with Linda and twenty-four or so in transit, I take lunch in the Namakdoon (Saltcellar) restaurant on the ground floor of the Laleh Hotel. I methodically select a table—I'm the only one in the place—and sit with my back to the long picture window that opens onto Dr. Hoseyn-E-Fatemi Avenue, as if to not look out at Iran might maintain my insulation from the looming ordeal to come. The crew has gone out with Hal Jones, and producer Denike is up in 801, trying to convince Hatam to permit us—the emissaries of benign, beneficent little Canada—to arrange our own itinerary among the suffering refugees. Behind me, as I tuck into my chicken kebab and an Elburz of long-grain rice, the traffic snarls and swarms and house sparrows chip their atonal announcements, flitting in and out of the hedgerows of a country I certainly never thought I'd see.

The entire process has been so sudden, so improbable, it is fair to say that I have not had time to do a lot of educational preparation for this shoot. I don't speak much Kurdish, and my entire Farsi vocabulary was taught to me by a taxi driver at the Tehran airport at two o'clock this morning: *masalei neest*, no problem; *Masalei bozorg*, big problem. Usually, someone else in our party would then ask the local word for beer, but in this case such knowledge would be moot.

In our business, what they have done to me is called a "parachute," which means that I have been shoved out of an airplane onto a story with somewhat less time to get ready than, say, Henry M. Stanley had at sea to mull over what he would say to Dr. Livingstone when finally he got to Ujiji. A phenomenon of jet travel and television's immediacy and wealth, parachuting is often decried, perhaps rightly, by observers of the media trade—what I don't know about the Near East, for example, will fill this book—but it has become especially common not only for reporters to be parachuted into crisis zones but also for famous anchorpeople and entire studio operations to be air-dropped into foreign locales, permitting, for example, Dan Rather to be in New York one evening and in Dhahran the next, his hair blowing in the Arabian breeze while, a hundred miles from the nearest battle front, he glares portentously into the camera and breathes, "the winds...of war."

My own experience may be atypical, because the usual practice at "The Journal" is to remain in the country for an extended period, then bring the tapes home to be edited in Toronto, according me and our other reporters the opportunity to get to know our subject before we have to commit a script to videotape. And there are other qualities a journalist needs in these situations besides pure academic backgrounding—doggedness, courage and a strong stomach are three that come to mind that I don't have. There is also the question of access. It was of little use to the CBC to have me, one of the world's ranking experts on modern China, in Beijing in the hours after the Tian'anmen Massacre when all the drivers and translators went into hiding and we couldn't get out of the Palace Hotel.

Arthur Kent, on the other hand, hijacked a rickshaw, grabbed a minicam and went to work.

A last resort, when sheer ignorance overtakes all obstacles, is to deliver a version of the All-Purpose Stand-Up: "With the situation in sharp focus, the people here can only wait and hope, for what will happen in the future, only time will tell." This is abysmal reportage, to be sure, but look what Henry M. Stanley came out with when, after all that rehearsal time, he finally found his man.

At the Namakdoon restaurant, as I polish off my kebab, a young man enters, and with him are two young women, in the requisite head coverings (*hijab*), of course, but not the black *chador*. The young women are actually wearing quite colorful paisley scarves and long trenchcoats (*rupoosh*) with slightly cinched waistbands that surprise the heck out of me when they end just above matched pairs of Air Jordans.

The male companion, who appears to be about twenty, is sitting between the two daughters of the Islamic Revolution, perusing the rather limited menu. (Chicken kebab, ground-lamb *chelo* kebab, sturgeon kebab, or combination kebab of chicken, ground lamb and sturgeon.) All seems normal, but then one member of the rather moth-eaten sextet of waiters idling at the cash desk comes over, says something to the young man, not angrily, but firmly, and the fellow dutifully, without a shrug or a grimace, gets up and goes to sit at the other side of the table from the two girls he has brought to lunch.

"Be damn careful having any relations with the women," the British traveler Ronald Sinclair was warned by a local businessman when he reached Tehran, by car, from idyllic Beirut, in 1927. "Believe me, it can be downright dangerous."

"That's true in more places than Iran," Sinclair replied. (He reports this in his book, *Adventures in Persia.)*

"That may be so, but I'm talking about this country, and take it from me there's still a great deal of religious fanaticism in Iran. As a visitor you may not be conscious of it, but it is there, lurking just below the surface. And there are plenty of religious fanatics only too ready to seize any excuse for making trouble. And on the subject of their own Moslem women, they are particularly sensitive."

The portrait of the Ayatollah, the DOWN WITH U.S.A. sign, the pointed rearranging of the *ménage à trois*—these gradually awaken in me the feeling that I'm not in Oklahoma any more. I've already been advised, by a Canadian diplomat who met us at the airport, to wear long sleeves and long trousers in public, not to shake a woman's hand in greeting and, furthermore, not to touch a woman at any time. (Getting women to keep their hands off me has never been a problem.) After the monotony of the long plane ride, the decent, if somewhat decayed, standard of the hotel, and the bland rice and chicken luncheon, these frissons of Iran-ness are electric, a stimulus to my inveterate traveler's brain that impels me to rise from my table, pay my bill of four thousand "goo-goos" (actually rials, but in "Journal" parlance, all foreign currencies are "goo-goos"), strut right out the front doors of the Tehran Tulip and get all the way to the intersection of Hoseyn-E-Fatemi and Hejab avenues—a good thirty yards—before the noise, unmuffled exhaust fumes and sheer impenetrable volume of the hurtling traffic sends me scurrying back inside, happy to still be alive. Then I go up to room 1134 and, sedated by all this excitement, take a three-hour nap.

In midafternoon, when Maurice and Chris return from filming Hal Jones's interview with the junior cabinet minister, and expecting that before dawn tomorrow we will be traveling toward the luckless Kurds, we determine to go off and see a bit of this capital that despite our combined experience of more than 150 countries, none of us has ever visited. The Islamic Revolution was achieved two years before "The Journal" was created. The long war with Iraq was covered by "The National." It has taken nine years and this monumental tragedy for our invitation, often solicited, to arrive.

Our transport is a small, burnt-yellow, Iranian-built, prerevolutionary Paykan—"Arrow"—sedan, copied, reputedly, from a fifties-era British Hillman Avenger, and under the command—for Brian has hired him to be our driver—of a small, shy man with apologetic eyes, balding with a receding wreath of dark curls, a non-English speaker called Pejman. As it is a sixteen-hour drive, minimum, to the nearest point on the Iraqi border where Kurds have encamped in large numbers, and since any one of our thirty cases of equipment would overwhelm both the trunk capacity and the superannuated suspension of Pejman's Arrow, he has been contracted principally for local travel, such as the run that editor Claydon will have to make much later tonight to the transmission facilities of Islamic Republic of Iran Broadcasting (IRIB) with Hal Jones's news report. If we're going to motor to the border, it will have to be in a bus.

"Bazaar?" I suggest to Pejman as a first stop on our tour. He doesn't seem to understand. I try again. "Bazaar? Bazaar?"

"Bazaar," Chris Davies growls, with a Persian accent.

"Ah," the driver grins. "Bazaar!"

So we set off, three of us compacted into the back seat, the elongated Claydon in the front with his knees on the dashboard. Producer Denike remains at the hotel, trying to wear down Hatam. I have a pang of guilt and think that my place is with him, but this soon passes.

We are heading south, down Hejab Avenue, descending toward a level plain that spills off the Elburz range toward the steppes of Central Asia. And Tehran spills with it, a lava-flow of urbanization that, like Los Angeles, spreads itself in seemingly infinite low-rise expansion with the mountains to its back, the emptiness of what must once have been a barren desert repealed by the crush of ten million souls. We are expecting the minarets of Cairo or the graceful domes of Istanbul; instead, Tehran, in these districts at least, presents a face of drab monotony, gray stucco shopfronts and colorless flats, almost Soviet in its purposeful ugliness, but without cathedrals or crenellated walls. South Tehran is commercial, but not prosperous; run-down, but not beggarly, an archetype of the Second World.

"Tehran is a city I liked particularly," the redoubtable traveler Freya Stark wrote in her diary in the Persian summer of 1931. "Neither western nor eastern, but with a character of its own, colorless but clear, like water—and I do not mean the Tehran drinking water."

But thirty-odd years took some of the glow off the metropolis. *Nagel's Iran*, published in 1968, a decade before the Islamic Revolution, labels Tehran "a capital designed mainly for motor traffic" and predicts that "the tourist will have some difficulty in finding the picturesque Oriental bustle he expects in a Moslem town." This urbanization, the little red book warns, "has created some appalling inequalities that are fraught with danger for the future."

The danger having exploded, then subsided, but with the motor traffic still a madcap freeway to hell, Pejman careers for half an hour down these charmless streets—we keep asking "Bazaar?" and he nods and rockets onward—until finally he pulls up at the curbside of a row of nondescript little food stores and tailor shops and makes a sign that we should disembark. Since I am anticipating the equal of the Great Covered Bazaar on the Bosphorus—or at least St. Lawrence Market in Toronto—it is no small disappointment that instead of a frenzied warren of clamoring dealers in carpets, worry beads, pistachios, *chadors*, dead goats, samovars, lacquerware, precious stones, tamarinds and myrrh, Pejman's finger is pointing to these humble little shops and saying "Bazaar, bazaar, bazaar."

The four of us get out and begin to search the small food shops for bottled water, which we certainly will need when we are in the mountains with the Kurds and which our hotel does not seem to stock. (The beverage list at lunch was nonalcoholic "Islamic" beer, orange juice with dubious ice, or cola served in old Coke and Pepsi bottles with faded lettering from before the revolution.) There are plenty of fruit juices in cans and foil pouches, and we buy a few dozen of these, but no mineral water or anything like it, be it elegant imported Evian or the Armenian abomination on which I once existed for two weeks in Leningrad—a liquid that appeared inviting and clear when first decanted but then, left to stand for an hour or so, began to rust, sending little red-orange flakes twinkling toward the bottom of the glass while a repulsive film of oil collected at the surface, as if some grizzled third baseman had spat tobacco juice into a mug of club soda.

We browse a bit more, surprised to be attracting not the slightest attention, friendly or otherwise, as if delegations from the Great Satan (and, in the case of the three Canadians with me, other, minor bedevilments) dropped in all the time. When we squeeze into a tiny menswear shop and Maurice purchases a blue dress shirt for six thousand "googoos," the merchant is the picture of politeness and good humor, and it is not until we get back to the hotel much later that Maurice discovers that the body of the shirt is adequate but that the sleeves—described by the proprietor as *"bozorg, bozorg,"* big, big—conclude just below the elbow.

It is now about three-thirty, and the few shops that were open have begun to shut down, whether for the dinner hiatus or because this is the beginning of the Islamic weekend, I don't know. The main body of the bazaar, if this in fact is the bazaar, glimpsed down a narrow, covered alley that leads inward from the street corner, is inert; one old man is sleeping in a doorway of a vacant butcher's shop, while another is moving his trays of raisins, dates and spices to the rear of his green-painted stall.

We are just about to give up on the mineral water and this rather far-fetched cross-border shopping when a young man comes trotting up to us from a small food store we had passed by earlier. It already was closing, the lights were out and nothing remained in a refrigerated display case but a single lonely yellow cake. In halting English, he asks our nationality—in China, a good way to disperse gawking crowds was to reply, "the Soviet Union"—and when we tell him that we come from Canada, he begins to get mist in his eyes.

He is speaking French now, asking about Montreal and the glories of old Quebec; he has read about these, he says, in books. Maurice is enchanted—he's stumbled upon a fellow francophone in a country with no English signs except for DOWN WITH U.S.A.

"I am sorry," the Iranian says. "I have not spoken French for ten years."

"That is all right," Maurice consoles him. "Your French is beautiful."

Back in the little yellow car, we try to inquire of Pejman the driver whether or not it would be a long journey to the tomb of the Imam Khomeini, or to the Cemetery of Martyrs where the fallen heroes of the Islamic Revolution and the eight-year war with Iraq lie entombed in their hundreds and hundreds of thousands.

"Khomeini okay we go," Pejman assents. And the cemetery? The word washes over him like a spring shower and falls to the ground, uncomprehended.

"Cemetery," Chris attempts. "Iraq. Saddam. Bang-bang." He makes a pantomime of a rifle being fired and a soldier falling dead, in this case, in my arms.

"Iraq. Bang-bang. Dead. Cemetery," the sound man reprises.

"Okay we go," Pejman says.

"How far?" I ask. "Minutes? Ten? Thirty? One hundred?"

"Okay we go," the chauffeur smiles, turning the key, starting in motion and making a brisk U-turn, the Iranian way, without looking.

Heading even farther southward, away from the snowcapped mountains and the Tulip International Hotel, we circle in front of the main railway station, leading me to imagine, for an instant, what it would be like to try to drag all our gear onto third-class carriages and to ride from here to Hyderabad and Hong Kong, watching the human pageantry, sipping tea. Then we find ourselves passing by a large vacant lot where, apparently, a great building once stood, for Pejman is pointing to it and saying, "Shah, Shah," and running his index finger across his throat.

Suddenly, Tehran ends. Just like that, after a forty-five-minute ordeal of lurching, crawling, tearing down avenues and side streets and even alleyways in an insane greyhound race of cars, trucks and buses, the city is finished. One minute, we're still in the charmless mess of apartment blocks and storefronts, but then Pejman executes a suicidal left turn from the right-hand lane, and in an instant we're among green fields, and at the side of the road peasants are peddling carnations.

It is still a mile or more to the mosque that holds the holy man's remains. I can see the dome gleaming golden in the sun now, as we approach the site along a straight, southward boulevard. There are even some directional signs in English—To the Tomb of the Imam Khomeini—and, as we turn off into the parking area, quotations from the scholar's inviolable writ: "A nation founded on martyrdom can have no fear of imperialist aggression"; "We should learn foreign languages to spread Islam."

The area has the feeling of incompletion and newness: scaffolding climbs a minaret high above the domed mausoleum; earth-movers and engineers' trailers are still on-site, and an exhibition of the Ayatollah's life and work is crammed into a small, cinder-block outbuilding that hardly befits the oracle of a flaming revolution. Yet thousands of cars and buses are parked in neat rows in the gravel, their passengers drawn, as we are, to the shrine.

At the men's entrance, Pejman takes our shoes and, brandishing them over his head like severed scalps in an old Western movie, carries them to a long, flat counter to have them deposited against pilferage. The small anteroom is solid with dark-dressed, pressing pilgrims waving little numbered tags, more interested in their footwear than in the four aliens in jeans and T-shirts who stand backed against the wall, trying to look inconspicuous.

The grand hall we enter, in an explosion of sound and filtered sunlight, is a fairground of gaiety where I had expected tortured grief to reign. Khomeini's funeral in June, 1989, had been the wild stampede of a bereaved, abashed nation—a million mourners, slapping their temples in ritualized self-punishment, nearly beating the coffin to splinters, hurling the ghostly body out of its sateen nest. I had watched it on CNN in a hotel room in China—the Ayatollah died on the same weekend as the Beijing horrors—and it seemed that Asia was coming apart at east and west, bookended by great national upheavals.

Now I am at the very heart of a revolution whose apostle commanded the annihilation of my country and my creed. It is not an easy room to walk into, not from physical fear of an angry mob—we would not have gone this far had non-Muslim foreigners not been welcome in this building—but because my presence seems to betoken some personal acceptance of the man herein entombed. I have had the same feeling at Chairman Mao's refrigerated mummy case and at the blown-up concrete shell of Hitler's Eastern Front command post in northern Poland, as if to *not* attend would somehow negate all history.

Imagine, then, to carry this baggage into the great hall—a towering hangar of crisscrossing girders and ventilation ducts, a Persian Pompidou Center—and to discover knots of peasant families picnicking on the marble floor while little boys kick at footballs, feinting around the supporting pillars as playmates run roaring in pursuit.

There is even a band playing. A hundred men in khaki dress uniforms are at the far side of the mosque from where we enter, brassily pumping out martial airs that bellow up to the flat metal ceiling and bounce back in disharmony upon the crowds below. This stationary parade has a purpose—it is Army Day, and this army has this year not been called to battle, though all around it, war has raged. Peacetime in Iran.

At the center of the mosque, below the dome that is held up by eight yellow-greenish marble pillars as thick as redwood trees, is a brilliant, pendular chandelier, and underneath that is Khomeini. The tomb itself is an enclosure about the size of a two-car garage, fenced in by a lattice of white woodwork that is covered, up to a height of about eight feet, by clear plastic, like a hockey rink. Inside the little house, covered in plain green baize, the color of Islam, is the bier itself. What is remarkable about the sight is not just the fame of the man who herein lies, but also the fact that the whole entombment room, about four hundred square feet, is knee-deep in coins and paper money.

Along the four sides of the mausoleum are a few dozen people who actually are chanting and moaning obeisance to the Imam, though these, too, are far outnumbered by ordinary sightseers and gawkers. Even at this point, jostling with the crowd to peer inside the little white-framed squares to see the catafalque and all the money, we are the object of no curiosity, hostile or otherwise. It is almost disappointing.

There are five, perhaps six thousand people in the building; of these, as far as I can see, we are the only foreigners, palefaced beacons among the dark, rough woolens and black *chadors*. We follow Pejman around the floor, grateful for his presence—I wouldn't have wanted to come here unescorted, though now it is clear that it wouldn't have mattered—until, after about fifteen minutes in the noise and the stifling heat, we reenter the swarming hive of the shoe depository and stand along the wall again while he shoves and butts his way to retrieve our sneakers.

Back in the Paykan taxi, we act out the show of the rifleman and the falling casualty to indicate that we still would like to visit the Cemetery of Martyrs. This turns out to be just across the road—though it takes nearly half an hour to wend through the asphyxiating rush-hour traffic jam—as if the eternal proximity of the spiritual guide in the green-decked coffin might make even more certain the immortality of the young men who, in his name, marched gladly unto death.

Pejman circumnavigates the area and parks on a tree-lined street that is quiet and uncrowded by cars. Along one side of this passage is a row of dozens of large, garage-type doors set one after the other in a single-story building that runs the length of the block. These seem to be the tombs of senior officers who fell in the glorious cause, though all the doors are closed and I cannot see inside. They are too new to hold the remains of military men of the former regime, executed in their royalist hundreds when the religious took control.

Across the street from their commanders lie the humbler million whose deaths in the great war with Iraq, in the end, gained nothing—no territory, no national treasure, no rising of the enemy populace against the tyrant, Saddam Hussein. Under the trees, now, we walk to meet them, hushed in this hallowed place.

In the Cemetery of Martyrs, no bands are playing, no boys are playing ball. The graves are marble slabs set flush in the concrete pavement, so that you walk on them without meaning to, then step back, with silent apology. Above each gravestone—these are inscribed with names and dates and perhaps a Koranic verse—is a small display case similar to a medicine cabinet, with a hinged glass panel, that contains some mementos of the dead warrior. All the cases are locked, to protect the priceless value of each family's memories.

Walking slowly down one row of these plebeian shrines, I see flags, pocket-sized copies of the Koran—perhaps carried into the last battle—candles, dried and plastic flowers, wrestling trophies, sports-club pins. And of course photographs—graduation pictures, sports outings, posed family groups and, commonly, a snapshot of a young man beaming as he sits in the turret of an antiaircraft gun or shoulders his rifle, invincible and proud.

As I turn the end of the corridor, I halt. Just ahead, a slim, gray-haired man has opened the door to one of the display cases. I watch him take a small candle from his pocket, light it, then place it among the photographs, as the flickering plays on his face.

The cemetery seems limitless. The young trees and the corrugated metal roofs that protect the gravesites from the elements make it impossible to see very far in any direction, imposing a sense of privacy on what must be a mile-square garden of closely packed grief. Only a few visitors are about, late on the afternoon of Army Day, with the sun about to plummet behind the reflective cupola of the Ayatollah's monument, on the flat plain to the west.

Through all of this, the tomb and the cemetery and the long ride from the bazaar, Pejman has said nothing, as if indifferent to both the frenzied driving and the sacred destination. But now I notice him at the end of one of the long, long rows of graves, looking into a humble display. There are school pennants and photographs of a boy of perhaps eighteen.

The driver turns to me.

"My brother," he says.

18 APRIL
Tehran

The little man from Welsh television is standing in the hotel parking lot, wide-eyed, looking for someone to complain to. He finds me. He says, "It was terrible. I don't think we were there for twenty minutes. Every time we tried to do something, they came running over and stopped us. Then they herded all of us back on the bus and made us sit there for an hour while they tried to chase down two fellows who just wandered off and got lost."

The little man from Welsh television—I visualize slate miners and their families glued to the set in Blaenau Ffestiniog—is telling me about the media trip to Ourmiyeh and the Kurdish camps organized by the Ministry of Islamic Guidance. He is older than I, stocky, the Welsh crew's sound man, and quite fed up with the whole experience. He says, "We're going home. That's it. We've had enough. I don't think we got a minute of decent pictures."

The BBC team has had much better luck, but to get it, they drove in a minivan crammed with gear and gasoline for sixteen hours, each way, to avoid the package tour and get some pictures no one else had. These images, in fact, have already appeared on "The Journal." On the very night we left, while I squirmed in my window seat, blindfolded and bleary, trying to sleep, our program was running a dramatic report from the Iranian highlands by BBC's Charles Wheeler.

"Life is a lottery," Charles Wheeler reported. "It favors the agile and the few."

(When producer Denike heard that "The Journal" was going to broadcast a first-rate BBC documentary from the precise location we had, at that point, not yet taken off for, his reaction was: "Then why are *we* going?" A senior editor told him, "For Maurice's pictures and Allen's script." I said, "Why don't we fool them and give them my pictures and Maurice's script?" Brian said, "Because then they'll never send us anywhere again.")

The miracle worker who got the BBC up to the mountains on their own time is an Iranian journalist named Kamran Farzal. In the lobby of the Tehran Tulip, Denike introduces me to Kamran, a clean-shaven, dark-haired man in gold wire-rimmed glasses who, smoking and grimacing, evinces a reporter's bone-bred distaste for bureaucracies, interference and red tape. Brian is trying to hire him to be our "fixer" to grease the wheels of Islamic Guidance; to accompany us to the Kurdish exodus; and, most important, to decipher for us a country about which we are as ignorant as jackasses and as innocent as lambs.

But Kamran Farzal has already been to the mountains. His reports of unimaginable suffering and death along the road, published in London, were among the first to alert the West to the Iranian aspect of the tragedy. In the hotel lobby, Kamran tells us that he has not slept in three days. When he comes to, after his need for sleep and his commitment to the BBC have been satisfied, he will work for us. Until then, he advises, we should decline all government junkets and try to reach the mountains on our own.

The revolution fired by the holy man whose scowling portrait, wreathed in mournful crepe, now hangs adjacent to the formulaic DOWN WITH U.S.A. in our lobby, once burned beneath my window, room 1134. John Simpson of the BBC—he was staying in 1119, just down the hall, where today a grizzled shoe-shine man squats plumply, soliciting business, brush in hand—was out in the road in front of the hotel the night the Islamic rebels triumphed, "making light conversation," he later would write, "with would-be martyrs."

By the light of a flaming automobile tire, Simpson made his notes:

"Barricades scarcely strong; 1 large old US car (Buick) dragged up, tipped on side...smoke and sparks go up from fires in streets all round... Ambulance sirens go, but nothing passes us. Some cars and m/cycles still on streets even now. Gunfire? Rare. Waiting. When will tanks come?"

It was February 11, 1979. The next morning, the front page of the Toronto *Globe and Mail* carried this headline, six columns wide: "Hundreds dead in Tehran bloodbath." The story said: "The end came after more than 40 hours of bloody fighting in the streets as troops of the army's Imperial Guard, loyal to Shah Mohammed Reza Pahlavi, clashed with thousands of followers of Ayatollah Khomeini.... The gaunt, grey-bearded religious leader, who has been the inspiration behind the tide of revolt that forced the Shah from the country, returned to Tehran earlier this month after 15 years in exile. He has vowed to create an Islamic republic...."

(Just below this dramatic report of fervor and death in a far-off land, the *Globe and Mail* used a photograph, four columns wide and ten inches deep, of the stellar hockey forward Guy Lafleur trying to steal the puck from a dancing Russian bear named Makarov. The story that accompanied the picture was under my byline, datelined New York. It began: "Before the tears and the cursing, the soul-searching and the long, lingering hurt set in, one thing must be said. Last night at Madison Square Garden, playing with a green, gold-haired goaltender, with two of the world's best forwards and one of its best defencemen out with injuries, the national hockey team of the Soviet Union played a perfect game, beating Team NHL 6-0." Such were the epochal events in my little universe at the time of the terror in Iran.)

February 11, 1979 was styled on the ancient Persian calendar the twenty-second day of Bahman. For that reason, on the national flag of the Islamic Republic of Iran, the inscription God Is Great is repeated twenty-two times along the margins of the white stripe of peace that separates the red of heroic sacrifice from the bright green of Islam.

In the middle of the flag, where once a monarchial lion had posed, there now is a new coat of arms, four holy crescents to represent the worldwide struggle of oppressed peoples surrounding an upright sword, for strength and fortitude.

Now these vastly disparate worlds have merged, under the tricolored banner. In the *New York Times*—I've brought the clipping with me—Judith Miller has recently reported the waning of the fundamentalist state. "The revolution is finally over," she quotes a diplomat. The headline says: Islamic Radicals Lose Their Tight Grip on Iran.

"Nevertheless," the report continues, "fear and suspicion of foreigners and one another are still pervasive."

The hockey writer, who has lost his way, walks into the breakfast hall. There is a buffet: boiled eggs, flatbread dotted with burned sesame seed, salty cheese, orange juice from tins, fresh, juicy pink-red grapefruit as big as bowling balls. I sit at a table and scan the room, studying the staff, on the lookout for fear and suspicion. But all I get is a lanky, lazy waiter with a steel jug in each hand who finally approaches and asks, "Tea, coffee?" and, invariably, pours the wrong one.

19 APRIL
Tehran-Bakhtaran-Do Ab

"I'm laughing as I write this," I write, laughing, and why not? A Yankee boy, bar mitzvahed, flying over the sere, forbidding fastness of Revolutionary Iran...in a private jet!

Denike has pulled it off. We are in a twin-engine Falcon executive aircraft, the gear—only fourteen cases of it—is stacked on the seats and in the narrow aisle, and for a moment giddiness overtakes my trepidation at the horrors that await us when we land. Four days after leaving Toronto, roaring through the desert haze, we finally are keeping our appointment with the Kurds.

The arrangement our producer has made with Hatam, the francophone official from the Ministry of Islamic Guidance, is for this plane to deposit us in the city of Bakhtaran—formerly Kermanshah, the capital of the Iranian province that borders Iraqi Kurdistan—whence a van and a "minder" will take us high into the mountains, where a million desperate refugees perch in a fragile sanctuary of canvas and cloth. On Sunday evening, the plane will return to Bakhtaran to pick us up. The price of freedom from the journalistic mob is thirty-five hundred dollars in United States cash.

Our cozy little jet has been chartered from a domestic company called Asseman Air. The pilot, a handsome, businesslike air force veteran named Rad, crawls over the packing boxes to shake our hands and wish us happy landings. And happy we are—Chris Davies, especially, is tickled by the company's name.

"Oh, man," he growls, groveling in luxury, exchanging the Australian accent for the approving argot of the South Bronx. "Dis be one bad-ass-man airline."

Only four of us are making the excursion this morning. Claydon has remained in Tehran, his editing equipment unneeded since, without our own satellite up-link, we have no way to transmit a story from the refugee area. We can only plan to edit a short documentary in the hotel on Monday, four days hence, and feed it from Tehran, through the studios of Iranian television. Also left behind in the capital is the huge blue duffel of sleeping bags and tenting. Two mornings ago, in our jet-lagged somnambulations, we had brilliantly forgotten to claim it from the baggage carousel. Now it is sitting in the Customs hall, entangled in a briar patch of paperwork, and when I consider that we have nowhere arranged to sleep tonight and not even a blanket to cover ourselves, I cease laughing. But at least I've brought along some tuna and a packet of fig newtons. When another American, Lt.-Col. Oliver North, flew to Iran on his secret arms-for-hostages crusade, all he had was a cyanide capsule.

Everything below is a sandy blur, lifeless, ungreened. I press my nose to the window and feel the sun's warmth; the vibration of the engines makes me tingle. I wish this flight would never end, that we'd just keep flying, flying, over the beautiful, ugly wastes.

Behind me, the boys are talking about small planes and frightful flights in dreadful places: Denike trying to get from Costa Rica to Panama during the Yankee invasion; Chabot at the North Pole, Davies in Sudan. Brian tells the story of our attempt to fly to an isolated Inuit encampment off the coast of Baffin Island in the Canadian Arctic. The landing strip was marked by oil drums lined up in the pinwheeling snow of a frozen fjord. The Twin Otter came bottoming out of the sky in a gale-force crosswind; "testing the conditions," the pilot said.

A woman began to scream—"We're going to die! Don't land! Don't land! Don't land!"—and, next to me, another Inuit woman softly cried, holding a baby girl who quietly gulped vomit into her mother's hands. We were flipping like a leaf in an autumn squall. I could see a snowmobile, towing sledges, heading toward the landing zone, its driver looking up at us, the helpless captives of the tempest.

We came tumbling down toward the furious snow and, at the last instant, the pilot aborted the landing and the plane reared upward again, straining to clear the sheer rock walls of the canyon. The screaming halted; the child slept. One day, I thought, the planes will kill me. But that was not the day.

On the tarmac at Bakhtaran International Airport is a big transport plane, in camouflage colors, with a German flag painted on its belly, and a Soviet-built Tu-154 jet with red-and-white Interflug markings that formerly, Rad the pilot says, was the personal aircraft of Erich Honecker, the East German commissar. It, too, now bears the banner of the newly amalgamated German state. Some officials have flown in it from Bonn to be photographed supervising the distribution of the relief supplies that came in the giant khaki cargo ship.

Inside the terminal, which is modern and clean, we see another mountain of television gear and, near it, Charles Glass, a renowned journalist for ABC News, once held hostage by Lebanese terrorists cheered, if not expressly commanded, by the Iranian mullahs. He also is trying to reach the Kurdish encampments. It's his second trip.

"How much did you pay Hatam for the charter flight?" Glass asks, and Denike tells him. Thirty-five hundred.

"So did we," Glass says. "Then I checked how much it cost to fly here commercially, on Iran Air. Not that they would take our gear. But guess how much—eight dollars! The taxi from the Laleh to the airport was more than that."

After an hour in the terminal building, waiting for the promised minivan and the ineluctable "minder," we are beginning to get the sinking feeling that the package offered by Hatam Holidays may not turn out as advertised. We drag the gear to the curbside and sit on the boxes to await our fate. Across the driveway, in a patch of greenery that gives the airport a homey, small-town feel, a dozen women in full black drapery are grouped around one of their number, embracing her, touching her shoulder as the woman wails and bleats and cries. The two teams face each other: a quartet of electronic interlopers from the alien West; a choir of villagers evoking the sorrows of all our immemorial grief.

And now a vehicle arrives, summoned, it seems, by some airport official eager to get the foreigners off his land. A lean young driver hastens us to the municipal headquarters. He takes the traffic circles on two wheels, and at one three-block straightaway, I peek over his shoulder at the speedometer and it registers 130 on the metric scale.

(At any rate, there's not much to see. *Nagel's* advises that the city "contains no old or modern building of interest." The energetic Briton Ronald Sinclair, driving down from the Iraqi frontier in 1927—we'll be going the opposite way—at first found this place "reasonably impressive, viewed from a distance." But when he entered, Sinclair discovered it to be "just as drab, dirty and uninspiring as the great majority of towns in this part of the world.")

At City Hall, we are plunked in four padded chairs in an antechamber to a suite of offices. On the wall in front of us is a large photographic mural of a rural idyll. A small boat floats lazily down a still, straight canal beneath a caressing crown of willows, somewhere in Britain, I'd guess, maybe Kent. Outside, midtown Bakhtaran on a Friday noon—I suddenly realize it's the Muslim holy day—is quiet. But I hear no calls to midday prayers.

A bureaucrat named Yousef emerges to greet us. He is tall and powerfully built, in his thirties, upright and proud. He speaks excellent English. He takes my hand in greeting and, barely squeezing, crushes it in a death grip that evokes simultaneous cries of pain from every bone, joint, ligament, tendon, artery and lymph duct. Then he recommends lunch, before we set off.

This is a man after my own stomach. My semiserious First Law of Journalism has been: "No story is more important than lunch." I've even learned the phrase in Russian: "*po spyervah nam nada pazavtrakat,*" though lunches in Russia usually turn out to be something I wish I'd skipped. The First Law is glib and often broken, but I cling to this trademark insistence on regular food and sleep, not because I can't live without them for a time, but because the imposition of routine seems to ease the strangeness of the worlds to which I am dispatched. Normality is my crutch.

Yousef leads us a couple of blocks in the sun, past a bank and a few shops shuttered for the sabbath, then down a stairway into a basement restaurant. The room is cool and uncrowded; a clot of waiters and busboys, leaning at the cashier's table, outnumbers the seated diners. Yousef and a few acolytes who have wandered over from the town hall with us order some grilled mutton and bowls of tangy, garlicked yogurt through which slabs of flatbread are swiped. Producer Denike protests at the relentless shrinking of an already waning day, but the Bakhtaranians have their priorities, and nabbing the occasional morsel, we wait while they fill themselves.

Politely rejecting a guided tour of the city, we return to our van just in time to catch the arrival, by car, of a certain Ali Ramzi, one of Hatam's men from Islamic Guidance. We assume that he is going to come with us to the mountains, but soon we find ourselves casting off from the curb while Ali Ramzi, immobile and unmoved, waves us godspeed.

Now we are bound for the town of Paveh, the last Iranian city marked on our map before the border outposts where the refugees are encamped. In the overloaded minivan, at unconscionable velocities, we tear across a level plain, featureless except where long, narrow plots have been irrigated and the first brilliant shoots of grain have emerged. Then, after more than an hour, we begin to ascend the acute, meandering switchbacks that mark the climb toward our unhappy goal.

The highway, flat and smooth at first, takes us past only a few settlements, and these are visions of antiquity, low, weathered enclosures of adobe houses and outbuildings surrounded by dried-mud walls. Some of the compounds include a small domed building, a humble mosque that could have been erected in the seventh century, when Islam first rode out of Arabia, wielding the sword of revealed holy truths. But then the pavement crumbles and now we are winding along the unprotected cliffs of a twisting alpine avenue, the flatland stretching far, far below us, then disappearing as we take a curve that reveals even more awesome mountains to come.

"We were following one of the great highways of history," Ronald Sinclair wrote of his passage here, sixty-four years ago. "Along it, in the course of successive millennia, invading armies had marched down to attack the fertile lands of the great rivers, while others had fought their way up to overrun the uplands and the great plateau.... One could see that the road had once been in good condition, thanks to the British engineers who worked on it in 1918. But since then no repairs had been carried out."

This has not changed. The driver, a small man in brown who speaks very little English, navigates the treacherous defile with confidence and altogether too much speed, squinting into the sun, cocking his ear to an on-board radio that is bellowing out what must be a mullah's Friday harangue. On the half-hour, for Iranian time is three hours and thirty minutes ahead of Greenwich, Denike extends the antenna of his little shortwave set and tries to audit the news from London, the only link to our own belief-system of unassailable veracity. But reception is defeated by the terrain and the roar of the engine, and the first English words we hear are the driver's, reading off a sign that says "Welcome to Paveh. Most Beautiful Place in Iran."

This is mere boosterism, because Paveh, though blessed with a peer-less situation in the folds of the high peaks—Freya Stark's beloved "tumbled mountains of Kermanshah"—is no St. Moritz. It is, instead, the very picture of Asia: pairs and trios of dark-haired men, standing and smoking and staring as we hurtle by; women in black, tugging wide-eyed, wonder-struck children past market stalls from which tumble oranges, apples, washbasins, scrub brushes, sandals, dollies, toy guns.

Just before we reach the center of the metropolis itself, we see, to the north of the highway, a cluster of low, gray, cinder-block dwellings very much unlike the traditional Iranian farmsteads we have been passing since Bakhtaran. Some of the buildings are roofed and permanent, but others are enclosed in plastic sheeting and patchwork cloth. The entire complex is fenced, and a small guardhouse stands at the entrance.

It is, the driver says, the increasingly permanent temporary refuge granted by Iran to the surviving Kurds of the Iraqi village of Halabja, gassed on Saddam Hussein's orders in 1988. The name of the hamlet brings back a single, haunting snapshot: two infants in a dusty street, eyes still open, mouths agape, frozen in the arms of their father, a family of death. Now, already, another insurrection had been smashed, and again, we would remember the tiniest victims, the ones we had come not to rescue, but to record.

The core of Paveh circumscribes a roundabout in front of a bus terminal, but instead of going halfway around the rotary and proceeding westward, the driver takes a narrow side alley that leads, through a big iron gate, to a driveway that comes to an unceremonious dead end in a ten-foot-high road-block of potatoes. This, it is clear, is Paveh's administrative nerve center, and the driver, explaining that his responsibilities do not extend into this prefecture, means to leave us here. He bounds up the steps into the three-story concrete pile and is gone.

Four days ago, assigned by our superiors to report on one of the most evocative tragedies of our time, we flew off, destined, it seems now, to advance no farther than the impenetrable wall of spuds that now restrains us. We are impelled to start heaving the tubers through the windows of Paveh City Hall, but just when I have picked out a nice meaty one, the driver limps back down the steps with orders to take us to the Kurds. He backs out and we rumble on. At the town exit, another sign, but it does not boast of the city's charms; no one except the Iraqi army ever would have entered Paveh from the west. The placard here, the driver translates, reads: "Saddam Is Wolf."

(In fact, an army of Iraqis did enter Iran through this lofty gate. They were Mojahedin guerrillas, many of them women and young girls, sent across the frontier by Saddam in 1988 in yet another fruitless attempt at an endgame in his war with the Iranian clerics. A report of the aftermath of the Mojahedin incursion describes the route we now ply lined with thousands of corpses covered in early-winter ice.)

The road, bare dirt now, continues to climb toward the frontier. We are on the inside lane, hugging the Zagros Mountains. Looking leftward, there is nothing but air, a drop of two thousand, three thousand, four thousand feet. Brian Denike takes one glance and says, "It's like driving on the edge of a thirty-story building."

Thirty minutes later, two hours out of Bakhtaran and its Friday air of repose, we begin to see the first of the straggling émigrés we have come all this way to shoot. First a few, then hundreds, the road clogged with them and their bundles, the intermittent meadows we pass becoming campsites, life-sustaining water rushing across the gravel road from melting mountain snows, women kneeling at stone-circle cooking pits, slapping whitish pancakes of flour onto heated iron pans, red-faced infants sleeping in sheepskins on the ground. Below us, coming closer now as we begin a steep descent, a brown-foaming river, traversed by a heavy, ancient-looking stone culvert that we now slowly motor across, the bellowing of the waters all that we can hear. We climb up a steep path toward a cluster of buildings and, once again, we halt.

It is an army base. Young men in olive-green fatigues cluster around the van, some with small color portraits of the Ayatollah Khomeini in protective plastic holders attached to a shirt pocket with a safety pin. A larger rendering of the deceased sage is mounted on a pole at the entrance to the area. There are a couple of sturdy green tents, a squarish, stucco main building that serves as offices, barracks and mess hall, and a latrine at the far end of the compound that none of us wants to even think about. Stepping back, looking at the way the buildings oversee the valley, I surmise that this has always been a pretty good spot for a fort. The place is called Do Ab—"two rivers." The more furious of the twin torrents that conjoin in the canyon below this camp is the Sirvan—"water that roars like a lion."

Denike stands on the steps of the command post and speaks in English and sign language with a round man in thick spectacles and civilian clothes who seems to have the run of the place. I walk into the building—the entrance hall is dark and empty, save for some political posters, but down a corridor to the right I pass a couple of sleeping chambers, each with several double-decker iron-frame beds. A few soldiers are snoozing on their cots, and I expect that, shortly, the officer of the day will burst in and roust the recruits, announcing that this is where the foreign friends shall sleep.

This almost happens. We are to be given a place to lie, but it is not in this building. It is in one of the tents I noticed driving up, and as we labor toward it with some of our baggage, out of its door flap springs a peppy little Red Buttons of a concierge, yapping, "Hallo, meester," to each of us in turn. The quarters are dry and clean and, at this hour, empty. The floor is laid with multicolored blankets, more are neatly folded against the rear wall, a single bare bulb and a gas lantern serve for enlightenment, and tacked to one corner is a piece of paper inscribed with flowing Arabic script.

While I am inspecting our green canvas accommodations, an ambulance heaves up in front of our tent. But it brings no casualty. Inside is a muscular driver, tending to fat, with two fully ripe cauliflower ears, and a lean young man in a brown plaid shirt who introduces himself as Sami, a medical intern, and whom, in our flippant way, we immediately rechristen Doctor Sammy.

In the fading hours of day, we prevail on Doctor Sammy to take us to the refugee camp where he has been treating the innumerable sick, though this, he says, is a twenty-minute drive deep into the valley and he already has labored since dawn. I ride with him in the front seat of the ambulance and ask whether the hombre with the vegetarian earlobes might, perchance, have been a champion wrestler. As this is the Iranian national sport and such damage is a common hazard of that game, it is not a very wild guess, but the supposition proves correct and absolutely delights the chauffeur. With an exchange of *kheili khoobs*—"very good," half my Farsi vocabulary—and with the rest of the CBC "Journal" Sirvan Valley Documentary Unit following in their van, it is in high spirits that we wind around a twist in the road and there before us is Hell on Earth.

It is a metropolis of white and green tents, thousands of them, arrayed in serried ranks on a shelf of the mountain that tilts down, as if wanting to spill its load, toward the river in the gorge below. Each pointed canvas roof frames whole families squatting on tiny patches of soil, cooking, crying, children in the road now, running beside us—"Hallo, meester"—and above it all, a plume of blue-gray smoke from a thousand little brushwood campfires in this vast, urgent jamboree.

But this is not Doctor Sammy's camp, and we drive on. He tells me that he is a medical graduate of Tehran University, once the impassioned fountainhead of the Islamic Revolution, but quieter now, and that when he heard of the Kurds' desperation, he made his way up here, though he is not of their nationality.

The third camp we come to is his. Just beyond a water truck at which a hundred men, women and children jostle in a brigade of empty buckets, we turn left, mount the packed-earth slope, and at the summit of the entire encampment, we reach a couple of soiled white tents, and this is the hospital.

Doctor Sammy corrects me: "This is the *new* hospital," he says.

"What happened to the old one?"

"It fell down the mountain in a storm."

For now, at least, the storms have ceased. The camp is bone-dry, except where passing water trucks, leaking life, have left a trail of round, dark spots in the dust. Compared to the panic and desperation of the first few days of the exodus, with Iraqi troops in murderous pursuit and no escape but to climb the naked, impossible peaks, this valley is a godsend.

In yet another convolution of the twisted history of this region, the Iranian government has furnished nearly all the shelters, foodstuffs and water that keep these Kurds alive, helping to save thousands of members of an ethnic minority that, within its own territory, it has long persecuted and despised. (The Grand Ayatollah Khomeini declared a jihad, a holy war, against Iran's Kurds in 1979.) In the Shah's time, and again during the long war with Baghdad, Iran had helped Iraqi Kurds in their frequent, violent attempts to gain an autonomous state, reasoning, perhaps, that the dismemberment of Iraq would set off an emigration of the Iranian Kurds, solving two problems at once. In 1980, Kurdish rebels had claimed dominion over one hundred thousand square kilometers of this mountainous territory, but a month of aerial bombing took care of that. And now Islamic Iran was giving the Iraqi Kurds a sanctuary, a restorative pause until they could return across the mountains and again try to destroy Saddam Hussein.

But the eyes of Doctor Sammy reflect not geopolitics, but love. He is sitting on a cardboard box now, holding someone's infant daughter, pulling down the eyelids, probing the belly, feeling the thickness of the hair. On small squares of brown wrapping paper torn off some carton of supplies, he and several other physicians are writing out prescriptions, and patients—there is a line of them, soundless except for coughing and snuffles—are taking these precious shreds to another little tent, which is the dispensary. Emptied boxes of medicines, many stamped with instructions for careful handling in Italian, are strewn about this makeshift pharmacy, and Doctor Sammy says, "We are out of almost everything."

There is brought to him a baby boy in too much agony to cry. The child—he is about a year old—has been badly burned in an air raid; Kurds cluster around us and claim that Saddam's planes dropped napalm on their town. The boy's face is nearly torn away. Patches of raw red skin contrast with oozing, yellowed wounds. Maurice takes his picture. Finally, we are at work.

We beg another of the doctors to stand off from the crowd and talk to our camera, but the crowd follows him and we are enveloped in the throng. His name is Ahmad Mansour, an army physician from Kirkuk who, sent to Kuwait City in the first days of the August occupation, deserted and made his way back home, and from his home to the Sirvan Valley camps. His wife has come with him, but his father and two brothers, when last he saw them, were in prison in Kirkuk, their probable fate too awful to discuss.

Dr. Mansour is a smallish figure in a hooded khaki jacket. He looks around at the tents, the mountains, the crescent of countrymen that enclose us, and says, "What I feel for these people is my condition also. First I am sad. Then I am very angry. I can do nothing for them."

"Aren't you safe here now?" I ask him. "Are you still afraid?"

"What I am afraid about," he replies, "it has already happened. That my brothers have been taken away. That a lot of people died. That our revolution failed...it is all finished."

We have arrived in the valley, the medical man says, in the trough between two great episodes of misery. The deathrate here has been slowed; Doctor Sammy notes that only five children have perished in the past week, a wonderful refutation of the reported "thousand dead a day" that launched us from our Canadian base. Most of the bodies have been sent to Bakhtaran for autopsy, a probing for the first microbiological

evidence of the epidemics that Dr. Mansour expects will begin to deci-
mate these people when the full heat of summer arrives. Only a couple
of small gravesites have been carved from the side of the mountain,
high up in a field of poppies where women are scavenging for stems and
twigs of kindling wood. It is beginning to get dark. We can do little
more today.

But as we fold our tripod and begin to descend toward the van and
the ambulance for the ride back to the fort, we are corralled by two
young men who seem to have been dropped here by spaceship. They are
about twenty years old, dressed not in turbans and ballooning Kurdish
pantaloons, but more like college kids from Carolina. They are square-
jawed, light-skinned Europeans, and presently they are joined by two
pretty enough girls in hastily arranged head scarves who smile and say,
"We are the Christians."

(The existence of Christians among these people should be unsurpris-
ing. Marco Polo: "In the mountainous parts there is a race of people named
Kurds, some of whom are Christians and other Mahometans. They are all
an unprincipled people, whose occupation it is to rob the merchants.")

The Christian girls, Hannah and Linda, and their brothers (or
boyfriends—this is unclear) are indeed Iraqis, residents of the fire-
bombed city of Suleimaniyah who joined the frantic getaway but who
now seem to wish they hadn't.

"Here, the Christians and the Muslims are all forced together,"
Hannah says. "It is no good. And I hate this scarf."

The boys also are looking for escape. They tell us that they have relatives in North America, in Philadelphia, they think, and somewhere in
Canada. I go down the list: Montreal, Toronto, Winnipeg, and so on, and
they stop me when I get to Vancouver. That's the place, definitely, maybe.
We explain that the best way for them to reach their kin is to appear on
Canadian television. Like city couples casually arranging a night of dinner
and dancing, we agree to meet on the morrow. Then they go back to a
donated tent in a metropolis of misfortune and I climb in the ambulance and
ride away. At the army barracks, the driver who has brought us all the way
from Bakhtaran in the van declares that he will go back to cosmopolitan
Paveh for his rest, but he promises to return at five o'clock in the morning,
to drive us to the Iraqi border, westward and upward still.

At dusk, back at our square green tent, in a community of divided loy-
alites and common exhaustion, we apportion the blankets and sleeping

space to ourselves and to a pair of Iranian guardsmen, whose eyes never leave us and the extraterrestrial wonders we have brought along. These include Denike's shortwave radio, tuned now to the BBC, tins of Del Monte fruit cocktail, long, spicy links of Tiller's Hungarian Sausage, made from the meat of forbidden pigs, and little tetra-pack boxes of orange juice.

I offer up a carton of juice to the two soldiers, which causes them to wave their hands furiously and to pass an index finger across their Adam's apples. They think it's alcoholic. *"Jumhuryeh-e-Islami,"* they say. This is the Islamic Republic. The Islamic Republic will cut their throats, and ours.

20 APRIL
Sirvan Valley

On each side of our tent, two small openings, perhaps ten inches square, have been cut into the heavy canvas and the flaps have been folded up and buttoned, creating tiny windows in the taut green walls. The entrance pleat has been drawn into place and sealed with wooden toggles. The lantern has been put out, the stove extinguished.

Unable to sleep, my eyes latched open by fascination and fear, I fumble in the knapsack for my glasses, and through the portholes, I search for the first signs of day. It may be only midnight—I don't know. To my right, the cameraman, the sound man and the producer sputter and whine like chain saws attacking metallic trees. A signal on Denike's digital watch emits a tinkling peep-peep, tolling the hours. I hear it five times.

But I hear no dogs, no cock's crow, none of the satanic cries of jackals on the mountainside that once, in Islamabad, woke me, shaking in terror, reaching for the phone to report that little babies were being murdered in the hills above.

As my eyes adjust to the yellowish dimness—outside, a bare bulb has been left on to illuminate the poster of Khomeini at the barracks gate—I detect more huddled bundles on the floor beyond my feet. I must have slept, a little—three more soldiers have crept into our tent to pass the night.

Though the sky beyond the little cutouts betrays no hint of dawn, one of the military men rises, noiselessly. My partners never even flinch as he steps over them. Turning to the lettered sheet of paper pinned at a corner of the southern wall, he begins his devotions. I realize now that this is the camp mosque, that the calligraphy points the path to Mecca, toward which the Iranian soldier, kneeling and bowing, whispers verses that only Allah and I can hear. I am sorry to be trespassing on his faith. Like ancient pilgrims on some holy quest, we irreligious wastrels of the jet-plane age are sleeping in the very shrine.

Here, the linkup to the circuitry of our own century is as tenuous as I have ever known. The umbilical is a sickeningly steep and narrow highway toward which, if he keeps his promise, our driver should just be starting out now on a windless, crystal morning. We have a radio that magically amplifies words spoken, in our language, a million miles away, but we possess no equipment—though such has been invented—with which to make a reply. The sense of disconnection and invisibility is dizzying. As I lie in the swaddling, on the moraine of an unnamed mountain, I imagine Linda at home, turning the leaves of my old, worn college atlas, and on the page marked "The Near and Middle East," a tiny light flashing to mark my sleeping place, a radar echo of our dislocated lives.

Today is our seventeenth anniversary. We met, each vacationing with a friend, a couple of years into our working adulthoods, beside the swimming pool of a small hotel on the Caribbean coast of Venezuela. She was a hospital dietician from Kingston, Ontario, working in Montreal, intrepid enough to attend home games of the Club de Hockey Canadien by herself, in standing room. I was a sophomoric sportswriter with a college-town paper, salaried at fifty-four dollars weekly, plus fifteen bucks more for reading the scores at noon and five-thirty on the lowest-rated AM radio station in New York State.

A year, a month and a day after we met, when we both were twenty-four, we were married in the living room of what once, long before, had been the handsome brownstone home of a mayor of Troy, N.Y. The house retained little of its turn-of-the-century elegance: the mahogany wainscotting was still in place, but squirrels staged all-night nut-bowling tournaments in the crawl space above our bed, and a couple of times, small bats invaded the living room, sending Linda diving for a closet while I set after the creatures with a hockey stick.

The episodes with the flying rodents mark the only times I've ever seen her foolishly frightened, though fear has been the measure of her life since long before she was burdened with my wanderings and me. When she was thirteen, a lanky, long-haired stripling growing up just a few yards from the Lake Ontario shore, she began to suffer terribly from the cold, shivering, turning blue and weak, clearly unwell, yet her malaise was indefinable. Her teachers even forbade her to wear slacks to school, though she walked freezing miles each way. They thought her complaints mere sniveling.

On the evening of her sixteenth birthday, after long spells of exhaustion, she fell into a coma and her parents were called to Kingston General Hospital to make their goodbye. It was not expected that she would live the night. But it was just then that a young intern drew some inference that her sickness might be identifiable. Blood samples were sent to the Mayo Clinic. A course of corticosteroids was begun. Three days later, she was awake.

The diagnosis, spectacularly correct, was systemic lupus erythematosus, a chronic, sometimes fatal, disease of the connective tissues—the joints, the lining of the heart and lungs, the kidneys, the skin—that the writer Flannery O'Connor, dying in the nineteen-sixties of its unpredictable malice, called, simply, "the Wolf." There was no cure then and there is none now, though the steroids—Linda has been taking them, daily, for twenty-six years—mitigate the inflammations. Much more is known today about lupus: it is a classic autoimmune disease, similar to rheumatoid arthritis, in which the body's defenses are turned, for no known reason, against its own organs—a silent, internal, civil war.

I once interviewed a man who had put down a five-thousand-dollar deposit toward a seat on the first passenger flight into space. He'd been everywhere else. The man said, "Some people get homesick. I get sickness for going away." So it has always been with me, and with Linda; why else would we have collided, like atoms in a cyclotron, in Venezuela, of all places? The disease has never kept her bounded, despite the occasional retreat. In 1975, she wound up in the hospital, on iced sheets, with a fever of 106°F after being given a contraindicated smallpox vaccination. (We were going to Guatemala to see the Mayan ruins, and did anyway.) In 1981, I was covering the Toronto Blue Jays on a road trip to Oakland when my office called in the seventh inning to report that my wife had collapsed at the Eaton Centre with a violent convulsive seizure. Bobby Doerr, a Hall of Fame infielder, drove me to the airport for the anguished flight home.

From these episodes, and others, Linda recovered sufficiently to walk into a doctor's office in Kowloon in 1983—we were on our way into China, with me still greenish from the swing through India and bloody Sri Lanka—and to be told, cheerily, by the Canadian-trained physician, "Oh, so you are going to live in Beijing. Well, be careful. Beijing is very filthy. If you get hepatitis, you will die."

Linda had decided, long before, that she'd rather perish in the course of a life of edifying travel than cloister herself fearfully in the foyer of the Wellesley Hospital. Now we were headed toward the proving ground of her convictions. Shaken by the doctor's glib warning, we met the Beijing correspondent of the Washington *Post*—he was in Hong Kong on leave— and asked about medical care in the People's Republic. He answered, "The only thing you can get in a Chinese hospital is sicker."

Our first few weeks in China threw us down a spiral of reciprocal delirium. Linda saw some green stains on the inner lid of a tin of orange juice and, having already swallowed some, thought she had poisoned us. She gasped from the hideous air pollution, found dark spots on her tongue and gums, and each time, Dr. Hong Kong increased her dose of steroids. And when this overmedication made her dizzy, she felt that she was about to have another seizure and took even more of the pills.

Just after New Year's, 1984, she learned that her father would need major surgery for bowel cancer and, the same day, that a fellow patient she had known through the Ontario Lupus Association had suddenly and unexpectedly died. That night, ghost faced, she told me she thought she was having a heart attack.

She slumped at the steps of our apartment building in the Diplomatic Compound while I raced behind to the tiny garage and, backing out, hooked the fender on the door frame and tore the front bumper off the *Globe and Mail*'s Toyota hatchback. We raced to Capital Hospital to the east of the Forbidden City. I had memorized the Mandarin words for "lupus erythematosus" from the dictionary: *hongban langchuang,* meaning "red-patched wolf." In a curtained cubicle of the Foreigners' Wing, a doctor gently took Linda's pulse and assured her that there was nothing wrong. She knew, of course, all about lupus; I'd gotten the Chinese tones wrong, anyway. Five years later, I'd stand in the courtyard of the same grand hospital, in a crowd of parents, friends and relatives pleading to learn who had been brought here, dying, from Tian'anmen Square.

This was life with someone living with lupus: in Taiwan, another mad dash to a hospital with pains and palpitations, a long wait among the gashed and baffled clients of the emergency room, then a large, beaming man approaching us and saying, "Hello. I am Dr. Dai." In Kowloon, an American missionary physician, a drawling Louisianan, telling us, "I'd burn chicken feathers in the corner if I thought it would help." He didn't have to. Linda yanked herself out of it. She and the Wolf are an even match. What she really had was hiatus hernia.

Two months after these unnerving scenes, we flew from Calcutta to the reclusive Himalayan kingdom of Bhutan. (Linda was probably the first lupus patient from Kingston, Ontario, to go there.) We were installed in bare-walled, concrete quarters and fed millet porridge and boiled milk.

A couple of hours after I'd returned from an interview with the tiny nation's young, forward-looking sovereign, leaving Linda buried under an avalanche of blankets, a knock at the door revealed a bearer in traditional Bhutanese costume of robe, boots and black knee socks. He held out parcels, a brilliantly painted Buddhist scroll, masks, an album of postage stamps.

"Gifts from His Majesty," the bearer said.

Then he looked over at the bed and saw Linda. Only her face was visible, pale as an egg, peeping from the pile of quilts. She was wearing the same toque I have on now, in the tent in Iran, mummified in my own woolen wrappings on another shelf of the great mountains of Asia, on our anniversary morning.

The porter gasped.

"Oh," he said. "Madame is suffering." Eight thousand miles apart on April 20, I am suffering, too.

Like Chico and Harpo Marx, assigned to shadow Groucho in *Duck Soup*, the driver fool us. He no show up.

By six-thirty, we've already been out in front of the tent for an hour, ever since first light, waiting, pacing, watching for the dusty white van to cross the bridge across the foaming Sirvan, far below the army camp. It remains cloudless and dry, an incalculable blessing for the Kurds, some of whom we now see walking along the gray gravel road on the opposite side of the valley, bent double under enormous bundles of bedclothes, burlap and wool.

Already, Maurice's plan to shoot the exiles as they awaken to light their cooking fires and bring out their dead is unachievable. The sun is arcing up to vault the lesser peaks. We are too late, too slow, too stupid.

"Did you really believe he was going to come back for us?" I ask Denike smugly. His attempt at independent coverage seems to have crashed in flames. We should have joined the pack as organized by Islamic Guidance.

"He said 'five o'clock,'" the producer snaps back. "You heard him. 'Five. Five. Five.'"

"He was just mimicking our English," I reiterate. "Maybe he thought we meant five in the afternoon."

While this pointless vituperation proceeds, Maurice and Chris stand aside, holding their tongues. They've seen this act before: producer and reporter, Chico and Harpo, a dialogue of morons.

Finally, Maurice begs to interject.

"Why don't we walk?" he offers. There is no alternative. The army camp is devoid of ambulances, freight trucks, jeeps. There is little sense in all of us waiting for the promised van. The driver need only be strangled once, should he ever arrive.

So we set off. Brian remains at the bivouac, to try to commandeer some vehicle, any vehicle, to take us on the absolutely essential run to see what is happening at the Iraqi border, which, according to the refugees we met last evening, is either ten, twenty, thirty or fifty tortuous kilometers west of here. Without even arranging a meeting point if he does locate some wheels, we strip down to the lightest possible amount of gear—about a hundred and fifty pounds of it—and start tramping.

The human traffic on the winding road is increasing now—whole families, with bedrolls and cooking pots, infants and hunchbacked crones—are coming toward us. For them, migration has become the only constant. We see groups of them huddled at the bridge where the roads and rivers converge. Now a truck halts at the crossroad and the crowd surges forward, heaving their swag into the cargo deck and pommeling their way aboard, some falling back in failure as the machine begins to roll toward the city of Paveh and greater Iran beyond. Yet others cross the stone abutment and start walking the other way, toward Iraq, searching, it would seem, for kinsmen encamped in others of these sudden, sprawling villages of cloth.

("It is a wonderful experience to see them on the march," wrote the British diplomat, C. J. Edmonds, CMG, CBE, in his book, *Kurds, Turks and Arabs* of Kurds on this treacherous trail in the nineteen-twenties. "...their tents, cooking pots, sacks of grain and household utensils piled up on the backs of ponies, cattle and women.")

Every few moments, Maurice spots something separate from the wider scene—a woman's weary face, a tearful child—and we stop and set up the tripod and Chris disengages the dead weight of the recorder from his shoulder. A thick black cable connects the camera with the deck; every time our march resumes, the attachment must be unscrewed and the wiring coiled like a cattleman's lasso at the sound man's left hip. Yet our presence invokes little attention from the people passing by. They are far too weak to be curious; we are hardly the first they've seen of foreigners come to document their dispersal; and the accoutrements we carry, so precious to us, are valueless to save even a single life.

Walking uphill, we are parading along the cusp of morning, following the sun as it plays along the cliffside. A switchback brings us around to face the brilliance and the effect is incandescent—the oblique rays illuminating the smoke from the valley campfires, deep in the roaring gorge; "the bitter and sweet," a Kurdish poem limns, "of the wayfarer's world."

We are trying to capture this bedazzlement when a truck approaches and I jump into the roadway to flag it down. It has not been sent by Brian—the driver and passenger speak no English and we get nowhere with a pantomime of a tall man with white hair and a beard. But they let us heave our equipment in the back and we climb into the flatbed, begging them to go slowly, slowly, so that Maurice can make a "traveling shot" of the tents and the people and the smoke and the brilliant blue sky.

We've gone about five clicks in the truck, through a couple of refugee camps, when it suddenly occurs to me that I don't know whether or not we've passed the place where we did the filming yesterday. I recall a medical tent at the high point of the community, and a water truck where two dirt tracks diverged, but, typically, I was too busy joshing with the ex-grappler with the extraordinary earlobes to gauge the distance back to our fort. And Chris and Maurice had been lying in the body of the ambulance and never saw the landmarks at all. We're lost.

Now the truck driver motions that we should get out. This camp—it might be the one we're seeking, or it might not—is as far as he goes. I request two more minutes, time enough to essay a stand-up—a "piece to camera"—from the elevated cargo bed.

I've had the words in my head, tumbling like laundry in the dryer, for hours. I've recited the sentences to myself at least a hundred times. Maurice angles Lucille the camera as far away from me as he can without falling off the truck. He gives me a wave and says, as he always does, "Go for it, cowboy."

This is what I say: "This is the second chapter of the Book of Exodus of the Kurdish people. The first was their escape—by foot, by donkey, by truck and by taxi—their flight from death, or toward it. Now—this instant Calcutta of canvas and plastic sheeting, where the Kurds are gathered, but still not free, not safe, not healthy...and certainly, not home."

(A "Journal" legend holds that I can recite, on command, every stand-up I've ever done. This was true for the first couple of seasons, but no longer holds. There have been just too many. Still, dozens of these ephemeral, single-use paragraphs remain in storage, burned in permanently by the process of forced memorization.)

When we dismount, and the truck rumbles off, we begin to walk back toward the last camp we've passed, accompanied, inevitably, by two dozen small, yelping boys. But this can't be the right place—there is no sign of the medical tent on the upper hillside, or the parked ambulance. So we reverse direction, three more vagrants on the dusty trail, climbing, climbing, with no ponies, cattle or women to carry our gear and no way of knowing if we've come too far, or not far enough.

Rounding one bend, I notice a small collection of tents far above on the mountainside and, parked in the roadway, a battered Datsun with a sign on the roof: TAXI. As I've noted in the piece to camera, many of the Kurds have escaped their ravaged cities by hack.

"Let's take a cab!" I announce to Maurice and Chris, who think I've gone dippy from the sun. But when I stand next to the little white-and-orange car, looking up at the refugee encampment and twisting my right hand back and forth as if turning the ignition, sure enough, a tall young man turbaned in the Kurdish habit comes stutter-stepping down the cliff, jingling a set of keys. He burbles something that I assume means, "Where to, pal?"

Ten minutes later, we are back at the medical tent we filmed last night. Doctor Sammy from Tehran is treating a man with what appears to be a bullet wound in the throat, and another fellow, a nurse, comes over and tells me that he has a brother in Toronto who works as a delivery driver for Pizza Pizza. (Had we traversed another few switchbacks, we'd have come to the camp ourselves.) Again, the cacophony. I close my eyes for a moment and take in the coughing, the crying, the children shouting, and when I open them again a small, twisted man is standing in front of me, holding up two mangled, fingerless hands. No one, we are told, has died overnight.

We are walking down the hill from the makeshift hospital, looking for the Christians, Hannah and Linda and the others, when I realize that only Brian has their tent number, their address in this expanse of gathered grief. There is a crowd of men around us now, and so I begin the familiar chorus: "Hello. We are from Canada. English—does anyone speak English? Hello." And I search the faces for someone with eyeglasses, which in many countries marks one who has been to school, and one who has been to school is most likely to have absorbed bits of the world's common tongue.

Immediately, three men—all without eyeglasses—chorus in affirmation. Announcing that we will interview each in turn, we follow the first man back to his tent. The setup is arranged: the man, a bank manager from Kirkuk, sits on a boulder with his tiny son between his knees. His wife, who also worked in the bank, and who attended university, is placed a few feet away, with her seven-year-old daughter. Maurice poses the family like cut flowers in a bowl. The children are admonished not to say a word, and never do, not even the baby.

We explore the encompassing aspects of their exile. These are not mountain people, not peasants, though they have been reduced to mendicants, dependent on the world's charity.

"We live," the husband says, "we live...like...." He struggles for the word, murmurs it in Kurdish.

"Like Neanderthal people," the woman explains. It is a brilliant simile; it condenses their sudden descent.

"Like cave people," I submit, reinforcing the idea.

"Cave people," the mother nods. And the husband adds, "No water. We cannot food. We cannot washing. We cannot do anything here."

I hear myself asking the woman, "Are you afraid that your children will die in this place?" I'm ashamed of the words before they're uttered.

"Of course I will be afraid," she replies. "We will die in thirst. My children will die."

"What do the children say?" I ask the banker.

"They say, 'Baba? Where is my toy? Baba? When we go to our home'?"

When I turn around to check if Maurice is happy with the framing of the picture, I see Brian Denike standing behind him. He has captured a government van—not "our" van; that's probably in Monte Carlo by now—and we will be able to proceed to the border. I have no idea how he found us.

The second man we have promised to interview is a surveyor who once worked for the Iraqi army, an unintentioned draftsman of Saddam's militarization. He, too, has been reduced to living in a prior millennium, queuing for water, scrabbling for food.

"When you survey the faces of the Kurdish people," I ask him, pleased with myself, "what do you see?"

"All are sad," the man replies. "All are angry. And all inside they are not happy. There is no happiness here."

Now we set off in search of the Christians, particularly the girls who told me last night that this life in the refugee camps of Iran was even worse than Saddam's Iraq, because at least with Saddam, you could get a drink.

We have their locator—tent number 44-9. In barely two weeks, the helter-skelter of the escape has been replaced by a rudimentary suburbanization, a segmenting into neighborhoods—the upper camp, the lower camp, the riverbank. Soon enough, I'm sure, there will be postal codes.

The Christians—Hannah and her sisters, and the two young men who have relatives in Philadelphia and Vancouver but can't remember their names—seem delighted to see us again. They chirp and giggle and make it absolutely definite that they will not appear on camera because, as Hannah says, "Saddam will see." We can't force them to broadcast their plaint. I wonder why anyone ever agrees to talk with us. In their shoes, I would search out a quiet corner and cry.

All this time, we have been doggedly followed by the third man we had promised to interview, a jaunty little English teacher from Suleimaniyah whose name, as he spells it out for us, is Safdi. We immediately decide not to question him, but to hire him as interpreter for the drive to the border. He seems delighted. Standing back to allow him to enter the "Journal" van, I bow and say, "Safdi first," and climb aboard. He gets my joke immediately. At least someone does.

Already in the front seat is a driver, solidly built, and his assistant, whose only function seems to be to occupy most of the rest of the cab. I am on a jump seat by the sliding side panel, Safety First is perched on the food hamper that Denike—bless 'im—has thought to bring from our tent, and the crew is lying on blankets in the back of the van, Maurice with his long legs cantilevered against the ceiling and Chris, shorter, braced between the tripod and the drinks cooler with his head on a battery bag. In the glove compartment are the business cards of Charles Glass and a dozen other reporters and producers, who were up here reporting this sad portrait of human suffering while we were still home in Canada, fat and warm.

In this humiliated posture, we begin the harrowing ascent toward the line in the atlas where Persia concludes and the Arab world begins. Every few minutes, the driver halts to greet some straggler along the road. In the customary manner, they loudly kiss each other's cheeks, usually three times, in one case an extraordinary six, and the recipient of all this osculation, a spindly geezer spewing gracious *al-salaams*, is invited to join us and seats himself *to the left* of the driver, making it four up front, and four behind.

We must be at least eight thousand feet up now, nearly as high as the snow on the magnificent peaks beside us, the river Sirvan, barely a glimmer, deep in the canyon it has carved. The road no longer deserves the title; it is a red dirt track, one lane wide, along which, as we travel, we are waved down by a woman in the center of the path, crying, holding a two-year-old girl who is bleeding from gruesome sores on her forehead.

"She wants a ride to the hospital," Safety translates, but the driver waves her off; no room. Angrily, I point to the associate chauffeur in the front seat, and the hobo squeezed flat between the driver and the door. But the helmsman dismisses my entreaty and starts up again, toward the border. I write in my notebook, "Imagine in Canada saying no to woman with wounded child"; but this is not Canada. It is Kurdistan, and there is misery enough for all.

The roadside settlements thicken—sheets of plastic wrapping held by sticks; piles of rocks supporting a carpet that serves as a family's roof. These are not organized camps, but rudimentary shelters erected by people too late, or too weak, to march the last few miles down into the cities of the Red Crescent, to join the cavemen with college degrees. One old man is simply sitting on a slab of bricks in the fierce noon sun, staring out at the spectacular canyon.

"That must be the worst part," Denike says as we pass him. "Waiting for George Bush."

We reach a place where a river of snow-melt surges across the road, born of a gay waterfall. We stop and the crew tumbles out of their contorted repose to capture the children splashing, the women wringing their meager washing in the foam of the rushing stream.

Bucking and heaving as we ford the rocky torrent, we turn another hairpin and here, finally, is the town of Nowsud that marks the end of Iran.

The village clings to the mountainside like a Tibetan lamasery, its brown, mud-brick shops and government offices crumbling into the roadway, the result, Safety says, of Iraqi bombing during the eight years of war. (The city also was burned to the ground by Ottomans in 1914, and sacked by various Umayyads, Abbasids, Hasanwayhids, Kakwayhids, Selcuks and Timurids, back through immemorial centuries of ceaseless war.) The effect is of a play-city of Lego blocks, kicked down in a child's tantrum. But everywhere, among the fallen buildings, the Kurds have found shelter.

And beyond Nowsud, in what must be Iraq, a serpentine of unmoving cars and trucks and buses snakes until lost from view around a corner, the vehicles piled high with bedding and belongings, a trailer park of emigrants for whom the highway has become home. The cars point toward Iran but are not bound there; proximity to the frontier seems to be sufficient. A small booth with corrugated metal sides stands at the Iranian side of the boundary. A couple of soldiers in green fatigues conduct a desultory frisk of people strolling into the Islamic state. On the other side of the dividing line—it is a few strands of barbed wire, tacked to wooden posts—what must once have been the Iraqi Customs house stands abandoned, its roof blown off, its walls collapsing and an Iranian flag flapping triumphantly from a pole.

Glibly crossing what must be one of the most murderously contested boundary lines on earth—millions have died in various struggles along its alpine sinuosity and its sea-level continuation into the head of the Persian Gulf—Maurice and I take a half step over the barbed wire and declare ourselves in Saddam Hussein's Iraq, but the humor is lost on Brian and Chris, who, a mere three months ago, were hell-bent to escape it.

Gazing around at the top of the world, I notice what seems a strangely familiar vista—a pattern of terraced farmers' fields carved into the sides of the mountain. Of course—this is the aspect I saw on CNN, back home, only last Monday, the report I'd cited as evidence that there was no reason for us to make the journey at all. But we had made it—via London, Vienna, Tehran, Asseman Airlines, taxicab, minivan and walking—to stand in the identical location on an absolutely splendid day with nothing of interest going on.

This enchanting, dismaying reverie is broken by two events. First, there is a loud detonation down in the valley that makes everyone jump. Then, I look farther up the hillside and there is the CNN base camp, still in place. Somehow, they have maneuvered a full-sized house trailer up this insane donkey path, plus an enormous satellite up-link dish, a smaller umbrella for telephone transmission, a line of pup tents and a Stonehenge of giant packing crates that makes our wimpish thirty cases seem as trifling as a schoolboy's pencil box.

And inside the trailer, which is filled with monitors and editing gear and gizmos, sits one of the stars of the cable-news firmament, Christiane Amanpour, a battle-hardened correspondent with one of the most beautiful voices on air. Timidly, for she is pecking out a script on a laptop computer as I climb the trailer's stairs, I introduce myself and mention that I'd seen her report last Monday morning. That's just great, she smirks; that was the day their up-link went out of order and they haven't filed anything since.

"We're waiting on spare parts," Amanpour says.

"How long will you be up here? Six months?" I tease the star.

"Screw that," the star replies.

Backing out of the trailer, recovering my composure, I find Safety First and ask him what the big explosion was.

"No problem," the English teacher says. "Is Iraqi mine blowing up horse."

Descending to the level of the furious Sirvan, crossing the stone bridge at the Do Ab confluence, I begin to understand why, in the midst of anguish and bereavement, a family clings to a couple of numerals chalked on the wall of a tent. There, just up the driveway to the army base, past the portrait of the Ayatollah, below the solid stone fort, is our foursquare canvas citadel that now, to me, is Home. Another lap completed, another traverse of the camps complete, I devour a can of chunk white tuna, Brian fiddles with his shortwave receiver, Chris pratfalls into the womb of blankets to begin what will be fifteen hours of uninterrupted sleep and Maurice bowlegs to the soldier's Neanderthal latrine, takes one step inside, turns around and says, "Ahhh—forget it."

As darkness falls, we gather the covers about us again and the little porter brews sweet, milky tea. Some soldiers, lolling outside by the water spigot, accidentally bump into the side of the tent, shaking the frame, and the superintendent, whose only English expostulation to this point has been the universal "Hallo, meester," leaps to his feet, sticks his head through one of the little windows and barks, "Shuttup goddamn fucking," and, delighted with himself, plops back down.

"Engleesh very good," he declares, slapping himself on the chest. "Engleesh too much."

Tonight, I awaken only once to look out through the cuts in the canvas at the Asian sky beyond. My crew, again, is performing its lushly orchestrated Symphony in Z. Again, a few Iranian soldiers have found a resting place on the hard, uneven ground beneath our gabled roof, and little Mister Shuttup Goddamn is balled up like a chipmunk in the corner.

These mountains have known war and invasion, the jangling caravans of ancient tradesmen and now the panicked flight of a shattered people. But tonight we lie together—Muslims, Christians, a Jew—and the thought takes me as I lie in the shadows that all men are truly brothers...as long as they're asleep.

21 APRIL
Do Ab-Bakhtaran-Tehran

$\mathbf{A}$t a little after seven in the clear, brilliant morning, with the sun just beginning to throw its gilded coverlet over the Sirvan Valley, Maurice announces that to hell with everything, he is going to go take a crap.

The rest of us are folding our blankets and searching our boots and shoes for somnolent scorpions and getting dressed in the same reeking duds we've had on since Friday morning. Breakfast, again, from the hamper: crackers, peanut butter, the last of the canned fruit cocktail. And now oranges are passed around the tent by our host, Mister Shuttup God-damn Fucking.

We are hauling the gear out through the door flap and counting it when a glint in the east presages Maurice's return from the latrine. It's his smile.

The government van arrives to haul us back over Pike's Peak and down to Paveh, where, in theory, the driver who stiffed us yesterday will be waiting to ferry us to Bakhtaran International Airport and the chartered jet to Tehran. There is no sign of Safety First, who, having already been paid off, does not seem compelled to hike twenty miles uphill just to kiss us goodbye. Doctor Sammy, the Grappler, the Christians—all are absent.

As we are stuffing ourselves into the vehicle to depart, Denike nimbly slips a rolled-up U.S. hundred-dollar bill into the mitt of Mister Shuttup, who makes an unconvincing show of refusing, pretends to decline a second time, then stuffs the greenback into the folds of his harem pants with deep bows and salaams.

It is probably worth a couple of months' salary in "goo-goos," if Mister Shuttup receives any salary at all. (He must have some dough, though; last night, he offered five dollars for Denike's four-hundred-dollar shortwave set.) But it is not unusual for us to drop a comparative fortune on our local aides. On a shoot in what then was Leningrad, when we paid off a fixer we knew as Olga from the Volga, she calculated the recompense to be equal to *nine years' pay* at the prevailing black-market rate, dollars to rubles. (She was only working part-time at her regular job.) Then she had the nerve to complain that our stipend wasn't enough to purchase a personal computer.

In the van now, ready to roll out, I can muster only a few, final pro forma *masalei neests* and *kheili khoobs*, and the tentman replies, his voice bouncing off the walls of the canyon, "Engleesh very good too much shuttup goddamn fucking meester," and then he is gone.

Heading southeast, into the rising sun, we are on the outside lip of the gravel road, the right-side wheels kicking pebbles over the precipice onto the rusted wrecks of smashed vehicles far, far below. The highway is clear—we've left all the refugee camps behind us, and only a few food and water trucks pass us going westward.

Suddenly, the road ahead is blocked by a lock-step convoy of oncoming cars. Getting closer, we see that they're not moving—it's a caravan of small coupes, taxicabs, lorries and even a white school bus, parked nose to tail, facing toward the border, two hours away.

Women and children are sitting in clusters in a yellow-flowered meadow beside the road, some of them hurriedly pulling scarves over their heads as we approach, and a carbuncle of men is growing next to the school bus, arguing and gesticulating as we slow down to see what's going on.

Three things become instantly obvious: they are Kurds, they are fixing to go home to Iraq, and for some reason they aren't moving. I wade into the knot of breadwinners and look for someone wearing glasses. He turns out, of course, to speak excellent English—he says he owned an electronics shop in Suleimaniyah, now looted and abandoned—and explains that they have been stuck here for three days because the officials of the Paveh district won't let them leave.

"Why will the Iranians not let us go?" the man asks me.

"I don't know," I tell him. "I'm not the Iranian government."

"Do you think Saddam is good man or bad man?" another fellow, a plumpish taxi driver, interjects.

"Very bad man," I offer.

"Then why did Americans not kill Saddam?"

"I am not the American government," I say.

"Don't tell me 'you are not,' 'you are not,' 'you are not,'" the electronics man snaps. "What can you do to help us?"

"Well," I reply suavely, "I can tell your story to my people." I give the high sign to producer Denike, who is getting the same treatment from another group, and he and the crew pick a spot and set up.

We knock off a couple of interviews. The men say that they've heard on the BBC that their leadership, meeting in Baghdad with the previously genocidal Saddam, has reached an agreement on significant autonomy and security for the Kurdish nation within Hussein's Iraq.

"And you believe that?" I ask each of the men, in turn.

"We must believe," says one. "They are our leaders. Yes, we believe."

This, however, does not solve the problem of the exit permit from the local prefecture. I explain that with tens of thousands of their brethen finally settled into camps a few miles up the valley, with adequate drinking water and provisions, the Iranians might be concerned that the sight of two dozen cars and buses heading confidently homeward could touch off another mad, mass migration.

"But we want to go home," the shopkeeper persists. "Why will Iranians not let us go home?"

"I am not the Iranian government."

Two hours later, we are back at the municipal building in Paveh, leaning on the dust-covered van and eating Fruit Roll-Ups while the driver, who speaks no Engleesh, goes inside and tries to rouse someone to decide how to most expeditiously get rid of us. At worst, I tell the boys, we can get taxis here for the descent to Bakhtaran on the arid plains. And we won't starve—the Matterhorn of unpeeled potatoes in the driveway is undiminished.

And unless Mister Shuttup was a government mole, we've been able to pull off what I never envisioned: wandering around the Islamic Republic on our own, without the Iranians' interference and, it is true, without much of their help. Now comes the best news of all: the driver, finding no one around with the authority to allow him to abandon us, is going to take us all the way to Bakhtaran himself, which is *kheili khoob*, indeed.

In this ebullient spirit, we inch through downtown Paveh in an aneurism of trucks and buses, crawling past a vest-pocket park in the center of a traffic circle upon which are encamped a dozen Kurdish families, these people having made the deepest penetration of Iran of any refugees we've seen.

Just east of Paveh, as the highway, paved now, begins to flatten out, we come to the complex we'd noted on the way up, the semi-permanent housing area for the survivors of Saddam's gassing of the village of Halabja in 1988. (The people of that village, it was reported, were being punished for their disinclination to fight back when an Iranian spearhead captured the area.) A chain across the entry road blocks our path, but when the soldier in the guardhouse asks if we're expected by the camp administration, the driver nods and says something and the chain is unhooked. We pull up next to a low, sandy, cinder-block slum and the crew prepares to take some pictures.

It's just the scene we need to end our piece: images to demonstrate how an exodus, once begun, is rarely reversed. We'll need to shoot some small children so I can write a line of script about how sad it is that they've never seen their homeland, and we'll try to find an English-speaker to tell us about life in this endless exile.

Maurice and Chris have gone up a hill at the west flank of the camp to get the wide shot, to "establish" the entire area in the viewer's mind. Then they'll descend to take the close-ups, the shacks of four bare walls with a plastic-sheet roof, the toddlers pooping in the muck near the water pipe, the idle men with vacant, hopeless eyes.

I'm trying to compose a stand-up in my head when I hear shouting from the hill. I turn to see Maurice jostling with a big man in a greenish uniform, and now they are carrying Lucille and the tripod down toward the van and I know we are in big, big trouble.

The soldier, or *komiteh* man, whatever he is, barks a few commands and we shrug them off with weak smiles: *no comprendo*. This is insufficient. Someone is found with a few words of the world language. We are asked for our papers, our invitation, our authorization. But all we can flourish is a plasticized card that says, "This identification is for the exclusive use of the bearer, an official representative of the CBC, which will appreciate courtesies extended."

It's even repeated in Arabic, a legacy, one suspects, of the Beirut years. But there's no Farsi, and, even if there were, the only courtesy extended here probably would be the offer of a blindfold before we are shot. Or it could be worse than execution: the officer may confiscate our videotapes.

I try to force myself in these excruciating situations to keep my trap shut and let more grown-up colleagues do the talking. The "Journal" annals are replete with tales of harrowing confrontation: a crew imprisoned in Argentina during the Falklands war; the unshakeable Ann Medina talking her way out of a PLO ambuscade in Lebanon by producing a photograph of herself with Arafat; another unit held hostage in Ghana and made to watch a film of a hapless tourist being mauled and eaten by lions. In January, it was Chris Davies who talked his team out of Iraq when, after the horrific dash across the desert in the opening hours of the air war, border officials at the frontier with Jordan wanted to send them all back to Baghdad, for target practice.

In 1983, on the very first day of my first whimpering foray into foreign correspondence, I was hauled out of a temple courtyard in Colombo by a Sri Lankan rifleman and plunked down on a bench in the sun. Also involved was a reporter from the Voice of America. We had been interviewing the terrified survivors of a massacre of Tamil civilians. After about an hour of just letting us sit there, they took the VOA man's calling card with a big smile, waved off mine from "Canada's National Newspaper," and hailed us a taxi. That was my closest brush with the law, until now.

It is difficult to know, in these cases, whether the detaining officer is curious, furious or merely looking for a bribe. The biggest fear is always that the tapes will be seized, as at the end of a month-long project called "Crime and Punishment in the Soviet Union," when a certain Captain Albin of the Leningrad P.D. told us he'd have to review all of our "raw" cassettes before giving us permission to depart.

We were afraid he'd want to confiscate our best stuff: the freshly butchered corpse of a Mr. Yuri Pautov, dispatched with one expert thrust to the aorta by his loving spouse, with a kitchen knife. But Captain Albin had an ulterior motive for his last-minute visit to our suite. He proposed an exchange of gifts. We would pay his way to Canada for what he called the "grand premiere" of the documentary. In trade, he'd brought each of us a wooden spoon.

While the debate with the officer proceeds, Maurice, the old pro, has left the camera running, never looking through the viewfinder but shifting position every once in a while to capture a different view.

I'm not thinking about wooden spoons. I am in the middle of the back seat of the ovenlike van, picking my lip till it bleeds. Suddenly, I am not so thankful that we've been let loose to prowl the Paveh district without a government handler. Denike's insistence that we not partake of "pack journalism" now seems about to have us imprisoned as spies. I'm pondering Bob Simon's forty days in an Iraqi dungeon; Farzad Bazoft hanged by Saddam for prying around a military base; the hostages of the Ayatollah and the Iranian "students" held for a year and a half.

In the heat and the silence, squashed between Maurice and Chris, my feet up on the drive shaft and my head resting back on a tripod case, I hear myself whispering "Oh boy. Oh boy. Oh boy."

Five minutes later—maybe it is ten—the officer says something to the driver and, mustering a couple of words of our lingo, he motions toward the guardhouse at the highway turnoff and says, "Go, go." I think that means we'll have to get out and wait there for some higher-ranking commandant to arrive, but before I know it, the chain has been let down, we've turned onto the pavement and we're rolling toward Bakhtaran again.

Maurice turns to me and says, "Don't worry—I got you enough. Couple of wide shots, some close-up. About thirty seconds voice-over."

At noon, we are back in Bakhtaran City Hall, cooling our heels in the same four armchairs in the same waiting room in front of the same photograph of the verdant Kentish canals. We are trying to get the same local official—Yousef, the English-speaker with the handshake like a leg-hold trap—to get a phone call through to Hatam in Tehran to make sure the plane is coming back to get us. Otherwise it is going to be another sixteen hours on the highway, longer if we have to go by camel.

The call goes through without delay and our cameraman is handed the orange plastic receiver, into which he murmurs Gallic endearments to a man we know has got us by the balls. *"Hatam, c'est Maurice, hein, Hatam, mon ami...."* We are hoping Hatam will advise Asseman Airlines to send the Falcon earlier—like, right now—instead of making us wait in Bakhtaran until the prearranged nine o'clock pickup.

I suspect this is not going to happen when I hear Maurice say, *"Eh bien, Hatam, oui, oui, dix heures...."*

This means that the plane is coming at ten o'clock. That's what we get for asking.

Still, we are in abundantly good humor as we walk out of the building and head for lunch at the same downstairs restaurant. Maurice is so happy to have survived the mountain roads, the detention at the Halabja camp, and the latrine at Do Ab, he decides to challenge Yousef to arm-wrestle.

"Are you nuts?" I yelp. "The guy's built like Mad Dog Vachon, and he's still got both legs."

"Well, yes, maybe you will beat me," Maurice tells Yousef.

"No maybe," the Persian replies, without smiling. "You will lose."

We walk on to the eatery, take a long, clean table, and I'm shaking all the waiters' hands, cooing, "Great to see you again! Hey, great to be back in Bakhtaran! Great to see you again!" It's been that kind of day.

Yousef orders bread, garlicky yogurts, a hillock of rice, the ubiquitous kebabs of ground mutton and a simply delicious fricassee of chunks of lean meat in a spicy, oily red sauce sprinkled with slivered almonds.

After we have eaten our fill, washed down with antiimperialist Iranian cola served in old Coke and Pepsi bottles, Yousef begins the postprandial conversation with the neighborly observation that he sees us as heathen scum.

"In Canada," he says, "I think you eat pig, yes?"

He pronounces it deliberately: peeg. We nod in a vague, non-committal fashion. I'm at the far end of the table, anyway. I pretend I can't hear him.

But Maurice, seated at Yousef's elbow, is friskier. He parries by inquiring why followers of Islam are not allowed to have a drink.

Yousef begins to explain that at the time of the Prophet, peace be unto him, there was a man who asked, "Why should it be wrong to take wine?" And the Prophet said, "You will see."

"So," Yousef deposes, "the man went out and drank two or three skins of wine. Then he fucked his mother, he fucked his sister, and when he woke up and found out what he had done, he killed himself."

"So *that's* why," I lean over and whisper to Maurice.

"Just one little fucking glass," Maurice replies.

I have wondered since we arrived how deeply the flame of Islam burns beneath the surface of the polished, cordial, educated men we've met. Yousef is beginning to give me a hint, a glimpse of the revolutionary fire. But he is a realist. On the walk back to City Hall, he tells me how the town's finances got messed up when the holy men started demanding supernumerary expropriations for religious schools and societies. He says that compromises have been reached; the banks, compelled to obey the letter of Islamic law, have done away with interest charges, but they've replaced them with "service fees" that keep the institutions solvent without trespassing on Koranic writ.

A week ago, we were still in Toronto, eating pizza and packing the granola bars and hoping—at least I was—that the shoot would be called off. Now I've had a great lunch, we've accomplished the trek up the mountain and down, and suddenly I'm the ranking expert at the CBC "Journal" on the Islamic Republic of Iran.

I propose to Denike that we ask Yousef if we can take the camera and go filming around Bakhtaran, to capture the flavor of life in a provincial capital.

Denike proposes that we find a bed somewhere and sleep.

Half an hour later, we have contracted two "day rooms" at the HO EL Bakhtaran—the letter *T* has fallen off the marquee—and I am twinned with the producer, who is flat on his back and droning like a cicada with emphysema.

We're on the second floor of the rattletrap hostelry, the equipment is piled in the lobby because none of us has the energy to carry it up the stairs, and the view from the window of room 9 is of a brick wall six feet opposite. But there is hot water, a toilet that does everything but flush, and here we pass the afternoon, showering, slumbering and shitting like civilized men.

At seven-thirty, we flag down three taxis for the transfer to the airport, which is no problem, except that when we pull up at the entrance, the gate is locked, the lights are off and nobody will let us in.

Yousef had assured us that Bakhtaran International is open twenty-four hours a day, Denike believed him, and so we are standing in the darkness and arguing with a policeman in the gatehouse when the barrier opens, not to permit our entry, but to let out a bus carrying German militiamen sent to aid and comfort the downtrodden Kurds, four hours away in the mountains. When the bus has passed, the gate closes again and we resume the gentlemanly debate.

Presently, a superior officer is sent for, he accepts our story about the chartered jet—or maybe he thinks we're part of the German army—and by the time we drag the gear through the deserted terminal building, captain Rad is already screaming landward, right on time. Under the flickering candles of the clear, black Persian sky, we soar home to Tehran. Bad-ass-man Airlines: We love to fly, and it shows.

22 APRIL
Tehran

The "editing process," which we now endeavor to commence in a salon the size of a curling rink on the eleventh floor of the Tulip International, involves carefully reviewing all the scenes and sequences that have been so laboriously filmed over the past three days, rejecting ninety to ninety-five percent of it, and then trying to make the remainder coherent.

In our absence in the Sirvan Valley, editor Claydon has established his equipment on a table at the western extremity of the room while, far to the east, there is a banquette on which producer Denike can stretch out and direct the editing through binoculars. Windows along the southern wall offer a boundless view of lower Tehran, its flat, dun-colored monotony expanding beyond Imam Khomeini's tomb and the flaming stacks of the petrol refineries until the buildings and the sky and the desert merge in a butterscotch blur.

The expansiveness of the suite—it goes on like a seraglio through rooms 1100, 1101, 1102, 1103, a kitchen, a couple of bathrooms and an office with a marble-topped desk, though it cost only a few dollars more than my plebeian cubicle—is a pleasant change from editing facilities back home, where Claydon is confined to a windowless confessional in which there is barely room for three people to argue. But here, room-service trolleys come and go, the fixer Kamran Farzal sprawls on a sofa and watches a film about storks on Iranian TV, and the maids' rounds are accomplished, all without being seen or heard.

On the big table, Claydon has set up a pair of video monitors, a pair of small audio speakers, two top-quality Sony VCRs similar to the "deck" that Davies has to lug around on his shoulder, and a controlling console from which both videocassette players can be operated. Though our editor was not with us in the Sirvan camps, his role now becomes crucial—a hand experienced enough to quickly make sense of a pile of raw tapes, yet an eye sufficiently removed from the shoot to be able to judge the audience impact of scenes that, to the rest of us, have become familiar and without weight. On one of the machines, Claydon builds a "master" tape, compiling scenes chosen from the reels we shot in the field—ten seconds of scenics from one, thirty seconds of interview from another, and so on. This is the solid-state version of the old film-editing mess of celluloid and sticky tape and splicing boxes. Video editing is neater, but the story still must be assembled in the head and the heart. The rest—film, tape, whatever—is carpentry.

If we work through lunch—and thereby flout the First Law of Journalism, a harrowing thought—we will have ten hours to edit what should be a ten-minute item, which is just about our average ratio of labor to finished product. Claydon already has arranged a satellite feed to Canada from the studios of Iranian television. Late tonight, he'll take our master reel uptown to a ground station from which it will be launched noiselessly through the ether, arriving instantaneously on a monitor in our Toronto office toward which knots of staffers, hearing my voice, will migrate to either praise or disparage the incoming work.

To compensate for our failure to record any scenes of Kurds actually dying, Claydon has been busy procuring several tapes of last week's tragedy from Iranian TV, and converting them to North American broadcasting standard through the facilities of the U.S. network ABC, which also is ensconced at the Laleh. I have often seen an ABC producer tearing frenetically across the vast lobby, halting once to take an urgent overseas call at the front desk and yelling into the mouthpiece that no, no, no! he didn't have anything new to feed for "Good Morning America."

From these reels, a compendium of the true horror of the exodus emanates: the shallow, shoebox graves of infants; the maddened scrum as food is thrown from open trucks; and the chilling rescue of mothers and children across a foaming, raging torrent by means of a high wire and pulley, a circus act at the edge of death.

We have captured no drama to compare with this. What we do possess—the panorama of the camps in the beautiful valley, the medical tent, the "Neanderthal" interview, the stalled queue of returning vehicles along the highway and the brief glimpse of the Halabja tenements—

adds in my mind to perhaps a three-minute item. Editor Claydon, having screened the material and compared it mentally to what the audience back home already has seen, night after night, of the Kurds' ordeal, agrees with my diagnosis. Only Denike is confident that we can fashion ten minutes of programming from our two-hundred-odd minutes of tape.

(The crew will not be needed during this day of intellectual fermentation. Mostly, they stay in their rooms and listen to the CD players they have brought along with them, Maurice soothing himself with classical strains, Chris preferring Ry Cooder and JJ Cale. But once, the parched duo arrives to enact a simpering pantomime of the waist-high refrigerator in the apartment kitchen. Maurice, down on his haunches, opens the fridge door and pretends to be burrowing through a veritable cofferdam of iced beer. "Hey, Chris," he calls out, "*Qu'est-ce que tu veux? Nous avons des Molson Export, des Labatt, des Carlsberg....*" Davies calls for a Blue, pretends to catch a can heaved from the kitchen, and then the two men exeunt, crying.)

"I have not found it a difficult transition," I wrote in the *Ryerson Journalism Review* last winter, asked for an essay on the move from newspapers to television. "Except for two elements. One is having to view my own stand-ups and the other is having to work with other people."

The first hang-up is not unusual. I know other television reporters, including well-known, glamorous stars, who leave the room when their face is due to appear, on tape, on the screen. It's true I don't like the way I look on camera. But then I don't like the way I look when I'm *not* on camera.

But "working well with others"—an echo from a grammar-school report card—is a different story. The successful newspaperman or woman comes to develop a haughty reliance on his or her own prowess. One grows to feel no necessity of outside assistance. Or, as the coach of the Toronto Argonaut football team once commanded me—the Boatmen had just lost their eleventh game of the season, against zero wins—"You saw it. Write it." Then he slammed the locker-room door.

In television, of course, when the door is slammed, all you get is a shot of a door. But the print guy is able to conjure—let us say "conjure" rather than "invent"—the scene beyond the barrier, the squinting through the keyhole of which journalism is born.

The solitariness of the profession can be felt even when a thousand other reporters are covering the same story. An entire Kurdistan of people may be assigned to the election campaign or the Super Bowl. The sights are identical, the subjects, the quotes. (At major sporting events, clubhouse comments are Xeroxed and handed out in the press box.) But then you are seated in front of a blank screen or an uninked leaf of foolscap, and you are utterly alone. You saw it, write it. Then give it to the copy desk and watch what *they* do to it.

(I usually enjoyed good fortune with the blue pencilers who handled my copy. Only one outrageous gaffe comes to mind. At Lake Placid in 1980, I was interviewing Lord Killanin, president of the International Olympic Committee, when a hotel bellhop rushed feverishly into his suite with a nosegay for poor Lady Killanin, who had slipped and broken her ankle while dancing. I called the courier "Buttons," a nickname for any liveried servant. The desk changed it to "Dick Button," the figure skater. One of the deskmen at the *Globe and Mail* used to remark that nearly all my columns contained references to death and the passage of time. That was fifteen years ago. I wonder if he's still alive.)

The traveling correspondent takes on an added burden beyond his single combat with the keyboard and the empty page. Not only must he write his own stories himself—always a good idea—he must also "produce" them, acting as researcher, travel coordinator, fixer, script assistant and all the other sundry aides-de-camp that are necessary to the procuring of the piece.

In December, 1984, the night after Linda's thirty-fifth birthday, I got on a plane at Beijing Capital Airport and took off for Karachi, Pakistan. The cockpit door was kept open all night; who would hijack a Silk Road caravan? I sat for a while in the first officer's chair and the captain looked down at the Himalayas and up at the full moon—he was navigating by the stars—and said, "This is the most beautiful flight in the world." And it was.

"A man walks down the street," Paul Simon has penned, describing my next morning. "It's a street in a strange world. Maybe it's the Third World. Maybe it's his first time around. He doesn't speak the language. He holds no currency. He is a foreign man. He is surrounded by the sound...."

So it was for me in Karachi—I didn't know a soul for two thousand miles in any direction.

From this bewildered confusion, over the next few days, I somehow single-handedly gathered, typed out and telexed—on an ancient, clattering contraption at the local Reuters agency—a series of stories on Pakistani life, governance and religion that included seemingly knowledgeable effusions on the status of women under Islamic law, the plight of the last two Jewish families in Karachi, the sorry state of horse racing in Rawalpindi and the political campaign strategy of President General Mohammed Zia ul-Haq.

From there, I went on to India, where I found myself in a Land Rover with the abdicated Maharajah of Jammu and Kashmir and his (only) wife. The former living god was running for the Lok Sabha, the lower house of the subcontinental parliament. He took me to a village of outcaste *harijans* and made a grand speech about democracy, but not in any language I could understand. People rushed forward to garland us with marigolds and necklaces of two-rupee notes. A holy *sadhu* slowly walked, all naked, by the side of the road.

To convey this, I was armed with my senses and a barely portable writing machine in a battered black case. (A Customs man in Katmandu once scrawled in my passport: "Holder has one typewriter which must be returned. Name of typewriter is Underwood.") I flew back to New Delhi to file and it made the front page. Headline: Petals for a Prince.

But nine months later, back in India for elections in the bloodied Punjab, I traveled not alone, but with a television correspondent named Jean-François Lépine, at the time the one-man Asia Bureau of the CBC. Together with a free-lance crew on hire in Delhi—the sound man was a Sikh who had cut his hair and removed his beard to escape the vicious lynchings that overwhelmed the capital in the wake of Indira Gandhi's assassination—we drove around the embattled state, following the dead prime minister's son. At the Golden Temple in Amritsar, in a seething crowd at a rally in Ludhiana, swatted by constables' brass-tipped bamboo lathis, I watched them make TV.

The presence of the camera brought the villages alive. A campaign procession near Patiala obediently turned around and marched the other way to take better advantage of the setting sun. We sweltered under a tent through a choleric exhortation by a white-bearded Sikh patriarch. The words were beyond our ken but the tautness of the faces of the old man's audience, their defiant postures, filled the lens. On Election Day, the photographer panned along the lines of nervous voters to reveal the soldiers and their heavy, wooden rifles, sand-bagged around the polling booths.

I watched Lépine do his stand-ups and thought, I can do that. Boy, was I wrong.

This was in the fall of 1985. By the next spring, having completed two years and a day at the *Globe*'s China bureau—the twenty-four-hour extension occurring because '84 was a leap year—and having given up on the idea of being the paper's Montreal correspondent after three whole weeks, still captivated by television's cosmic power, I mustered the gumption to ask the boss at "The Journal" for a job.

"If you do what we do," the boss riposted, "who'll do what *you* do?" He looked dismayed and pecked weakly at his lunch.

He hired me anyway.

"All right," he sighed. "I'm willing to roll the dice."

Armed with this vote of confidence, I was sent out to do dry-run stand-ups on Toronto street corners—on the very first day, a vagrant stood just out of camera range, crying, "Walter Cronkite! Walter Cronkite!"— and I was then hustled out-of-province for my first few stories, someplace the boss didn't have to see or hear me.

The first shoot, an oldtimers' reunion in an Albertan mining town that had elected a Communist council in the thirties, went well enough, but it was the second one that really ushered me into my career. On this trip to an assemblage of Second World War film cameramen in Victoria, British Columbia

—I was in the middle of an interview with one of the veterans on board a ferry when the producer pulled me away, saying "Here's how it's done," and then jabbed the startled septuagenarian in the breadbasket, demanding, "How's it gonna feel *right there in your gut* when that door opens and you see the guys...?";

—one of the unit's commanding officers passed out while we were filming him looking over an album of old photos;

—the producer suggested I take a whisky—or he'd take several— before I ever crawled in front of a camera again;

—the cameraman, affronted when a free-lance cinematographer was hired to make a "newsreel" of the gathering on grainy black-and-white film, declined to speak a word to the producer during the entire shoot;

—and it was explained to me, after another of my probing interviews, that there were only three questions appropriate to television newsgathering: How Does It Feel? Describe Your Emotions. What Is It Like?

This was my introduction to the world of "working well with others."

What is it like to perform a solo act for a dozen years and then to have to couple with a stranger? It was, at first, like me typing with one hand and someone else typing on the same keyboard with one of his hands—imagine the resulting miscegenetic mess. Personal relations were often strained, but then, Sullivan hardly spoke to Gilbert.

Still, I persevered—it was just coincidence that my first eleven producers all failed to notice my abundant talents—and by the end of the fourth season, the mantle of apportioned creativity began to feel comfortable. Denike had been a key player in this transformation. When he had the good sense to contract dengue fever in Panama, resulting in a two-week confinement, I was able to structure and write the piece unsupervised and it turned out to be a pretty good show.

And fame, one of the three principal reasons I had made the switch from print—money and power were the others—was beginning to arrive. Last summer, I was waiting for a ferry to the Toronto Island park when the captain of one of the vessels came steaming up to me. He was in crisp nautical whites with gold braid, a tall, erect, black-bearded freshwater salt.

"Love your column," he ordered, a short seven years after I ceased to author it. "Great column. Really enjoy it."

Another time, I called Revenue Canada to inquire why they kept charging me interest on taxes I'd paid months earlier, and when I gave my name, the woman—she had answered my call on the 154th ring—bubbled, "Oh, yes, Mr. Abel! The sportswriter! I do enjoy your column every day." This was only eight years after I'd given it up.

Still, my continuing absence from newsprint and the frequency of my television work—sometimes as often as once every three months—was beginning to make an impression. One morning on the Toronto subway, an elderly woman rose and insisted on giving me *her* seat.

"But, madam," I protested.

"Do sit down, you poor man," she sighed. "You're always being sent off to those awful disasters."

And it was just before our embarkation for the island that day when the ferry captain returned to where I was sitting and, squinting, said, "Come to think of it, I haven't seen you in the *Globe* lately."

I said that was understandable, as I'd quit the paper fifty-one months earlier.

"That's right!" the helmsman realized. "I've seen you on the TV. Listen, tell the *Globe* they've got to take you back. They'll pay you whatever it takes."

In the capacious suite at the hotel in Tehran, we begin to edit our story. Claydon suggests that we lead off with a flashback to the worst days of the Kurdish migration—the terrible scenes he acquired from the Iranian network. To this I accede readily, as does Denike, when word of our proposal finally reaches him by wireless at the far end of the pavilion. So we'll open with a minute or more of the images, now familiar, that so shocked the world only a few days ago. It seems the best way to remind the viewer of the disaster while allowing us to make it clear that we are moving on with the tale, that those first, frantic hours already belong to history.

From there, we introduce "our" valley, with some of Maurice's magnificent visuals of the morning sun on the campfire's haze. We will lay in, unscripted, about thirty seconds of these panoramas. Back in Toronto, the graphics unit will superimpose our title here, and Denike's name, and mine. (On our program, the crew is not credited. "The National," at least, scrolls everybody's name, even the mail boy, across the screen at Christmas.)

For a title, we tend toward banal simplicity: "Dreams of Amazonia" in Brazil, "Legacy of a Tyrant" in Romania, and so on. Juggling various permutations of "blah-blah of blah-blah," we settle on "Valley of Despair."

After the titles, we have a shot of a cow walking alone down the mountain road with Doctor Sammy's camp in the background. Her sonorous mooing is followed by mine, on camera, from the bed of the pickup truck. It's the line about the "instant Calcutta of canvas."

It is a synthesis of pictures and narrative, far different from the solitude of writing, yet immensely challenging, the silences mattering as much as the paragraphs. In retrospect, what was most unexpected—what I knew least about television after thirty years of watching it—was the intricacy with which the images are maneuvered to fit the words that accompany them, and vice versa. A half-second's silence can yawn like a cavern; or I find myself snarling at the screen, "Shut up, Al, for God's sake, shut up."

While Claydon fiddles with knobs and buttons, rewinding tapes, watching scenes over and over and over, selecting just the right instant to begin and end each clip, Denike and I talk about the structure of the doc- umentary—What comes next? What will we end with?—and I try to scribble some lines of script on a notepad, to be voiced and added to one track of the master tape at the end of the editing.

As Claydon plays and replays what he has cut so far, I read the script out loud, honing the timing and the tenor of the phrases. (When heard at home, though, my voice will sound, as a reviewer in my own *Globe and Mail* once accurately reported, "completely monotonous.")

I'm trying to say as little as possible over the scenes of the Sirvan camps. After explaining where we are, and after demonstrating how vast is the expanse of the tent cities, we decide to use the footage from the medical hut, the doctors treating the morning lineup, an old man lying on the ground with an intravenous tube in his arm, the supplying bag of life- giving fluid pinned to the tent wall. Then, the boy with the burned face. It is by far the most compelling image we have; after this, we know we've shot our wad. I offer some lines about "individual agonies punctu- ating the shared community of suffering."

As I'm reading this melancholy aloud, I'm startled by someone behind me. It's Maurice—I didn't hear him come in. (The room is so huge, the Iraqi army could have come in with him.)

He hands me a sheet of paper on which he's written:

Tout ce qui se conçoit bien
S'énonce clairement.
Et les mots pour le dire
Viennent aisément.

("All that is well created flows clearly. And the words to be spoken come easily.")

Then we call room service and order chicken kebabs for lunch.

When we screen the finished product, after eight hours of editing, I pace around the room, holding my nose. It hardly seems to justify the enormous expense of our transatlantic, tri-continental shlep—eleven-odd minutes of television that will seem pretty tame compared to the mad, macabre scenes our audience has been seeing for a fortnight. We haven't even used the lovely segment of the motionless convoy of Kurds who want to go home, discarding it as too confusing. (We have taken pains here to draw the Kurds as terrified refugees fleeing genocide and horror;

it would violate the thrust of the piece to introduce, nine minutes into the story, a group heading assuredly the other way.) And the Halabja camp also has been dismissed, though the shots Maurice surreptitiously took while we were being detained by the army certainly were usable. Without an interview with someone there, it just doesn't work.

"The ordeal of the Kurds may be just beginning," I write to close the voice-over. But in the dry, warm sunshine of the Sirvan Valley, it doesn't look that way.

But the Second Law of Journalism is this: If you don't get the story, for God's sake, get *something*. So Chris Davies strings a microphone cable from the recording deck to a table in an adjoining bedroom—our makeshift "sound booth"—and I sit in there with a headset on and deliver the narration with as much passion as I can engender. Then Michael Claydon takes the tape off to Iranian TV headquarters and Brian Denike goes down to the lobby to bribe the operator into placing a call to Toronto, to advise them that our item is done.

23 APRIL
Tehran

Buoyant with a grand idea, full of fresh, plump grapefruit and salty white cheese from the breakfast buffet, I jitterbug impatiently around my room, exercising manfully with my lightweight, portable, rubber-hose chest expander, until ten o'clock, which seems sufficiently advanced an hour to dare to wake up Denike.

He is already about. I am ready to spill my brilliant plan for salvaging the shoot and our reputations when Kamran Farzal, the Iranian journalist (and our contracted fixer), appears behind Brian and informs me that the BBC television unit is being expelled. This news mixes with the noxiousness of Denike's Benson & Hedges and Farzal's Winston to create in me a miasma of depression, which is never far from the surface anyway.

Why is the BBC crew being booted from the Islamic Republic? Their visas have expired; an extension has been denied. They've already been working beyond their original seven-day permit, flying back and forth almost every day to the refugee areas. But with the situation stabilizing on the Iranian side of the frontier, and with Western troops beginning to escort some of the Kurds who fled to Turkey back into "safe haven" within Iraq, the Beeb has asked permission to work on a piece about life, culture, politics and religion in the twelfth year of the Islamic Revolution, two years after Ayatollah Khomeini's death. This has been flatly turned down.

"Well," Denike sighs, having noted that our own seven-day visas expire tomorrow, "I might as well ask. What was your idea?"

"I thought we should do a documentary about life, culture, politics and religion in the twelfth year of the Islamic Revolution, two years after Ayatollah Khomeini's death."

We adjourn into the living area of Denike's apartment, which, compared to my little room with the crash-banging window and the stench from the bathroom plumbing, sprawls like the palace of Versailles. Sunlight is billowing through the open windows and it is clear enough to see bare, brown hills rising from the flatlands to the southeast where yesterday there had been only dust and haze. The producer, our Sun King, lights another cigarette.

"That's the piece we wanted to do in January, just after the war started," Denike says. Stranded for seven weeks in Amman with Davies and Chabot after the escape from Baghdad—Maurice hadn't been in Iraq when the war began; he was assigned to cover Canada's air base in Qatar on the Persian Gulf—Brian had applied for Iranian visas, to cover the war from the perspective of Iraq's longtime adversary. He never got them. Only because of the Kurdish tragedy are we here.

"Don't you think it would be fascinating?" I reply. "Can't you see it—'Iran Today'—I'll do the stand-up at the Ayatollah's tomb: 'Good evening, I'm Allen Abel in the Islamic Republic of Iran, and behind me, the catafalque that holds the remains of...' "

"Fascinating," Denike agrees.

"It can't hurt to ask," Kamran allows.

The man to ask, of course, is Hatam, the bureaucrat from the Ministry of Islamic Guidance who procured our jet to and from the Kurdish frontier. We've not been in contact with him since Maurice's phone call from City Hall in Bakhtaran confirmed the return flight to Tehran. It was a bit of a surprise last night when he did not demand to review our "Valley of Despair" before its intraplanetary transmission; in fact, no one from Islamic Guidance oversaw the satellite feed.

Emboldened by this inference that Hatam might actually trust us and our work—by now, he probably has had a full report from Mister Shuttup Goddamn—Denike and Kamran head down three flights of the airless fire stairs to room 801, directly below us, where Hatam and his minions are based.

I hang back in the Hall of Mirrors while the two men go to plead our case. Hatam's English is not proficient enough to reap full value from the stand-up I'd perform for him to clinch the deal: "...behind me, the catafalque..."

Ten minutes later, they are back.

"He wants us to submit a request in writing," Denike reports.

"We'll ask for a nine-day extension," Kamran says. "Then maybe they'll give you seven, or at least five."

Producer Denike, wreathed in toxic smoke, takes a steno pad and a felt-tipped pen and begins to take down suggestions that I fire at him from the sofa. At the top of the list, the two evocative locations the crew and I have already toured, but not photographed: the Ayatollah's bier and the vast Cemetery of Martyrs. I can't remember seeing anything on our network from these powerfully moving sites. Then I think, Maybe that's because anyone who tries to work there with a camera is beheaded. But Kamran offers assurances that British crews have filmed at both places unhindered, as long as someone from Islamic Guidance comes along.

So we add to the list: the former American Embassy where the hostages were confined until their release at the instant of Ronald Reagan's inauguration; the campus of the University of Tehran, the seedbed of the seething rebellion that evicted the Shah; the "Holy City" of Qom, a few hours by road to the south, beyond the gray-brown horizon toward which we all turn, as if on cue, staring out the picture windows to the veiled nation outside.

"We need a holy man, a mullah," I declare. "Someone to decry the current opening to the West—even the acceptance of foreign aid for the Kurds—as a betrayal of the revolution."

Then I add: "What about Khomeini's son?"

"He won't talk to foreign journalists," Kamran answers. "But we can try to get Khomeini's daughter."

"And some members of the Majlis—the parliament," I throw in. "People on both sides of the debate over liberalization."

Ideas are beginning to roll out faster and faster, like the scene at the chocolate factory when Lucy Ricardo and Ethel Mertz have to stuff bonbons in their brassieres to keep up with the accelerating assembly line.

Before Denike has finished writing down "Majlis" and "Khomeini's daughter," I've already suggested a theatrical performance, a sports club—traditional Persian wrestling preferably—a newspaper editor, a visit to the oil fields on the Persian Gulf coast, a trip to a rural village similar to the mud-walled compounds we saw along the road from Bakhtaran to Paveh, a grade-school English class and an up-market carpet exporter.

"By the way," Brian asks Kamran, getting into the spirit. "Are there any golf courses in Iran?"

The fixer nods affirmatively but hastens to add that we'll be more likely to find Japanese businessmen teeing off than Iranian duffers. Still, the very mention of the ancient and honorable game energizes the producer. He moves to a clearing in the middle of the room and practices his short-iron stroke.

At this point, editor Claydon emerges from his bedchamber, which is in yet another part of the CBC zenana. He studies the scratch pad with all the listed elements and says, "Wow. That would be a great show."

We determine that Kamran should write the whole thing out in Farsi—"The Canadian Broadcasting Corporation respectfully proposes to be permitted, under the auspices of the Ministry of Islamic Guidance, to visit the following locations, etc., etc."

This will take some time, as will the filming, but the promise of the completed story outweighs whatever travails may be required to produce it. (How different from my ear boil and my "I don't want to go" of last Monday, at home.)

The thought is dazzling: "Iran Today." Buoyant with a grand idea, I take the elevator to the lobby, swagger into the coffee shop and devour two freshly killed, white-eyed trout. Only the thought of golf leaves me uninspired. The last time I played, on a par-three course in Brooklyn—I was in high school—my best friend proposed to show me how far he could drive a dimpled sphere. On the eighteenth tee, with our bus fare home fully invested in a deposit on the ball, he wound up and blasted it over the fence and, with one perfect bounce, into the back of a speeding dump truck. After that, I gave up the sport.

I used to believe that there were three qualities essential to the journalist's craft: curiosity, compassion, and serendipity, the ability to find what you are not seeking. If the first two could be cultivated, I would say, the third would certainly follow. Or, as the baseball executive Branch Rickey put it: "Luck is the residue of design."

This is the best example of serendipity I can summon: a couple of years ago, while we were trying to set up a shoot to commemorate the 150th anniversary of the invention of photography, my producer, Alan Mendelsohn, was looking to expand the story's Toronto focus by having parts of it filmed in Vancouver, B.C. We'd need some basic scenes of lensmen at work—weddings, baby pictures, even someone whose specialty was high-priced portraits of pets.

Thumbing through the listings in the Vancouver telephone directory under the prefix "photo-," Mendelsohn found this listing: "Phototherapy." I demurred, explaining that this was probably a form of medical treatment using ultraviolet light, or some such, but he persisted in calling the listed number. "Phototherapy" turned out to be a fascinating branch of psychology whose practitioner in this case, Judy Weiser, let us tape her while she discussed the innermost feelings of one of her clients by reviewing old family photos with her.

In this remarkable case, a woman brought in a twenty-year-old snapshot of herself, her sister and their mother at the beach. She thought it merely depicted a happy childhood outing. But in the corner of the photo was a rolled-up newspaper. The sight of this provoked deep memories of resentment of a parent who'd rather read than spend time with her kids. We made this part of the documentary "The Secret Life of the Family Album."

For a lone newspaperman, prowling around with naught but a notepad, they seemed enough: curiosity, compassion, and, in Karachi, serendipity again—heading for an interview with a government official and spotting, from the taxi, a faded Star of David on a yellowed stucco wall, a passing glance that turned into a successful search for the only surviving elders of this crumbling, abandoned synagogue: the Last Jews of Pakistan.

But the intercontinental television crew, burning money like jet fuel in a jumbo, needs to add a fourth ingredient: local help. This is as indispensable in free societies as in fettered, as requisite in Paris as in Paveh, Iran. Even in San Francisco after the 1989 earthquake, we wasted precious hours searching for the proper vantage point from which to take a panoramic overview of the blacked-out city. By the time we snaked up and down Nob Hill, Russian Hill—in our frustration, we would have climbed Benny Hill—the lights had come on again. A local could have steered us right in seconds.

In Toronto, producers keep on file the names of available agents in dozens of countries. These become part of the show's extended clan: Eduardo in Mexico City, Esther in Budapest, David in Berlin. When a story breaks, a crisis erupts, the first call goes not to the cameraman or the travel agent; it goes to the fixer, who becomes part of the irreducible unit for as long as the shoot lasts, and part of the "Journal" household, forever. This is why the despair in the office was so thick last autumn, when a young woman who had guided a "Journal" unit in Colombia was, for no damn reason, ambushed and killed.

The flip side of the dependence on a source of local knowledge is the realization, as Kamran completes his neatly flowing petition, that nearly everything I know about the current scene in Islamic Iran is what *he* has told me. (I am the show's "ranking expert" after barely a week in-country only because no one else has come here at all.) And now we plumb for even more of his insight, though this will not be included in the letter to Islamic Guidance.

He tells us of his fifteen-year-old son and his friends, a new generation too young to remember prerevolutionary Persia. The boy has bad eyesight and flat feet, but still he must report for summer military training.

"He's almost 'martyr's age,'" I say, and the fixer fixes me in his glare. Some Iranians, he says, did send their sons, willingly, to die in a futile charge from the desert trenches, to lie forever among the limitless rows of marble slabs, under the little aluminum picture-cases with the diplomas and ribbons and candlesticks, at the cemetery where the city of the living ends.

Yet the boy also harkens to American rap, even 2 Live Crew. "Fuck this, fuck that, fuck the police," Kamran quotes.

Will this generation uncomplainingly adhere to the dictates of the holy savants?

By midafternoon, the letter has gone down to Hatam. Maurice and Chris are fired up to start shooting "wallpaper"—visuals of traffic, shops, sky-lines, government buildings and so on that we can use anywhere in the piece. Pejman the driver has fallen asleep from the excitement in the front seat of his ocher-colored Paykan taxi, and I, while changing some dollars into "goo-goos" at the hotel cash, have glibly boasted to a reporter from *Time* magazine that we're going off to do a wonderful doc-umentary on Iran Today.

This frisson of activity is, well, premature. After a time, Hatam informs us that the application is problem free in principle, but that it will have to be booted up the bureaucratic line, they'll also need a cover letter from the Canadian Embassy, we are not to shoot a single frame—one-thirtieth of a second—outside the hotel (or even from the windows) without the presence of a functionary from the Ministry of Islamic Guid-ance, and wouldn't it be easier if we just chartered another plane and went back up the mountain and did another story on the Kurds?

No, we say, it wouldn't. That topic is fading—the lead item on the BBC World Service today is the Soviet economy—but we are at the mercy of our hosts and so the crew is ordered to bring its equipment back upstairs. Perhaps tomorrow.

24 APRIL
Tehran

As "tomorrow" begins, the crew is fixed in one inflexible resolve: tonight, to eat dinner somewhere else.

Last evening, we had chosen the Rôtisserie Française on the uppermost floor of the Laleh, going "French" especially to delight Maurice, yet all of us willing to make the ascent, as the alternatives were peanut butter on Stoned Wheat Thins from our food locker or yet more kebabs from the Namakdoon restaurant in the hotel lobby.

The Rôtisserie Française offered a considerably more imaginative menu, including Châteaubriand for two, roast duckling and grilled Caspian sturgeon, the slightest *soupçon* of which would touch off a fatal chain reaction in the bloodstream of M. Chabot. The view of the city by night was breathtaking, a plaque on the wall as we entered announced the joint as a (lapsed) member of the Chaîne des Rôtisseurs, and behind what once must have been a fully stocked wet bar a waiter now perched blankly on a stool, awaiting Repeal.

I chose a plate of thinly sliced roast lamb, which was even better after I sent it back to the kitchen to be cooked, and admired the surroundings. Appearances had been kept up rather nicely, I thought—the silverware was heavy enough to serve as jousting lances and the pewter plates might have been used in the discus throw when the 1974 Asian Games were held in Tehran, back in the Shah's epoch. But when I ordered a bottle of what the stewards called "Islamic beer"—an unfoaming nonalcoholic, uric liquid that tasted of sweetly soured prunes—my tablemates groaned in unison. It was cola, cola, cola for the boys; I'm surprised they didn't order coq au Coke. I stuck with my Molson's Iranian.

Gourmandise being a shared attribute of many of us who live on the road, I was dismayed to notice that the crewmen—especially the sensitive Maurice (sound men will eat anything)—were not fully satisfied, even when a dessert trolley halted at our station with cakes and a faultless crème caramel. Certainly, I informed the cameraman, this was no worse than the rooftop restaurant at a hotel I used to frequent in New Delhi, which featured pseudo-Italian cuisine and a squat, bald Hindu bandleader who'd hold his trumpet in one hand, a crumpled kerchief in the other, and growl out his Louis Armstrong impression to the appreciative Brahmins at table.

And, I continued, making everyone lose what remained of his appetite, tonight's repast was undeniably better than the meal service aboard the Chinese state railroad, especially the less glamorous routes. For example, luncheon on a run up toward Manchuria when everything had been struck off the menu—pork, beef, duck, chicken, panda—everything except "egg-drop soup," made of dropped eggs, sloshing and splashing over the lip of a shattered chinaware bowl to form rivulets on the plastic tablecloth, and from there down onto my pants.

(Breakfasts were worse. One morning, slavering in my hard-berth sleeper while billions of fellow travelers paraded out of the dining car with piping hot bowls of noodle soup for which they had paid the equivalent of three cents, I was repeatedly denied entry, only to be ushered in after everyone had finished and presented with a platter of cold fried eggs by a hostess who said, "Foreigners eat eggs. You are a foreigner. Foreigners eat eggs.")

But at least the Chinese had eggs. The first time I went to Moscow, with poor Linda in tow, to cover a hockey tournament in 1979, we and several other Canadian hangers-on were undiplomatically booted out of the dining rooms in a half-dozen hotels, told that there were "no seats" while all around us, prostitutes and their johns dined in Czarist opulence. Finally, when we were grudgingly admitted to the Starry Sky eating hall in our own hotel, we sat for ninety minutes waiting to be served, a situation that did not improve until the great Canadian columnist Jim Coleman, then nearly seventy, stormed right into the very kitchen itself, bellowing "All right, you Commie bastards, break up this cell!" and emerged with some pickles and a bowl of peas that were being dried for use as BB shot.

Still, I have my limits. In the Punjab, when J.-F. Lépine would ask a server to brush the flies off a rack of tandoori chick and bring him a piece, I stuck to bananas and rice. And in the sanctum of the Amazon rain forest, when the women of the Kayapo tribe, their skins slathered with a blue-black vegetable dye, unearthed the river-fish they had buried in hot coals and sand and handed up morsels, I politely declined.

But the sound man ate it.

Now, at midmorning, we remain a frozen tableau, a wax-dummy diorama from some ethnographic museum: the crew on a worn leather chesterfield in the lobby, their gear littered around them; Denike and Farzal and Claydon, slouched around the eleventh-floor apartment, glumly smoking; and myself, in black corduroy Chinese slippers—Mountain Goat brand, the finest—dumped in an armchair, listening to "News About Britain" on the BBC, all of us waiting for Hatam.

We already have laid out a timetable for the production of "Iran Today." As soon as Hatam gives the signal, we'll start to do our street scenes of Tehran and interviews with two members of parliament, whose secretaries Kamran already has contacted. Tomorrow, Thursday, we will drive down to Qom, the religious capital, returning in time to do my stand-ups at the tomb of Ayatollah Khomeini, at dusk, when the light will be best. Friday, the Sabbath, we will attend noon prayers at Tehran University; Saturday, we'll meet Khomeini's daughter, and so on.

As the clock ticks and hours vanish and our visas drain toward expiration, we hear a report on the radio that one member of the Majlis, reacting to Iran's plea to the West to send aid for the bedraggled Kurds, has thundered: "If America is putting honey in the mouths of Muslims, they must have put poison in it first." This is precisely the dichotomy we want to present, the tug-of-war between the forces of reform and strict religiosity.

But by noon, there is no word, no permission. So I go down to the coffee shop and polish off two more dead trout.

At three o'clock, when Denike and Kamran finally decide they can stand the wait no longer, they descend to room 801 and return with Hatam's decree. The Ministry of Islamic Guidance has decided that since we were admitted to Iran to cover the flight of the refugees, that's what we should be doing. So please go do it.

It is a crushing blow, but Hatam, the devil, has left open two small windows. If we want to interview parliamentarians in Tehran about the refugee situation, and nothing else, this will be allowed. And if we still wish to produce a full-scale documentary on "Iran Today," we should nip back to Canada and apply for visas to do that story and he'll guarantee that these will be granted.

"I'll go over his head," Kamran exhales, back in the CBC suite.

While the fixer goes to the telephone to try to reach contacts in various government departments, Denike repairs to his boudoir where, beside a short stack of golf magazines, there is another phone. He calls the Canadian Embassy and asks an attaché there to please contact the Foreign Ministry, ostensibly a more liberal branch of the regime than Islamic Guidance. We don't like to beseech the diplomatic corps for aid; we try to do our own work. But a lot is riding on this proposal: money, minutes of air time, and, most deeply felt, the knowledge that beneath the picture windows of the Rôtisserie Française, a vast and compelling nation, one of the world's most venerable civilizations, lies curtained, and the drawstrings are held by one lousy little wise guy, in room 801.

At five o'clock in the afternoon of the eighth day of our seven-day visa, Maurice, with his precious camera Lucille, Chris, with his forty-pound "portable" video recorder, and I, hauling the tripod and a canvas bag of spare batteries heavy enough to serve as ballast for a supertanker, stagger out of the lobby and into the parking area to wake up Pejman the driver. We are, at last, going to go shoot some wallpaper. Hatam has okayed it—he's sending down one of his agents to "handle" us while we drive some of the main boulevards. We'll need some exterior shots of the Majlis, a shopping district or two, maybe the railroad station. The man from Islamic Guidance will ensure that we don't get any footage of anything interesting. But at least we're under way.

After half an hour of idling in the enervating heat—what with the editing on Monday and the list-making yesterday, it's the first time I've been outdoors since we returned from the mountains; it feels like the seasons have changed—we see a familiar figure strolling toward us. This is Ali Ramzi, the government man who was supposed to guide us up to the Iraqi border but whom we last glimpsed waving goodbye from the sidewalk in downtown Bakhtaran. Still, I'm glad to see him. At this point, I'd be glad to see the Ayatollah.

Without breaking stride, Ali Ramzi nods a brief greeting, walks right past us, exits the driveway, turns right and joins the queue for a southbound city bus.

Back to the eleventh floor. During our absence, there have been more disputations. Denike is now insisting that we pursue our story without accompaniment from Islamic Guidance. Either we roam your country as we choose, he tells Hatam, or we go home. But Hatam has been pacifying. He doesn't want us to bolt. Maybe one of Kamran's phone calls got through.

And there is word from the Foreign Ministry, via the Canadian mission. A feature story on "Iran Today" is precisely what the ministry would like us to accomplish. The minister himself, the personable Ali Akbar Velayati, will give a press conference tomorrow to call for even more help from the once-reviled West. Surely, sympathy for Iran's appeal for contributions to Kurdish relief, this tentative emergence after a decade of vehement withdrawal, all would be aided by a realistic portrait of the republic and its people. Perhaps tomorrow.

In the taxi, driving back to the Laleh after a flavorful dinner at an Indian restaurant around the corner from the compound where the American hostages were humiliated and confined, Maurice says: "When Brian called me last Sunday and told me we were going to Iran, I jumped at it, eh? A new place, a new country. I still get excited, eh?"

I tell him that I remember traveling around Asia, the confusion of airports and hotels and interviews and then, sitting down to the typewriter and the sudden epiphany as I pecked out the dateline—HONG KONG; CALCUTTA; SHANGHAI. The letters cemented my relation with the place; I had been there. Even a second trip to Tehran would be redundant. I'd have no trepidation, little thrill. It would just be work.

On the boulevard between the restaurant and the Tulip International, we pass a plaza with a splashing ornamental fountain, gaudily lit by colored lights playing into the spray, around which families with children sit and chatter, absorbing the sultry night. At the base of the fountain, in somewhat chipped and fading scenes, are paintings of the Dome of the Rock in Jerusalem and an Israeli flag with red streaks across it, and, in Farsi, what I assume are rallying cries for the extirpation of my people.

A few blocks away, under a portrait of the Ayatollah Khomeini at least three stories high, painted on the flank of an office building, a minor public rally of some sort is in progress. As we approach the scene along an elevated freeway, astonished that any sort of protest might proceed here, we see that the demonstrators—about a hundred men and black-robed women—are milling in front of a church. Some of their protest signs are in English—what on earth for?—and these, it becomes clear, are Armenian Christians, commemorating the mass murders of their country-men, seventy-five years past, at the hands of Ottoman Turks, their still-burning anger unthreatening and convenient to the present regime.

The U.S. Embassy itself, now a training school, is nearly invisible in the darkness. We see only the low wall that encloses it, festooned with slogans in Arabic and Roman fonts, and the florid faces of Khomeini and the spiritual leader Ali Khamenei and other long-bearded prelates I do not recognize, but these seem merely formalistic, like the leftist hoard-ings in India that proclaim Chairman Mao Is Our Chairman Too or the walls in Toronto on which have been sprayed Tories Out and Make the Rich Pay. Here, in Tehran, on a soothing spring evening, the fury that once raged seems distant and unreal.

We've divided into two cars for the ride to the restaurant and back. Pejman has the three nicotine fiends with him in the yellow Paykan. The crew and I are in another taxi, black, with a driver we don't know and a big decal on the dashboard that says NBC News—London.

Tomorrow, we may motor to Qom, or we may be evicted from the country. So, when the chauffeur offers to take us on a tour of the more fashionable uptown districts we haven't seen, we gladly agree. This has us on a six-lane motorway, zooming past the nationalized old Hilton, the seized Sheraton, toward the slopes of the Elburz Mountains and North Tehran. We meander along the commercial avenues with fantastic flower shops and fluorescent-lighted pharmacies, then down the side streets to wonder at the secrets kept in high-walled, stately houses.

Dreamily, gazing at the passing scene a million miles from home, Chris Davies turns around from the front seat and says, "I love my job. It's the work I hate."

25 APRIL
Tehran

Foreign Minister Velayati—it is accented on the final syllable, vel-ya-*tee*—opens his press conference by declaring that the government of the Islamic Republic of Iran sees "no obstacle" to the admittance of American personnel who might accompany relief supplies for the Kurds. The care and feeding of the exiles will cost Iran three hundred million dollars a month, and help is badly needed, the minister says. He is a trim figure, neatly bearded, smallish, presenting himself to us in the woolen waistcoat and the dress shirt, buttoned to the neck, but without a tie, that the post-revolutionary elite wears as a purposeful abandonment of the Western cravat.

The audience is being held in a small pavilion—called "The Pavilion"—at the Tehran airport, as the minister is about to fly off to Saudi Arabia. This in itself is an extraordinary voyage for the chief diplomat of a country whose propaganda billboards once cartooned the arch-villain Saddam Hussein as a mere pipsqueak hiding behind the flowing robes of King Fahd of the Saudi royal house. But these are extraordinary times in the East, an hour of shifting allegiances and a new ordering of things. Cozying to the Saudis, accepting succor from the Great Satan; Velayati and the Iranian president, Hojatoislam Ali Akbar Hashemi Rafsanjani Behramani, seem to be testing the envelope of the mullahs' vulnerability, the limits to the holy men's power to keep the revolution pure. Ayatollah Khomeini seems very dead, indeed.

It is a stifling morning, the summer seeming to press down harder, a vise being tightened, every day. Denike has stayed back at the Laleh for a final assault on Hatam and the intransigent weight of Islamic Guidance. Kamran was supposed to ride with us from the hotel, but he missed the scheduled "wheels-up" time, and he arrives at The Pavilion in a separate taxi long after we have gained admittance through a gauntlet of guardsmen, wordlessly, by flashing the same CBC identification cards with their imprinted gratitude for "courtesies extended" that got us nowhere with the soldiers at the Halabja camp.

Only one other Western television journalist has turned out for the news conference. It is Christiane Amanpour of CNN, descended, to her eminent relief, from her pup tent on the barbed-wire border with Iraq, where she and her crew and her satellite dish and her career had been stalled for more than a week, owing to a faulty transponder linkup and the decaying of the Kurdish tragedy story as the tragedy slowly eased. Amanpour's heritage is, on her father's side, Iranian. This enables her, when an airport official presumes to nudge her shoulder toward the corner of the room where we are supposed to stand, to erupt in a tirade of imprecations in the local language that sends the poor man squirreling for cover.

We send Kamran off in search of a panjandrum who might be able to beg Velayati to answer a few questions in English at the conclusion of the event. But by the time he returns, the minister already has been ushered to his place on a sofa under a photograph of Khomeini, a phalanx of Iranian journalists is poised to take notes, and Ms. Amanpour, wasting no time, has rocketed her first inquiry on the subject of American aid.

For the next twenty minutes, as the Iranian press corps waits its turn with more amusement than impatient frustration, Christiane, in a head scarf and trench coat, lassos the minister on U.S. assistance, the prospect for diplomatic relations with the Great Satan and the fate of American hostages in Lebanon, while I feebly heave in a couple of supplementals about reaction within Iran to this opening to the West. When, finally, someone does call out a question in Farsi, Amanpour verbally bowls him over, and grinning, the foreign minister keeps going, in English all the while.

I ask about the member of the parliament who remarked that any relief America would send to the Muslim Kurds would surely be laced with poison.

Velayati coolly shrugs off any hint of domestic dissonance. He says, "We have confidence in what we are doing. *We* are the government."

As the press conference ends and we all pack our equipment to leave, Amanpour follows the foreign minister into the VIP lounge where he will wait until his flight to Riyadh is ready to depart. She asks, respectfully, if Velayati has managed to catch any of CNN's satellite transmissions from the border ridge. (This was the first time the Islamic Republic permitted a foreign network to broadcast live from Iranian soil.) The minister nods and says, "Yes, some of it," and this thought— that even the leaders of Revolutionary Iran check CNN to see how things are playing in Georgia—makes all the old gee-whizzing about the "global village" seem somehow understated. The power and arrogance of CNN is widely reviled by my colleagues—Denike, in particular, vilifies their Baghdad correspondents for refusing to share the only phone line out of Iraq on the night of January 16.

But I'm merely in awe. Even the Iranians watch them. No wonder they've never answered any of my letters of application.

After "no problem" and "very good," the next phrase we begged to learn in Farsi was the universal command: "Come on! Come on! Go, go, go!" This, we were told, was simple: "*Zoot, zoot, zoot!*"

Wheeling back to the Laleh after the press conference with the foreign minister, we try out this latest addition to our repertoire of foreign imperatives and curse words, which already includes my limited knowledge of Chinese insults and Chris Davies's encyclopedic grasp of Russian terms for the female pudenda.

"*Zoot, zoot, zoot!*" we chant in unison and Pejman, laughing, picks up the pace, if this is possible, for he already is hurtling along the six-lane airport expressway in the customary local style, weaving in and out of the prenoon traffic, claiming proprietary rights to two lanes at once by straddling the fading white lines.

Maurice and I are in the rear seat with the camera steadied between us, and Chris is up front.

Suddenly, I feel Pejman hammering the brakes. We are sliding, slowly, the tires screaming, but still in the left-most lane, skidding forward, when I look straight ahead through the windscreen and watch us slam into a woman in full black *chador* who has tried to walk across the road.

The impact is heavy and full. The woman—I've caught just a glimpse of her face—has just started to open her mouth to scream when the Paykan rams her, in the left hip. She is thrown upward like a rag doll—one of her shoes flies off—and then she falls, her robe billowing, and she's on the ground in front of the car and I can't see her any more.

The taxi is stopped, shut off. Maurice reacts first—"Get out! Get out!" he gasps. "We'll get hit from behind for sure!" He opens the door at the left rear of the vehicle, grabs the camera, climbs out, and I follow.

I walk to the tail of the car and lean against the metal railing that divides the motorway, looking away. We are in a neighborhood of small apartment blocks. A few hundred yards away, the highway is surmounted by a pedestrian overpass that no one uses. I want to throw up. But nothing comes.

Pejman already has moved to the front of the car. Now, so does Chris. After a few moments, I take a deep breath and turn around.

The woman is lying, motionless, on the pavement, but there is no blood. She is alive. Some local residents scramble across the roadway— traffic has slowed, but not halted—and gently drag her into a sitting position on the curb of the median strip.

"She's alive," Chris says softly, incredulously.

I see her better now. She is elderly, puffy, her face the color of coffee with cream. She breathes in measured gasps, opens her eyes once, then closes them.

From out of nowhere, Kamran materializes. His taxi, traveling a few minutes behind us, is parked on the right shoulder of the road.

"You guys better leave," he says. "If they find out there are foreigners involved, her family will want more money."

All this has taken perhaps ten minutes. No policeman has arrived. Pejman is standing in front of his vehicle, quiet, dim eyed, in shock. We gather up our equipment from the trunk and carry it to Kamran's cab. It is not until we reach the sidewalk on the right side of the highway that I see them—a schoolgirl, about ten years old, and a much younger boy, holding hands, transfixed in horror, watching the old woman on the ground.

In July of 1979, in San Juan, Puerto Rico, I went swimming one torrid afternoon with a fellow sportswriter named Doug Gilbert. It was a rare hour of relaxation in the middle of the Pan American Games, a quadrennial festival of athletics in which the United States generally thrashes everyone else (except Cuba) in just about everything.

The water in the pool of the Holiday Inn was as warm as consommé. Gilbert and I lolled in the tepid shallows. He was a rare man—a professorial student of sport, especially the "miracle machine" of Communist

East Germany, about which he had written an excellent book. Yet, only a few years earlier, the tall, lean journalist had been a swift middle-distance runner on Canadian national teams.

That evening, most of the reporters walked over to the stadium to watch some of the track and field. Doug said he'd be a little late; he had some writing to do at the hotel. An hour later, trying to sprint across a six-lane boulevard in a hurry not to miss the final races, he was hit by a Volkswagen Beetle and, after surgery that night, he died. I hadn't thought of this for years, until today.

Driven back to the Laleh—"slowly, slowly," we make out to the driver by hand sign, as this is a phrase we've not thought to learn—weighted by this awful morning, we find producer Denike at wit's end. The trip to Qom already has been called off—no "handler" was available, Hatam claimed; all were tied up taking foreign journalists to see the refugees. Our documentary is melting away, our visas have expired and now, we hear, Pejman has been arrested.

At his work area on the big table at the eastern end of Denike's living room, editor Claydon is inserting cassettes into one of his player-recorders. These are stock shots of the Iranian parliament he has obtained from the local television network. At least, he reasons, if we can't produce a thirty-minute treatise, we could cut and file a two-minute story for "The National," our nightly news, using the Velayati press conference. Still, we'd have to shoot something ourselves—the tomb, the cemetery— to make even a brief item come alive.

By late afternoon, even this small effort seems beyond us. As if to reinforce the mood, a wild sandstorm gathers to the southwest and, hurriedly sealing the windows, we watch it rip into the downtown core, whistling and whirling, a cocoa-powder tempest that in China would be heralded as the portent of profound events, a shift in the Mandate of Heaven.

It is now midmorning in Canada. Wearily, Denike picks up the telephone. Instantly, cheerily, the long-distance operator picks up—he has been well suffused with cash for several days now—and asks, "You wish call to Toronto, Mr. Dee-nike?"

Indeed, he does. He reaches a senior editor at our office and, bearded chin in hand, reports, "The last three days have been the most frustrating days of my life." This, after Baghdad and more than a month of nothingness in Amman, not to mention the dengue fever.

On the phone, Denike seeks the mandate of heaven to consider an alternative plan. We could go to Jordan and, from there, try to drive into Iraq, to report on the state of Saddam's shattered realm. We could come home, having produced nothing but a weak eleven minutes on the Kurds in their dry, green tents. I throw in some other offerings: Beirut, where Syrian dominance seems to be underwriting a lasting peace; or Kuwait, where hundreds of oil wells remain ablaze and where Canadian troops, in the blue beret of the United Nations, are arriving to patrol the Iraqi frontier. Toronto will make a decision, we are advised, and call us back. Perhaps tomorrow.

Just past midnight, having finally figured a way to get some fresh air in my room without the window banging and clanging like a Cantonese opera—I've stuffed the tightly folded cardboard from a box of Christie's Onion Thins into the hinges—the phone rings. Late-night calls have always terrified me, but this turns out to be only CBC Newsworld, English Canada's twenty-four-hour information network, inaugurated last year with wonderful intentions and virtually no budget.

I am connected to the anchor desk in Calgary, Alberta, for a "phoner" on the plight of the Kurds. The interviewer, Whit Fraser, begins, as all intercontinental parleys begin, with bewilderment at the time difference.

"It must be an ungodly hour there, Allen," he says.

I am in no mood for this kind of banter. The woman on the airport road...Doug Gilbert....

"Well, Whit," I reply. "It's a godly country." I wonder what the komiteh, should one of their men be condemned to audit the conversation, makes of this gibe. We go on to talk about our experience on the cliffs of Kurdistan, about the refugees living "like Neanderthal people" and about the carloads of those who are ready to go home.

"We spent two nights in a tent up in the mountains," I tell the anchorman.

"So did I," he says, a voice from a saner world. "Last weekend. But I was ice fishing."

26 APRIL
Tehran

Our secret weapon in the assault on the Ministry of Islamic Guidance is our charming francophone cameraman. After breakfast, convinced more than ever that one solitary bureaucrat is blocking our route to an important, attainable story, we deputize Maurice. He is to go down and speak to Hatam in the language of Voltaire. He is to tell him of The Dream.

This is what Maurice has revealed at the morning meal: that last night, he dreamed that he and Lucille (that's his camera) had been in the beautiful Elburz Mountains, shooting a scene in an idyllic peasant village, with the snow-whitened peaks all around. Then someone had come up behind him and had started whapping him with a big, heavy stick.

This was Hatam.

So Maurice, pregnant with symbolism, goes to see Hatam to make a final appeal. Maybe bonhomie will achieve what neatly lettered petitions could not. I wish him luck—"*Tout ce qui se conçoit bien...*"

While Maurice works on one branch of the mandarinate, I am dispatched in a taxi to another of its tentacles, to begin the laborious process of applying for permission, not to remain in Iran, but to leave it. As we have overstayed our official seven-day welcome, it is necessary now to attend a specially designated Police Bureau for Foreigners, to have fees paid, photos submitted, forms filed and passports stamped with a visa extension valid until midnight and an exit permit. If Hatam does allow us to work, we'll have to come back and do this all over again.

For one hundred and nineteen minutes—that's how long it takes for one American and four Canadian passports to be inked and scribbled in and a perforated stamp affixed—I am back in People's China. The setting, the scene, is evocative of Cathay: a corner office with bare concrete floor and whitewashed walls; unkempt young militiamen padding about in boots with fraying laces, rooting around in old wooden desks and producing aluminum plates, then vanishing into some unseen commissary in the back of the building, to emerge later, furiously eating as they walk, with heaps of steaming rice. Even the application forms are held together with straight pins made in Shanghai—Three Geese brand. But at precisely noon, the loudspeakers crackle to life and then issue, to my amazement, a recording of the midday chimes of Big Ben. This would not happen in China at noon. At noon in China, everyone goes to sleep.

At noon on the Muslim sabbath in Tehran, Iran, I am handed the five passports and ride back to the hotel Tulip, passing, on quiet, tree-lined streets, the block-long compound of the Soviet Embassy and a graceful Italianate church, hung with scaffolding, that turns out to be the Papal Nunciature, closed for repairs.

Maurice's crusade has been only partially successful. Hatam now allows that he will have a guide available to escort us wherever we want to go, perhaps tomorrow. But Denike stands firm, and insists that we be allowed to travel on our own. Kamran offers to resign from our employ; "Maybe I'm the problem," he says.

Whatever the problem, it's too late. Toronto has called. They want the Canadian fire fighters in the deserts of Kuwait. Iran is over.

(But "Valley of Despair," we are informed, was a hit. It even was rebroadcast by PBS in the United States of America.

"I told you so," Denike waggles at me. "Don't be so hard on yourself.")

This time we all go down to the coffee shop and—except, of course, for Maurice—we all select No. 21 on the menu, trout with almonds, but there are no almonds, and there never have been.

After lunch, I return to my room to pack. I'll miss 1134—the view of the mountains through the brown-gray soup of sky, the fading Pepsi-Cola billboard on the building across the street, the shoe-shine man sitting on the floor in the hallway, lathering some businessman's brogans, and the kindly old gentleman who would timidly tap at the door and inquire softly, "Any washing?" All across Asia—in hotels, on trains—you meet people like these, persistent in their antique manners despite the fire and fury of their nation's reigning polity. They will outlive all the ayatollahs.

Sorting my things, trimming for travel, I leave the chambermaid a bag of almonds, a sack of raisins, a tub of all-natural peanut butter that is leaching oil, and four pairs of surgical gloves. I'd taken them from the CBC nurse, in case I had to hold a dysenteric infant in a Kurdish mother's tent.

Gracious in victory, Hatam reiterates his promise that new visas will be issued as soon as we go home and reapply. Then he assigns one of his men—this is yet another exit formality—to come up to our editing chamber and screen all of our tapes before they'll let them, and us, out of the country.

We suggest that the fellow begin by viewing "Valley of Despair." He gazes at the opening scenes, then, just after I've weighed in with my poetry about "the shared community of sorrow," he reaches up, hits the fast-forward button, rubber-stamps all our tape boxes and leaves.

For our last supper in the Islamic Republic, we are taken at a driver's suggestion to what appears, at first, to be just a blank iron wall. (Pejman, we hear from the captain of the taxi rank, has been released from custody, negotiations with the victim's family are beginning and the old woman, incredibly, is still alive, but with her hip and leg shattered.)

Behind the wall, as we push the iron gate open, is a stairway that leads to a carpeted foyer with chandeliers and a stately grandfather clock. There is wallpaper of golden chintz and a languorous, roller-rink melody is issuing from speakers in the wall.

To the right, the lobby issues into a large, formal dining room. Sixteen tables with crisp white cloths have been set for dinner service. Three waiters in identical gray shirts and blue neckties stand forlornly against a wall. No one else exists.

We are seated at a table in the corner, adjacent to an air-conditioning unit that is pumping out a hurricane of arctic air. Already on the table are flagons of oil and vinegar, a tureen of mustard and an ice bucket. One of the waiters hands each of us a menu with no prices on it.

In Moscow in the Brezhnev years, a patron often would be handed a menu of Tolstoian thickness, with literally hundreds of dishes listed—fish, fowl, game. But only a couple of entries would have prices handwritten beside them, and only these specific atrocities—often, only one, such as "pressed chicken tabaka," a halved fowl, first grilled and then sat upon, or vice versa—actually would be on sale.

This experience leads me to suspect that maybe the restaurant we are in now is out of everything except oil, vinegar and mustard. But the waiter removes all suspicions.

"What is good?" he asks rhetorically. "All is good."

Ordering beefsteak, charmed by the *belle-époque* surroundings, I am just settling in with my frosty Islamic beer when a party of eight enters the dining room. This includes two young mothers, pushing baby strollers, who are dressed in stylish, oversized sweaters, tight jeans, earrings the size of lacrosse balls and—I do a double-take—nothing to hide their exuberant, lightly tinted hair.

"Where are we?" I gasp at the waiter, who has brought fresh lettuce and blood-red tomatoes.

"Armenian Club," he replies. Perhaps it is better to stay at home. The more you see of the Orient, the less you understand.

27 APRIL
Frankfurt

Twenty-four hours later—twenty-four!—we are in the press tribune of the Waldstadion in Frankfurt, Germany, awaiting the start of the game between the Galaxy and the Montreal Machine in the World League of American Football. A red sun is setting behind the electronic scoreboard, cheerleaders in purple-and-tangerine knickers are high-kicking at the fifty-yard line, and four of us—Denike has begged off—are up in the grandstand, having talked our way in. About forty-five thousand other idiots are here, too.

What the hell are we doing at a football match in Central Europe? It's a long story. When the office in Toronto determined that we should proceed to Kuwait to cover the Canadian fire fighters in the blazing oil fields, it was left to us to figure out how to get there. By air, as the Scud flies, it wouldn't be more than a ninety-minute flight, directly from Tehran to the tiny, rescued emirate. But there are no direct flights.

In the colossal living room of Denike's apartment at the Laleh, we tried to work out the logistics. To enter Kuwait, we'd need a Kuwaiti visa. This could be obtained anywhere in the Persian Gulf region: Dubai, Riyadh, Bahrain, etc. But to get to any of those places, we'd need a visa for *that* place. And you couldn't get any of those visas in Tehran, Iran.

Dubai, one of the splendiferously wealthy sheikhdoms within the United Arab Emirates, seemed a possibility. We might conceivably be granted visas on arrival and be permitted to enter while we applied for Kuwaiti papers. And there was a way to get there: deposit hard-currency payment for tickets at a Tehran bank, go to the airport with all our baggage at three o'clock in the morning, line up for a domestic Iran Air flight to Shiraz, sit around Shiraz all afternoon and then hope to get on the short international hopscotch across the Gulf to Dubai, the very flight the U.S. Navy once mistook for an Iranian fighter jet and shot down, killing innocent hundreds. This notion we dismissed, after much debate, as unwieldy.

The process eventuated into one of those brainteasers that used to run in the *Reader's Digest*: the lion lives next door to the chimpanzee; the brown house is owned by the same man who owns the llama; Mr. Smith and Mr. Wilson are cousins, so who owns the zebra? What was left to us, alas, was a weekend in Germany, the only country obtainable from Iran for which we *didn't* need a visa in which we *could* arrange a visa for Kuwait.

This had us in a squadron of taxis, and the equipment in a battered blue pickup, hurtling insanely down the same Tehran motorway where Pejman ran down the old woman, heading for the airport and the convenient 2:00 a.m. departure for the West, wine and unsequestered women. Iranian Customs, which we had been warned would be a nightmare of search and seizure, turned out to be a breeze. The inspectors asked for a few cases to be opened, saw no carpets or caviar, and waved us through in minutes, wham, bam, thank you, Imam.

When we walked out on the tarmac to board the plane, it was ten days to the moment since we had landed from Vienna, full of the weighty expectation of a roundelay of death and misery. It hadn't turned out that way at all; only the accident on the freeway had put us in proximity with our fears, though that incident, replayed ceaselessly in my mind's eye during the cab ride, last night, was enough horror for me.

Once, in a rainstorm on a superhighway in Ontario, driving Linda and her parents home from a family visit, I had lost control and skidded across the median and a tractor-trailer barely missed us before we slid to a halt, unhurt. Once, heading out of New York with four college buddies on a camping trip—to Alaska—my roommate had swerved to avoid hitting a yellow dog and had slammed us into the guardrail, but, again, though the station wagon was demolished, none of us was injured. Now I was taking from Iran not the memory of the dreaded Kurdish holocaust, but the indelible sight of the grandmother on the highway and the sound of our metal meeting her flesh.

When the door closed, the plane took off, the liquor trolleys were wheeled out and some of the Iranians and other nationalities on board began to get pissed, I was in another of my glowering snits, facing a sleepless night in a roaring plane.

I put on the blindfold and hid under a blanket and tried to sleep. Two Euro-businessmen across the aisle to my left were smoking unfiltered Gitanes. In the corridor to the right, lined up for the toilet as we descended toward a refueling halt in Istanbul, a German and an Iranian hurled invective at each other in English, the world language.

"You are a...uh...uh...a shit!" the red-faced German spat.

"No!" the Persian hissed. "You are a shit."

"You are a shit."

"You are a shit...."

Amid this gleeful atmosphere, Claydon noticed in *USA Today* that the Frankfurt Galaxy would be home on Saturday night to the Montreal Machine.

At seven-something in the morning, Central European Time, we landed at Frankfurt Flughafen and began anew the labors of Hercules with the thirty parcels of gear, humping some of it into storage, the rest into a couple of Mercedes-Benz taxis for the supersonic cruise along the autobahn to the InterContinental Hotel, downtown on the River Main. The Third World was history, at least for the weekend. I checked in with my MasterCard, gave the clerk my frequent-flyer number, zipped up to the twelfth floor in the spotless, mirrored lift, unlocked my door with the computer-coded key, flicked on CNN on the satellite television, pranced into the bathroom to draw a gorgeous flagon of cold tap water, and found a big brown cockroach skating blithely along the toilet seat. Then I went to bed.

For an old hand from journalism's toy department—*TV Guide*, reprinting an antique hockey column of mine, once labeled me a "veteran scribe"— talking four freeloaders into the Waldstadion has been no challenge at all. I collect identification cards from Michael, Chris and Maurice and saunter over to the *Eingang für Presse*. Shrugging and smiling while a woman from the home team's media office goes up and down a list of prearranged credentials that I know we're not on, I keep saying "Kanada tee vee, Kanada tee vee," and she apologizes for whatever stupid bugger left our names off the comp sheet and hands us each a ticket and a pass for free food and beer.

It's a long, long hike from the gate to the grandstand through the forest for which the arena is named. Just outside the barriers, hordes of teenaged Germans are swilling can after can after can of pilsener, trying to get suitably legless before they pass through the police checkpoints at which all cans and bottles in a fan's possession are being taken away. The drinkers stack their empties in neat pyramids—five cans on the bottom row, then four, three, etc.—attempting to lure the female of the species in much the same manner as the bower bird of New Guinea struts around his "lawn," displaying shiny bits of glass and metal.

The leitmotif of the evening is sex, beer and rock music. The World League of American Football, or WLAF—the *W* is silent—is midway through its first season, an experimental agglomeration of major-league rejects in mostly minor-league cities in North America, plus London, Barcelona and Frankfurt. Back home, in such metropolises as Sacramento, Raleigh-Durham, San Antonio and Birmingham, Ala., the league hasn't made much of an impact, but over here, among the dazzled uncognoscenti, it is the rage.

There's a thumping little group playing at a tailgate party in the parking lot, a marching band from an American army base is stomping along the sideline, the cheerleaders are forming into parallel columns for the *"Einmarsch der Gladitorien"* and here come the players—and a helicopter.

Out of the chopper, looking terrified, a young boy alights at midfield. His name has been drawn in some promotional giveaway, he's handed Galaxy souvenirs and, up behind us, the fans are batting big red balloons. One of them suddenly explodes with a bang that would have sent us diving for cover last night, in Tehran, Iran.

But this is just a punctured plaything and we wlaf it off, and the big tele-screen on the scoreboard shows us a close-up of the cheerleaders, none of whom is wearing a veil, or much else. It is a stupefying moment, to compute, as the players take the field, the power we possess to flit about the globe from Mideast to midfield, disaster to dalliance.

"A week ago tonight," Chris says, "we were at the refugee camp. And now a football game, with all the cheering and the music, and, the funny thing is, we're not out of place at either one."

The public-address system is blaring Dion's, "The Wanderer," as if on cue: "I hop right into that car of mine, and drive around the world...."

Mike Claydon answers, "That's sad. That's really sad. We're not really at home in either scene. They're both just transitory. We know we're going to leave the refugees, and we know we're going to leave the stadium, after a few hours."

I didn't expect philosophy tonight; I just came for a ballgame, dropped off the magic carpet for a while in a universe I used to inhabit full-time. Screaming to be heard above the music and the roaring fans who are up and doing the Wave, I tell the boys about a night on Long Island during the Stanley Cup finals, ten years ago. Next to me was a man and his wife, both decked out in Islander jerseys, Islander toques, Islander wristbands, pennants, pins. Mike Bossy scored a goal to go ahead of the Flyers and the man turned to me, delirious, hollering "Isn't it great! Isn't it great! Isn't it great!"

And I looked up from my notepad and, deadpan, stared him in the eye and said, "Just another night at the office."

For a professional sportswriter, it had to be that way. I remember the instant I flicked off the switch of fanaticism—and as a boy I had been a first-rate fanatic for the baseball Mets and hockey Rangers, though never one to haunt the dugouts and locker rooms, begging for autographs.

It was Willie Mays Night at Shea Stadium in the late summer of 1973. Mays was retiring—no one knew at the time that the mediocre Mets, barely above the .500 level, would win the National League's East Division and go all the way to the World Series, prolonging the rather pathetic last acts of the great center fielder's deteriorating career. He went to the microphone and delivered a generally incoherent valediction that ended with the tearful hero commanding himself: "Willie, say good-bye to America."

At this point, some fifty thousand worshipers and nearly everybody in the press box, too, was moved to stand and applaud, but I told myself—I was covering for the Troy (N.Y.) *Record*—"You're a pro now. Sit down and shut up," and I did. After that, win or lose, home or away, it didn't matter. I rooted for something to happen that would be worth writing about. You cheer for the story.

Now the football game is about to begin, and Davies and I are going through an imitation pregame radio show:

Abel: "We have a very special guest with us tonight, ladies and gentlemen—he flew in all the way from Eye-ran just to be at the game tonight—Chris Davies, ladies and gentlemen...."

Davies: "Really great to be here, Bruce, really great...."

Abel: "Well, Chris, it's a great matchup here tonight in Frankfurt—Canada against Germany—it's a great traditional rivalry—a lot of history between these two countries...."

Davies: "That's right, Bruce, it's like that time Germany defeated England in the World Cup of Soccer and the German players were laughing at the English, saying, 'Ha ha, we beat you at your national sport.' And the Englishman said, 'That's all right. We beat you twice this century at yours.'"

The Montreal Machine is on the second stop of its European tour, the WLAF schedule having been arranged so that each North American club need make the expensive Atlantic crossing only once in the season. The Machine, trying to win football back into the hearts of a city that drove its formerly beloved Alouettes into extinction, takes the pitch tonight fresh from a narrow 45–7 defeat by London Monarchs, making it perhaps the only team ever to lose at Wembley Stadium by forty points in any sport.

The setback in Britain was explainable, though, by the fact that the Machine still was reeling from a heartbreaking 44–0 loss to New York the weekend previous.

This sequence of emotional blows to the groin has left the Machine apparently unable to ever score a touchdown again, but the Frankfurt Galaxy, whose head coach is the father of the famous Denver Bronco quarterback John Elway, seem no better. (Almost all the players and coaches in the league are Americans.) At the end of the *erste Viertel*, the score remains 0–0, which may be yet another promotional ploy, nil–nil being the only score the soccer-fed European understands.

Football with helmets may be foreign here, but the stadium is nearly packed with wailing, chanting young Germans—I seem to be the only one here who is over forty—and a huge number of U.S. servicemen from nearby bases, many of them in full Desert Storm camouflage fatigues. There are more American soldiers at the Waldstadion tonight than there are in Zahko, Iraq, protecting the homecoming Kurds.

"The Americans just come over here with their game and all this music and the cheerleaders and everything," Clayton sighs, "and they just lap it up."

Meanwhile, after ten plays from scrimmage inside the Montreal twenty-yard line, including two pass-interference penalties in the end zone, Mike Perez, the Galaxy quarterback, finally flips a little twelve-inch pass in for a touchdown, the joint erupts in frenzied celebration, fireworks are shot off, the moon rises, and so do we.

29 APRIL
Frankfurt-Bonn

As the business week begins, we are knee-deep in diplomacy. Producer Denike and I work the phones at the InterContinental while watching CNN, MTV, "Tic Tac Dough" and "Supermarket Sweep" to keep our minds sharp and stay abreast of our industry. Cameraman Chabot and sound recordist Davies have gone off to Sachsenhausen, the sudsy playground of the Frankfurter male.

The staff of the "Journal" documentary desk informs us that they have contacted the Kuwaiti Embassy in Washington, forwarding passport details, etc., thereby enabling us to pick up our visas in Germany and dash off to Kuwait, via Cairo, which is the only place Kuwait Airways is dependably serving at the present time.

But a call to the Kuwaiti Embassy in Bonn reveals, as I expected it would, that they have heard nothing from Washington, they know nothing about any Canadian television crew, they are not issuing visas to anybody, and please go away.

It is always like this. Last November, Denike and I were assigned to India, where Hindus and Muslims were engaging in an agony of reciprocal murder, and we read and researched and packed and got our antimalarials and I bought a carton of Fruit Roll-Ups, but we never got the visas in time. The same thing happened with the Armenian earthquake in December, 1988. By the time the Soviets came through with the visa, nobody was dying any more. So we didn't go.

Visas for the Amazonia shoot in Brazil came through only after each of us obtained a notarized affidavit from the Metropolitan Toronto Police stating: "I am directed by the Chief of Police to certify that a search, based on the above name and birthdate, failed to disclose any such person with a record of criminal convictions in the national repository for criminal records in Canada."

At the bloody height of the Romanian revolt, border guards at Nadlac issued visas on the spot and waived the mandatory currency exchange. Going back the other way, to newly democratic Hungary, you had to line up, fill out papers, buy "goo-goos" and have photographs taken, developed and cut to size.

Most of us got into China, before and after Tian'anmen, on tourist visas—marked with a capital *L* for *luyou*, "wandering traveler"—hefting our twenty or thirty cases of "personal effects" through the Nothing to Declare channel at Beijing airport with shrugs and smiles toward the indifferent Customs men. (Flying in the day martial law was declared, my producer and I shredded our CBC identification cards and wrote "entrepreneur" as our occupation on the landing forms. Another fellow at our show puts down "TV repairman.")

Visas for the Soviet Union usually were issued on the afternoon of departure, to prolong the suspense. A couple of times in 1990 the office went through the tiresome rigamarole of applying for Soviet visas for me and a crew; we were going to do stories on the space program, women's issues and food shortages in Siberia. Both times, it took so long to get the visas, the higher-ups lost interest in the projects and called them off the day we were supposed to leave.

This was embarrassing. The food editor of the *Toronto Sun*, learning that I was once again off to Mother Russia, had sent a photographer to snap me stuffing my satchel with granola bars, President's Choice chunk white tuna in spring water, pitted prunes and Fruit Roll-Ups. The photo spread had to be pulled down at the last instant. Another shot at fame's sweet embrace, lost forever.

"Visa problems," usually cited as an excuse for Latin American ballplayers to arrive late at spring training, have more than once deprived me of immortality. Had the Saudis not been so lethargic about letting me in as a relief pitcher back in February, I could have been the first man into liberated Kuwait, instead of Bob McKeown of CBS. Thus, rather than a Canadian reporting for a U.S. network, there would have been an American working for the Canadians.

Eventually, I was awarded a Saudi visa; I had put down "Christian" on the application, as the kingdom maintains a statutory prohibition on the admittance of Hebrews. But, as the ecumenical West was at the moment deeply involved in saving the Saudi's bacon, the rules were relaxed. Then the ground war commenced and our man in theater stayed on.

I don't like to lie on application forms. When Linda and I planned a trip to Burma in 1985—this was before the horrible annihilation of the democracy movement in that beautiful, benighted country—I wrote "journalist" on the questionnaire and the consular attaché handed it back and said, "Cross that out and write 'teacher,' or we won't let you in."

A few months later, preparing for our long peregrination homeward from China, we applied in Hong Kong for visas to visit South Africa, purely as tourists: Table Mountain, Kruger Park and so on. Under "Profession" on the application, recalling Rangoon, I put "teacher."

The next time I talked to Toronto, the *Globe*'s foreign desk told me there had been a call from the South African Embassy in Ottawa. It had rejected my visa application because officials "didn't like what I wrote the last time I was in southern Africa."

I had never set foot on the continent in my life.

And six months after Tian'anmen, Mike Browning of the *Miami Herald*, who harbors the most profound sympathy for the Chinese nation (though certainly not for the Chinese government) of any of the correspondents I knew there, was denied a renewed resident's permit because, at the height of the troubles, he had reported from the People's Republic after entering on a visa stamped with a capital *L*.

Around the corner from the InterContinental, in a restaurant facing a sudden square of greenery amid the skyscrapers of Germany's financial nucleus, Brian Denike and I take lunch at the tasteful Park Hotel. The dining room is busy and attractive, and we are led to a cozy table for two on a riser next to a gleaming black piano. A soft melody plays.

The piano lounge at the Park Hotel is where Brian's wife used to sing, late at night, for businessmen and wanderers.

Two years ago, Brian and his wife bought a nineteenth-century farmstead three hours northwest of Toronto complete with a handsome stone house. They bought three horses, even found a nearby town where Brian could buy his size-thirteen sneakers.

Then came the Berlin Wall, Panama, Germany again, Panama again, Baghdad, Amman and now this excursion, which, if the Kuwaiti visas come through, will take Brian Denike in exactly the opposite direction from Frankfurt than one would travel to go home.

We tuck into our shrimp salads, sip our Perrier, change the subject, talk about our plans for Kuwait.

Sometimes, at home, if she thinks I'm not listening, Linda will be singing "Heavenly sunshine, heavenly sunshine, flooding my soul with glory divine."

At this point, we feel compelled to enlist the aid of the Canadian Embassy in our attempt to get into Kuwait and salvage the shoot, the budget and our chances of ever being sent anywhere again. (One of our bosses once was put before a firing squad in El Salvador. He doesn't want to hear how much woe we're going through to get a simple story on some Albertan firemen.)

The Canadian Embassy enters the pursuit with customary enthusiasm. Someone agrees to put me through to someone else who puts me through to a woman who promises to call the Kuwaitis and tell them that we are bona fide reporters and unblemished in the national repository for criminal records. This takes all day.

Late in the afternoon, we are told by the Canadians that a Mr. Faisal will meet me at nine o'clock tomorrow morning in Bonn to grant the necessary visas. When I call the Kuwaiti Embassy to confirm this, the receptionist, recognizing my voice, hangs up as soon as I say hello.

So now I'm on the train. It is InterCity Express number 128—"the Karwendel," named for a peak in the Tyrol—sliding out of Frankfurt Hauptbahnhof, beginning the two-hour run to Bonn, the little capital on the Rhine. The other men stay back in Frankfurt; they'll meet me tomorrow at the airport for the flight to Kuwait City, via Cairo. They've got my suitcase, I've got their passports, everything is arranged and the Karwendel is crossing the river at sunset, the churches at Mainz silhouetted in the afterglow, and scullers scaling easily the ripples in the golden glass.

It is a perfect hour—rolling beside the sinuous river, beneath the ruined castles, free for the first time in fourteen days from the rest of the goddamn crew. I'm deep in a thick red armchair, the only man in *Erste Klasse*—there are no women in this carriage—who is not wearing a suit and tie. The reverie is broken only momentarily when a blind man being led down the aisle is knocked off balance as the speeding train shifts and an armrest hits him right in the crotch.

The last time I rode this route, I was not in *Erste Klasse*. In 1971, just graduated with a degree in physics from a university I knew as

Unfathomable Tech, I Hebrewed around Europe with four other guys and one stupid, inflexible rule: we wouldn't spend more than five dollars to sleep.

This meant that we existed most nights either in flophouses—sometimes five to a one-bed room, for economy—or in the compartments, corridors and even toilets of second-class trains, our passports and wallets stuffed in our underwear as we lay on the reeking tiles.

We endured one of those passages along this very route, trying to sleep sitting up on the local shuttle from Frankfurt to Mainz and back again and again, then slatted on a park bench on the riverbank and finally aboard the milk run up to Düsseldorf, where we bedded down on the waiting-room floor. The next day, we took a tourist steamer down the river and one of the boys fell in love with an English girl from Hemel Hempstead.

Of the others on that penurious excursion, two are successful chemists in New York and one is an environmental engineer in Louisiana with twins by his second wife. For them, Tech was, in the end, not Unfathomable. What happened to the fourth guy, or the girl from Hemel Hempstead, I have no idea.

The Karwendel settles into the Bonn station, a cozy, small-town terminal quite unlike the enormous sky-domes of Frankfurt, Munich or Berlin. Across the street is a three-star Hotel Continental—not Inter-, just Continental—and I saunter in and take a room without even bothering to ask the price. It is not 1971 any more.

Behind the hotel, in a neat little plaza in the pedestrian zone of his hometown, a statue of Beethoven stares grimly out in grimy bronze toward the Kaufhof department store. A middle-aged couple lies loudly snoring at the deaf composer's feet. She is in jeans, her patterned blouse unbuttoned and open. He, passed out, is sprawled on the pavement with his head resting gently on the lady's right tit.

I step over them and dine at Pizza Hut. Then, blissfully alone, I take the tiny lift to room 32 in the Continental and burrow under a down-filled duvet as warm and soft as an expense account.

30 APRIL
Bonn–Frankfurt–Cairo

At 0610, to the splashing of traffic in the Bahnhofstrasse, I awaken nearly strangulated by the sinister foreign bedclothes. We are tied up like the combatants in a famous wrestling match at Maple Leaf Gardens in the nineteen-fifties when the two monsters, pythoned in complementary "scientific" leg-locks, had to be carted off to hospital while still entangled, their separation being beyond the abilities of the studiously flabbergasted ringside crew.

It is likely that I am the only person in the breakfast salon who tonight will sleep in Cairo, Egypt. The four of us are booked at 1400 on Lufthansa out of Frankfurt, Claydon the editor having returned to Toronto yesterday with six of the packing cases and my long underwear, his services unnecessary in Kuwait as we will bring our tapes home and edit them in our base on Carlton Street, a block from Maple Leaf Gardens.

There are six others in the lacy dining room, embedded in newspapers. The ambience is so still I let my cornflakes go soggy, lest any crunching break the Teutonic silence. Then I pack the red knapsack, pay the bill—about ninety dollars—post a Mother's Day card to Brooklyn, slosh across the streetcar tracks and set out in a taxi for the Kuwaiti Embassy. I've got two hours and twenty minutes to pick up the visas, come back to the station and entrain for Frankfurt Flughafen, to meet the boys at Cairo check-in. It should be easy.

At 0859, I ring the bell at the Kuwaiti Embassy on Godesberger Allee and the metal gate slides open, operated by a sumo-sized Arab with a pistol in a holster on his hip. He tells me to wait in a small anteroom until Faisal arrives.

In the room are some tables and chairs, smiling portraits of the emir and the crown prince, and a papier-mâché scale model, apparently made by children, of downtown Kuwait City with many of the buildings toppled over and blood spilling over the seawall. There is no sign of Faisal.

At 0930, an attaché enters to inform me, in German, that the Kuwaiti Embassy has never heard of me or "The Journal" and that I should fill out application forms for each of us, in duplicate. There is a line on which to enter "Father's Name." I know that Denike's father's name is Emerson—it's the only thing he's ever told me about his antecedents. For the other two crewmen, I just make it up: Marcel for the father of M. Chabot, and for Davies, naturally, Bruce. Under "Religion," after considering "infidel," I put "non-Muslim."

At 1005, I find the man who gave me the application forms in a rear office, reading the *Herald Tribune*. He takes the paperwork and places it on his In pile.

"Go sit down," he says.

Now four businessmen arrive in a taxi, hydroplaning through the gateway in the increasing downpour. They join me in the waiting room and fill in forms. The eldest, an impeccably tailored old-timer who is using a fountain pen and blotter, breaks off his scratching to speak to me in Arabic.

"Sorry, I'm from Canada," I tell him.

"Oh," he replies, in a perfect BBC World Service voice. "I'm from the Middle East. But you look more Middle Eastern than I do."

At 1020, I go out to tell the man reading the *Herald Tribune* that if I don't get the visas by 1045, the Canadian Broadcasting Corporation will be out seventy-five thousand dollars, the people of Canada will be unable to view the proud reconstruction of the proud nation their proud Canadian Forces risked their lives to liberate, and I'll get fired.

I am beginning to get a bit unstuck. In flawless German, I tell him that *ich müss ein Schnell-train am elf uhr machen für wir haben Reservazionen in Cairo diese Nacht.*

This means that I have to make the eleven o'clock express because we have a booking in Cairo tonight.

"Oh," the diplomat says mockingly, "you go by train to Cairo?"

At 1035, I phone Denike at the hotel in Frankfurt to tell him that it doesn't look cheery.

At 1050, I try to sneak up the stairway to the second floor to either find "Faisal," whom I suspect does not exist, or make a direct appeal to the ambassador, but I am blocked by the behemoth with the pistol. I skulk back to the waiting room. The four businessmen have got their visas and split.

At 1057 on my one-dollar watch, Mister Go Sit Down pushes open the door to the waiting room, smiles and hands me the four passports, with visas for a two-week stay in Kuwait. He says, "You find taxi, outside." Outside, the monsoon has begun. There is not a second to spare. I run out onto the Godesberger Allee and begin semaphoring energetically for a cab, but the avenue is being torn up by construction, traffic is at a standstill in both directions and I am getting soaked. My train leaves in twenty-one minutes and the station is twenty minutes away.

There are *Strassenbahn* tracks down the center of the boulevard and I start running along them to a station-stop a few blocks away. At 1103, a trolley slides in and, assuming that it must wind its way toward the Bahnhof eventually, I board it, and it does head downtown, toward Cairo, Kuwait, home and Linda.

At 1116, the streetcar halts and I start running again, through the tunnels, plowing through a Hitchcockian menagerie of *Schulkinder* in Benetton raingear and up the stairs to *Gleis* 2 just as the 1118 express to Frankfurt sails up to the platform and docks.

It's the Amsterdam–Innsbruck Limited, exactly on time. I have not, to this point fretted about telling Denike I have the visas, because last night there was a mobile phone in the club car of the Karwendel and I figure I'll just call Frankfurt from the train.

But there is no phone on the Amsterdam–Innsbruck.

I have been through all fourteen cars of this hurtling sausage-link and now I wend resignedly toward my reserved *sitzplatz*, in a glass-walled compartment quiet as the tomb. Seat 25, I find, faces backward. My mother always told me that if you ride backward, you'll throw up.

"I must change seats," I tell the frozen features of the executives who occupy the two forward-facing chairs. "If I ride backward, I'll vomit."

One of them makes a great show of getting up and switching sides.

At 1130, slumped stupefied against the fogged-up window, I envision twenty-four cases of television equipment being manhandled toward the lobby of the Frankfurt InterContinental while the crew gets the day started in the lobby bar and producer Denike, in room 1818, lies fidgeting and chain-smoking, staring daggers at the unringing phone.

At 1147, the Amsterdam–Innsbruck Limited pauses for 120 seconds at Koblenz. Grabbing the knapsack—that's all I'd need, to have the train pull out with all our passports aboard—I run along the platform toward a vacant yellow phone booth, fire in two one-mark coins, dial the Frankfurt city code, then the hotel exchange, get the operator, beg for room 1818, and listen to it ring and ring and ring. No answer.

Back on the train. Next stop, Mainz, in thirty-nine minutes. So—why not some lunch? I go to the diner and select boiled beef, parsleyed potatoes, beetroot salad and a bottle of mineral water. Very nice. The First Law holds.

At 1236, or eighty-four minutes before the departure of the Frankfurt to Cairo jet, I explode off the train at Mainz Hbf toward two yellow telephone booths placed conveniently seven miles away at the other end of the platform. One of them is marked International Calls Only and the other is an empty cubicle with prettily colored wires coming out of the wall.

At 1257, the train arrives at Frankfurt airport. I take my knapsack and my macho leather jacket from Istanbul and, sighing heavily for effect, disembark. At the first phone I see, I call the InterContinental to tell the boys I'm sorry that it didn't work out.

There's no answer in anyone's room and no response to a page at the lobby bar. I ask the front desk if they've checked out.

"Computers are down," the clerk says. "I can't get that information."

So I filter up the escalator toward the gargantuan international check-in zone to look for my companions, who might, after all, have decided to take the twenty-four cases of equipment to the continent's most congested terminal, even though they aren't flying anywhere today, just for practice.

At 1307, I have the crew paged. This produces an amplified snoring from the loudspeakers easily conquered by the din of the thousands below. Then I see Maurice.

He is loping toward me in slow motion, arms open, as if we are lovers in a field of daisies, which, at this moment, I guess we are.

"You are de only one who could 'ave done dis," Maurice says, a big man gently caressing the visas, and me.

Ninety minutes later, we are airborne, I have country music on the headset and the Kentucky Headhunters are singing "Oh Lonesome Me." On the video screen a few rows forward, Lufthansa is showing a British documentary on the death march of the Iraqi Kurds.

1 MAY
Cairo–Kuwait City

Sixteen hours is not very long to devote to the wonders of Lower Egypt—even less so when eight of the hours are spent at Cairo airport and seven of the others, you're asleep. Fortunately, I have been here before, with Linda, as part of our direct route home from Peking to Toronto via Manila, Borneo, Thailand, India, Zimbabwe, the Dead Sea, the Maldive Islands, Gibraltar, Nairobi and Spain. We took a trans-Suez "youth" bus from Jerusalem to Cairo—a trip heartily recommended to devotees of cigarette smoke, satanic-worship music played at life-threatening volume, and three-hour border crossings—but the fun didn't end there. Our hotel room window opened directly onto the bullhorn of a particularly enthusiastic muezzin—first call to prayer, 4:42 a.m.—and then, after retreating in claustrophobic panic from a slither up into some pharaoh's secret treasury deep inside one of the pyramids—the room was empty, anyway, and had been for four thousand years—I prevailed, after a frank exchange of views, in convincing Linda to take a short camel ride to the Sphinx, the first few paces of which were accompanied by an outburst of ghastly bellowing, braying, neighing and spitting, though the camel never made a peep.

Also, while packing for our Egypt Air flight to Madrid—it was the same day that an Egypt Air flight was hijacked to Malta and dozens were killed in a botched rescue attempt, but, hey, were our families back home worried?—I inadvertently left behind a nice pair of sheepskin mittens Linda had bought in the Old City of Jerusalem. Now, en route to Kuwait, we were booked to spend the night at the same airport Novotel, and I was looking forward to retrieving the lost gloves, which I presumed the hotel had been holding for the past five years in case I ever set foot on this continent again.

This was not to be. During the restful two and a half hours it took for Maurice and Chris to get permission to bring Lucille the Forty-Thousand-Dollar Camera, and the forty-pound videocassette recording deck through Customs for the night—the twenty-four checked pieces were left in storage for onpass on Kuwait Airways—the boys decided to change to the Mövenpick, leaving me unable to retrieve Linda's lonely mittens and leading Brian into a hive of baksheesh-begging hustlers trying to arrange a lift to the new hotel while, hour after hour, I watched the Novotel mini-van circle around and around the arrivals loop, empty and forlorn.

And during the brief pause for the necessary entry formalities—the crew counted thirty officials in the Customs clearance area with them, and claimed to have been interrogated and made to fill out forms by every one of them—I was able to once again enjoy one of the aspects that had made my last trip to Cairo so unforgettable: the persistent belief held by every person I met from here to Karnak, and in Israel too, that, from my looks, I must be indisputably Egyptian. Over and over, I heard it, back then—"Ah! You are Egyptian man!"—and now, in the airport, it was happening again, despite my assurances that as far as I know, the last of my ancestors to live in Egypt was Moses, and he caught the trans-Suez "youth" bus going the other way.

On top of all this, there was the matter of the time change. According to the Lufthansa *Flugplan,* this was the night that Egypt set its sundials ahead an hour, to summer time. Wanting to confirm this locally, I approached nineteen people in the arrivals lounge and got the following results: seven said it was the night to change clocks, four said it was not, and eight said, "Ah! You are Egyptian man!"

The check-in lineup for the Kuwait Airways 747, nonstop to the flaming desert, includes, besides us and our twenty-four packing cases, several prosperous-looking Kuwaiti businessmen in full, flowing *dishdasha,* the entire diplomatic representation of the Republic of Ghana, returning to the liberated emirate for the first time since the war, dozens of "guest" workers and their wives, children, parents, grandparents and great-grand-parents, each of them—even the diplomats—pushing great pharaonic monuments of luggage, piled on flimsy wheeled carts like the stepped pyramid of Saqqarah.

We four breeze through in relative ease—we are flying "Oasis Class," after all—and have completed formalities by seven-thirty for a takeoff that is scheduled either at ten or eleven o'clock in the morning, depending on whether or not it is Egyptian summer time.

As it turns out, it is summer time, and at precisely the scheduled hour of eleven o'clock EST we are seated comfortably in a forward cabin, a hostess is proffering melon and dates, and the twenty-four cases of television equipment are waving at us from a wagon that has not yet been brought anywhere near our plane. I can see them from my starboard window, as can my agitated seatmate Maurice, who otherwise might be enjoying his issue of *Time* that contains an excellent piece on "Iran Today" by the reporter to whom I had boasted back at the Tulip International of our plans to do the same thing, which, of course, we didn't.

When mention is made to the flight crew that our baggage remains quite obviously unloaded, reassurances follow that this is not a crisis— *none* of the baggage has been loaded yet. This announcement results in more melon and dates—they are magnificent, the fruits of victory—and, swatting aside the curtain from First Class and slumming back in Oasis, a visit from an American water-quality expert who has been in and out of Kuwait, assisting the reconstruction of the desalinization plants. (We had met at check-in.)

The waterman is a fountain of information. Though I am not nervous at all, compared to the lip-picking neurosis of the takeoff to Iran, two weeks ago, it still is encouraging to hear him say that Kuwait is well supplied now with food and bottled water, and that the hotel where we will be staying—the Kuwait International—is up and running in grand style, except for the higher floors, which were torched by the sore losers from Baghdad. When I inquire about the quality of the air, which in newsmagazine photographs is an opaque goulash, the American says, "If you can see it, breathe it."

Regarding the water now beginning to flow through Kuwait City's mains, he is equally comforting. "I performed the standard scientific test," he says, balding and brassy with a Virginian drawl. "I drank some, and didn't die."

"Bedouin ways were hard, even for those brought up in them, and for strangers terrible: a death in life," Lawrence (of Arabia) wrote in *Seven Pillars of Wisdom*. He should have flown Oasis Class. Below us now (we finally have taken off) are the Martian expanses of the Najd, the northern Arabian desert, in places a blackened red, as if the blood of the world had dried, elsewhere the pink of a Creator's nursery, and, from this altitude, seemingly impossible of life, though the British explorer Wilfred Thesiger, traveling by caravan in the vast quarter we now survey, found "cold streams in forests of juniper and wild olive"; he climbed "steep passes, where baboons barked at us from the cliffs and lammergeyer sailed out over the misty depths." That was in 1947.

As I look down, as if from Phobos, on the craters and the lava flows, the sense of space travel lulls me into an ethereal sort of trance, sometimes focusing on the powder-puff sandstones below, other times going blank, dreamily watching little gelatinous "floaters" gliding across my pupils. I had felt the same rapture in the private jet in Iran—the suborbital gliding that, for a space-crazy boy born a few decades too early, must serve as a replacement for the commonplace cosmic voyaging I will not live to see.

And this flight, truly, is celestial; Thesiger's "brick-red downs, splashed with deeper shades," broken by county-sized patches of blue-black flatness that seem at first to be oceans but, at closer view, are only outcrops of stone. But, still, deep in their magazines and their portable music machines, my fellow travelers disregard the earth's display.

After an hour or so of this glory, the more germane and current aspects of the area begin to intrude. These, at first, are mere whitish scrapings on the increasingly flat, brown landscape—fingernail scratchings on a sunburned back—but then I see the trails merging, widening, the footprints of Desert Storm.

The sands are flat and featureless now, and there are no towns, no roads. But as we approach what must be the southwestern corner of Kuwait and overfly the Neutral Zone—what a fascination that strangely named rhombus on the map always held for me!—the evidence becomes irrefutable. These broad trails must be the leavings of hundreds of trucks, tanks, humvees; the horseshoes of piled sand must have hidden the heavy guns, before breakout; the big fenced quadrangles, empty now, must have been the staging camps.

Still at thirty thousand feet, we are over Hafr al-Batin, the last town in Saudi Arabia—a Scud hit here, I remember; maybe dozens did and they never told us—and here is the Kuwaiti frontier, the Iraqis' silly eight-foot berm and the "flaming wall of oil," so easily countervailed, that were supposed to keep the M1A1s out. And now more of the horse-shoes, south facing—Iraqi positions, their farthest forward, where the most expendable troops were abandoned with half rations and a mine field between themselves and surrender. I had hardly thought of the war for weeks, consumed with the Kurds, the battle with Hatem, the visa chase, but now the geography was coming to life. From here, the British Desert Rats must have swung left, around the Iraqis. Far to the east, at the coast, that must be Khafji, held by Saddam for half a day. At this altitude it is all a giant West Point blackboard; you can't see the dead boys from up here.

I had passed the conflict in my own country; my war stories were tales of civilian wounds. At first, I was assigned to the United Nations as the hourglass ran out. At the midnight moment of deadline on January 15, a fittingly vague and foggy evening in New York, I watched a few straggling protestors count down the seconds and then fall silent, as if listening for the echo of the first bombs' report. Crossing the avenue, I prepared to do a stand-up with the Secretariat building behind me—"at the great arena of diplomacy, there is nothing left to talk about"—but before these portentous words could be edited and broadcast, war had begun, invalidating all analysis by noncombatants like me.

Two of the men on this plane with me today were, of course, the first to know it; Brian and Chris remember lingering in their rooms in the al-Rashid tower for more than an hour, watching, hearing the missiles' unerring declarations of hostilities. Then, the long climb down to the basements, the crowded shelter shared with fellow journalists, hotel employees, dark-eyed men with guns, local citizens—an unforgettable life raft of mixed allegiances and fears. And Maurice had been in Qatar—at the air base fittingly and painfully christened "Canada Dry"—and if the Canadians had not exactly turned the tide of combat (they fired only one air-to-air missile...at a boat), at least he was "in theater," among stouthearted women and men.

I, meanwhile, had moved on to the Country Music Jamboree in Wheeling, West Virginia, part of a peripatetic rummaging through mid-America for the state of the national soul. A bluegrass bass player had heard the news of war's outbreak while driving—"I found myself crying in the van," he said—and if the resonance of American patriotism rang a little hollow among the sophisticated intellectuals of our Toronto office, in Wheeling the tears were real.

The trip went on: to Beallsville, Ohio, where seven sons of a single tiny hamlet had been killed in Vietnam, and a dozen more were active now, in the gulf; to Kent State University, where frat boys of the type who, in my college days, would have occupied a dean's office or burned down an army recruiting station were rallying on the common, chanting "Liberate Kuwait!" And onward: to Pittsburgh, to meet a decorated hero of Vietnam and a tortured POW of Korea, in whom this new war had reopened horrible places in the heart; and to a small town in Illinois, where a woman in the reserves had been called overseas, leaving behind a two-month-old daughter. The soldier's father rocked the infant and said, "This is like a cancer, eating away at me."

That was the breadth of my action; I was home by January 31, my birthday, when our budget ran out. Then came the abortive exercise with the Saudi Arabian visa and the liberation of the emirate, followed—preceded, actually—by the splendid reportage of the Canadian Bob McKeown, who once, a long time ago, had tagged along with me to a couple of Muhammed Ali's last, pitiable prize fights in Las Vegas, McKeown an eager idolater of the champ, and me a dispassionate old columnizing pro.

Sixty-three days after the first shock troops from CBS rolled north to free a captive nation, our big plane starts to bank and descend and suddenly, ahead of us, there is a stone wall in the sky. It is the beginning of the smoke from the burning oil wells, a deep black bruise in the blue atmosphere, and we are heading straight for it.

A slight buffeting on impact with the edges of the cloud, and the smoke is on us—the smell starts to intrude through the ventilation fans in the overhead racks—or maybe I am just imagining. Outside the window, night has fallen over us. How can the engines operate? How can the captain see?

But the plane keeps sinking and turning, lowering itself toward a runway that must, I fear, lie right in the terrifying shroud. And now, as the plane banks obliquely to the right, the first burning well appears, a flickering little Bic at first, through the blackness, then, as we drop through a layer of obscuring smoke, becoming brighter and brighter, a giant, seething cyclone of flame, the sensational vandalism of the beaten foe.

And then, more wells—two, eight, twenty—candles on a devilish birthday cake, blinking, blistering orange geysers punching up from utterly blackened soil, the man-made lava of the motor age. Maurice and Chris are at their windows now, hypnotized—I hear them softly murmuring, "Oh, fuck...oh, fuck...oh, fuck..."—and I assume that Brian is equally transfixed, but he is back in the smoking section where I can't see him, avidly prepoisoning his bronchial tubes before we have to land, and breathe.

The nightmare stretches as far as I can see, a Halloween costume draped on the desert flatland, orange fires, black pools of oil. I am gripped by a brilliant idea—why not just water-bomb the wells, send in big, dripping tankers heavy with seawater from the gulf? I visualize a scene from the movie *Always*, Richard Dreyfuss serenely hurtling through the smoke of a burning forest; John Goodman, his plane's engine on fire, about to crash, chortling into his radio, "And I was in *such* a good mood."

So was I, until we hit the wall. Now the death-world below us has me a little shaken—after all, we're coming here to *live*. But then, just as suddenly as we entered the darkness, we leave it, bursting into brilliant sunshine for the final approach to the landing field. On the ground, rolling toward the terminal, I see the airport control tower, blasted and blackened; the roof of one giant hangar torn off and shredded like tissue paper; American soldiers at a barricaded access road with a hand-painted sign—Turn Here or Die.

But inside, the airport works. There's an efficient check of the visas I had no trouble procuring yesterday—was that only yesterday?—in Bonn, the gear is making its way around the conveyor belt, and even a man from the Canadian Embassy is present to greet us with the news that in a few days' time, the Honorable Michael Wilson, minister for International Trade, is to come to Kuwait to discuss Canada's role in the reconstruction of the ravaged state and, the diplomat avidly hopes, to have his picture taken by us while doing so.

The Kuwait airport is as vast as Vancouver's, but only a small part of it has been repaired (or, having been needed for Iraq's "domestic" flights, wasn't too badly savaged). It is the same, we see, with the inbound motorway to the downtown core—the road surface scraped up a bit by tank-tread, but otherwise clear, the infrequent Mercedes-Benz sailing along at 140 km/h, while along the margins and median strip lie fallen light standards, burned-out cars, smithereens of furniture and dead appliances, big chunks of concrete fallen from the lane dividers, sandbags, ammunition boxes, soldiers' helmets, shell casings and great heaps of variegated household trash. Tattered flags flop wearily to welcome us, last of the liberators; we jet past the Lebanese Embassy, fittingly unscratched, and when we pass one big blue sign that indicates the next exit—we're on a six-lane, limited-access freeway—I notice that one of the rows of Arabic lettering has been obliterated by a bucket of white paint and the embassy driver says contentedly, "That was Baghdad Street."

But there is a Cairo Street, a Tehran Street—how familiar the latter name has become, and, of course, we have just flown in from the former—and, along these and other avenues, little sign, from a distance, of ruin and devastation. Coming out of Baghdad on the second day of the war, the "Journal" team had seen not one single building hit by what they knew had been two nights of intense bombardment—so precise was the "smart" weaponry, and so carefully chosen by the Iraqis was an evacuation route that bypassed all the targeted installations—and it is like that here, in Kuwait City, the damage seeming to have been caused more by cyclone than cluster bomb.

As abruptly as it began in the empty suburban sands, the freeway comes to a conclusion with a sharp, right-hand turn down a one-lane ramp in the middle of which has been planted, upside-down, a triangular yellow warning sign that we slalom to avert, the overloaded rear of the station wagon fishtailing under the strain. We now pass a Hotel Continental—Welcoming Back to Business, a banner declares—and tie up at the side entrance of the former Kuwait Hilton, now the International, though in this case the amendment in name was a result not of revolutionary antiimperialist nationalization, as in Iran, but of a Kuwaiti consortium buying the joint from Barron and Conrad and their kin, for pocket change.

Entering the Kuwait International, now, each of us, in turn, passes through a perfunctory security checkpoint in the lower lobby and emits a little stifled yelp of surprise. We are climbing a stairway to a spotless, air-conditioned, carpeted marble corridor that leads toward the plush and dignified main hall, the bookstore, the billiard room, the bowling alley, the menswear boutique and a French *pâtisserie* from which slim young waiters are waltzing with trays of cream puffs and nesselrode.

So far, our arrival in the emirate has been accomplished with considerably more aplomb than the greeting accorded Lord Curzon, when he became the first viceroy of India to slog onto Kuwait's dockless sands. It was in 1903, and when the procession neared the palace of the sheikh, Curzon noted, "It apparently became necessary for the cavalry escort to express their rejoicing not merely by war-cries of the most blood-curdling description, but by firing ball cartridge promiscuously either in the air or into the ground at the feet of their prancing steeds. Others hurled their spears frantically into the air. The result was the wildest confusion."

The International, by comparison, is a model of decorum. It seems to have everything: DHL courier service to and from all points; an AT&T office where calls can be placed, instantly, to any of the countries that joined George Bush's coalition; a car-rental agency with the wonderful name, after Iran, of Rent-al-Mulla; a government information office handing out free posters of the emir and the crown prince; two swimming pools, and a bank.

Unfortunately, it does not have any vacant rooms.

This we learn as Brian engages a friendly young woman at the reception desk. As with the visas, the "Journals'" Toronto headquarters has assured us that our reservations at the International are all set, though arranging them has been a difficult matter of getting NBC News in New York to contact their people in Kuwait by satellite phone to ask them to book four rooms for us. This has almost happened—there is a single reservation for a Mr. Bee-nike, which is close enough—but even this already has been given to someone else, and would we please luxuriate in one of the lobby sofas, or preferably, would we please go away?

The embassy vehicle has departed, leaving our voluminous cargo in the custody of a frantic little Buttons in a green uniform who seems to have been separated at birth from our Mister Shuttup Goddamn, up among the peaks of Kurdistan. While we wait, stewing, for four rooms to materialize through some creationist miracle, the porter pops up every five minutes—"Baggages, meester?"—and this does not end until the manager intervenes. The manager is a German named Hermann Simon who has not slept since Liberation and whose eyes now have receded into deep, blackened caves, leaving the impression, as he staggers about the lobby, tripping over millionaires, of a victim of voodoo, or Lon Chaney on Stimorol.

But Herr Simon comes through. We do get four rooms—Denike's, once again, is a suite large enough to host the Republican National Convention—and only one trifling obstacle remains. There are no keys to the rooms. Says manager Simon, sighing, peering out through the black holes, "Ze Iraqies took zem. Ve haf zree hundert rooms like zat."

So, in turn, Baggages Meester must accompany each of us to our chambers, which are in two separate towers of the enormous hotel, and each time we return from a meal or a day's shooting, he will, it appears, have to open the doors for us. This is rather infuriating to my cohorts, especially Brian, who will have to pop in and out dozens of times in the next few days, arranging fixers, vehicles and so forth. But it is less of a problem for me, since, when I arrive with my suitcase and my knapsack at room 522, I discover that my door has only a neat, round hole where the lock and knob used to be, thanks, it seems, to ze Iraqis.

Borrowing some inch-wide, reinforced gaffer tape from Maurice, I rig up a foolproof personal security system to safeguard my five thousand remaining United States dollars, my clothing and a treasury of Fruit Roll-Ups and canned tuna. First, I tape over the hole in the door so that no one can see me as I labor with my rubber-hose chest expander. Second, I call Linda back home—the line is so clear, so noiseless, she hears my hello and gasps, "Are you in Toronto?" and in her voice I hear her wishing I was.

Then I change clothes for the hotel's lavish buffet dinner and find I've got so much gaffer tape strung up, I can't open the bloody door.

2 MAY
Kuwait City

At half past ten, our inaugural morning in Kuwait City turns suddenly and frighteningly to midnight. At first, returning to my room after a sumptuous breakfast and some rummaging around the information offices on the ground floor, I have only the sensation of an approaching thunderstorm, a gathering closeness beyond the sheer, lacy curtains that are draped in front of the sliding doors that lead to my small balcony. I had gone out there last evening for a while, to look over the grounds of the U.S. Embassy just across the street—there, a besieged platoon of diplomats had mulishly withstood several weeks of the Iraqi occupation, living on rice and well-water—and beyond it to the bizarre Kuwait Towers, lauded as "visually exciting" in the 1984 edition of *Longman's Business Guide to Kuwait*, with their now-famous blue spheres skewered on obelisks like giant cocktail olives speared by toothpicks in some Brobdingnag of legal alcohol.

But now a blanket has been thrown over the city. The smoke is rolling in from the burning wells, twenty miles and more to the southwest. This is the pall through which we had descended yesterday, a windshift of just a few degrees casting it over the national capital instead of the empty sands. Moment by moment, it grows darker and darker, until I am certain that there is no more light to be sucked from the heavens and the sun has utterly disappeared. If Saudi Arabia was Mars, then Kuwait has become Venus, a shrouded planet of perpetual eclipse.

The streetlights come on, and swaying, loosely anchored strands of bulbs that hang down a dozen stories from the hotel's roof are lighted by some baffled photovoltaic cell. I am reluctant to yank open the balcony door and step outside, fearing that I'll let smoke into my room, thence through the hole in the door to the hallway beyond, but curiosity prevails and I step outside to discover, not a choking chemical stew, but a coolish, dry, breezy, comfortable dusk, lighted just at its farthest western fringe by the glow of brilliant daylight where the cloud's extremity must be. There is no smell of smoke at all—it is above me, wafting out over the Persian Gulf, to fall, some experts have predicted, as black rain on the plains of Iran or, blown even farther eastward, to smother the prevailing Himalayan air currents and disrupt India's life-giving monsoon.

Sliding the portal closed, I once again tear all the gaffer tape off my doorjamb and rush across the hall to get Maurice, who has not shot a single frame of video since the twenty-first of April, at the camp for the survivors of the gassing of Halabja where he was shoved around by the Iranian officer. He is already set up and filming—and worried, understandably, about what this air will do to his asthma over the next few hours and days and weeks. I suggest that the view is even better from my side of the hotel and so, with Chris coming up to join us from his room in the other tower, we assemble on my balcony, disregarding the Please— no photography decal on the sliding door, and for the first time in eleven days and five countries—Iran–Turkey (for refuelling)–Germany–Egypt– Kuwait—we are making television again.

Our assignment in Kuwait is, first, to report on the battle of the Canadians in the oil fields against the hellacious fires; and then, a general survey of life and politics in the emirate in the springtime of its deliverance. There already was a "Journal" crew in Kuwait City in late February, the day after the Iraqis stole away in full retreat, but theirs was a hurried visit at a frenzied hour. The pressures I feel now are not of time and certainly not of danger—the war is long over and it can take two full hours to do justice to the hotel's dinner buffet—but the more insidious, personal need to produce something of quality from this shoot after all this farcical, expensive traveling and all these wasted days. I know the other three men feel it also. I could sense during the landing in the 747 that the panorama of destruction outside the portholes represented a tiny nation's tragedy, and a cameraman's dream.

To the west, from my little balcony on the fifth floor of the Kuwait International, Maurice frames the silhouette of the downtown office towers against the narrow rim of golden sky. The rest is a thick gray-black ceiling, about five thousand feet above us, drifting toward the gulf. There is hardly a sound: only a couple of Marines lazily patrolling the perimeter of the American Embassy; the odd car traveling the beach road, oblivious to the traffic signals; and, once, a muffled kaboom that indicates that the French soldiers painstakingly combing the seafront have disposed of another Iraqi land mine.

Devoid of sound and movement, in this crazy midday darkness, the famous city whose fate had become intertwined with all those lives in Wheeling and Beallsville and Pittsburgh seems more like a cardboard model, a film-studio special effect, than a living-place of real people. In the borough of Queens in New York City, there is such an attraction—you ride in little gondolas over and around a scale model of Gotham, first in "daylight"; then, darkness falls and thousands of tiny lights come on. Kuwait City feels the same, a Lucas-Spielberg trick.

We get a call from Brian to come look at the view from where he is, in NBC's editing suite at the other side of the complex. There, a window leads onto the roof of the hotel's grand ballroom, where scions of Kuwaiti royalty once threw lavish balls, and soon will again. (When they get back from London.) Maurice and Chris walk out to get another shot, pointing back and up at the hotel tower, with the disc of the noonday sun just barely detectable, a faint circle in the gloom.

Doubtless, we are more energized by this display of magnificent pollution than are the guys from NBC, who have seen it too often before. (Their producer has been "in theater" since August 3, 1990, the day after Saddam's steamroller crossed the Kuwaiti line.) But even they rouse themselves to grab some tape of the phenomenon; this, they aver, is the worst it's been in weeks. Aren't we lucky.

For Brian, the whole draining ordeal is beginning again—all the planning and arranging and organizing that the viewing public, switching channels as soon as my face appears, never sees or appreciates. When we were in Frankfurt, we received from Toronto a folio of faxes as thick as a phone book; it contained articles and research about Kuwait and the fires and we have culled lists of names to try to contact. This is good—it would be even better if the local telephone system was working—but clippings from *Newsweek* and the *Economist* do not serve to transport all the gear or set up the interviews. So the producer knuckles down, determinedly, and is not particularly cheered by my report that Rent-al-Mulla in the hotel lobby is sold out of every wagon, jeep, limousine, dune buggy, rickshaw and sedan chair in its garage.

While our producer tries to find someone who knows someone with a van, the crew and I set out to photograph Kuwait City under its veil of preternatural night. This has us, minutes later, in the firm grip of Baggages Meester, who is leading us toward a round-faced, gap-toothed man in an absolutely filthy *dishdasha* who turns out to be a taxi driver in cahoots, no doubt, with the effervescent bellhop. The houseman—we love him immediately—is dubbed "Rochester," after the wily houseman of the penurious Jack Benny, and we settle into his dust-covered, battle-ship-sized, midseventies Chevrolet for a cruise around the world's wealthiest war zone.

We begin on the seaside corniche, heading for the "exciting" Kuwait Towers. Turning from the hotel ramp onto Arabian Gulf Street, the four-lane avenue that runs for miles along the waterfront, Rochester immediately plants the pedal to the metal, the eight-cylinder brontosaurus accelerates like a Saturn V booster and I, in the front seat, remembering the old woman in Tehran—and the fact that Kuwait, even under Islamic alcoholic prohibition, has the highest per capita rate of highway fatalities in the world—begin a rhythmic chant of "slowly, slowly, slowly" that the crew, and then Rochester himself, picks up in turn until it turns into something like a kindergarten rendition of "Row, Row, Row Your Boat" and the driver finally grasps what we are suggesting; namely, that 120 is a trifle swift, especially when the light we are just passing through is red.

The sky is beginning to lighten a bit as we approach the three towers, one of which contains a restaurant high in its big blue globule. (Another is a water tank and the third tower does not have a sphere attached to it.) Now, a pattern is set that will hold true all over the city—many buildings, seemingly little damaged from a distance, turn out on closer inspection to be hollow, looted, burned out. So it is with the Kuwait Towers—a couple of big shell holes are visible at their bases and the restaurant's panoramic windows have been blown out and stains of soot have oozed down, evidence of an awful torching.

Back at the airport, the man from the Canadian Embassy had warned us against walking on or near the beach—a half-dozen people, mostly children, were being blown up daily, he said, after triggering lightly buried mines—but beyond the towers on the plush yellow sand, some men are surf-casting, and not only have they trod on the forbidden zone, they've parked their cars at the waterline.

Perhaps recognizing that he is in the ultimate no-parking area—and that any fish he reels in are likely to come preoiled for easier frying—one of the anglers takes a small carpet from the trunk of his car, lays it gently on the sand and begins his noon prayers in the freakish smoke screen of the day. From here, I reckon, a pilgrim could motor down to Mecca and back in a weekend. Never have I been as near to Islam's holy nucleus.

From the beach, we drive through the downtown business district, which is virtually lifeless on a Thursday—the beginning of the Muslim weekend—and here also, though some shops appear to be well stocked but merely closed at the moment, are blackened shells of cars, heaps of garbage, looted storefronts and uprooted paving stones, as if nothing had been touched since the Liberation. The odd outpost of life—a pharmacy, an incongruous pizza stand serving some loitering G.I.'s—makes the scene even more mad, The Day After in a real place. Only at the Meridien Hotel, its copper-colored glass tower pockmarked here and there by blasted windows, with shredded steel cables hanging out of the obliterated rooms, is any work being done. In the charred wreckage of the opulent lobby, a couple of very dark-skinned laborers—probably South Indian— with gauze masks over their mouths and noses are wheeling barrows of ashes and shattered glass out of the building and dumping them—with a concerto of tinkling breakage that Chris carefully records—in big piles on the sidewalk. Yet the hotel—a few rooms, at least—is open for business.

The atmosphere has reached a grayish compromise between day and night as we drive—slowly, slowly, slowly—back down the harborside road, past two of the ruling family's larger palaces, gutted and raped, a deserted hospital, empty schools, the pillaged yacht club—many boats have been towed into the parking lot and set ablaze; only the charcoal hulls remain—and stretches of luxuriant beach-sand on which, defying fate, families are strolling and children are kicking soccer balls, as at the tomb of the Imam Khomeini. Every few blocks we halt to do some shooting, treading with nerve-tingling caution a few tentative steps onto the beach, though Rochester seems oblivious to all danger and goes flopping off in his torn sandals, kicking up little dust-devils of sand.

The strand is paralleled by sandbagged Iraqi fortifications, the front-line positions in which they concentrated their defenders when Operation Imminent Thunder—a masterful exercise in military sleight-of-hand and manipulation of the press—made it seem that the assault on Kuwait would come by sea, not land. The rows of trenches and redoubts stretch for miles along the coast, constructed with thousands of sacks of the abundant sand and bulwarked with red and green bricks torn out of the ornamental promenade. Secondary and tertiary positions lie along the median strip of the coast road and the first few inland streets, all of them still stocked with cases of ammunition that we deem unwise to take home as souvenirs, lest the bunkers be booby-trapped.

Farther along, we pass the seaside SAS Hotel, where a United Nations delegation is staying, and on the boulevard in front of the complex, another row of burned-out cars, their windows shattered, tires taken, ornaments stripped, seats and upholstery melted into a chocolate fondue of fabric and tar. A couple of days ago, one of the UN guardsmen says, a small truck exploded just in front of the hotel—right where we are standing—and six people were blown to bits. No one knows why.

Not far away, a small building has suffered the same kind of detonation. The roof has collapsed, big chunks of concrete have fallen from the walls, the furniture and interior decorations are a wrecked and twisted shambles, and the only part of the structure left unscathed is a tall tower, at the very top of which is a red-and-white barrel that bears the portrait of that great American military officer, Col. Harlan Sanders. From a bunker in the parking lot of the ravaged restaurant, long, narrow trenches extend north and south, as hasty and primitive as Confederate earthworks. One of the dugouts is right in front of a posted menu, priced in dinars, that must have marked the entrance to the drive-thru ramp at this Unlucky Fried Chicken shack.

From here, it is only a short ride to the one active center of life in liberated Kuwait, though the way Rochester puts the hammer down whenever I pause for half a second in my begging for mercy, even Saskatoon would be just an hour or so away. This is the grand, modern Sultan Center, a combination supermarket and department store that managed to remain open through most of the occupation, undamaged amid the spiteful wreckage all around.

The Sultan, entered through automatic doors and a quick, friendly frisking from an assistant manager, puts an end to whatever trepidation of famine and discomfort might still be lingering in me from the first hours of the shoot, two weeks ago. We have entered a mid-American shopping-cart theme park, recreated in a ministate that only a few decades ago was home only to several thousand pearl divers and desert nomads. (In Lord Curzon's time, it was even worse. To board his vessel and escape the sheikhdom, he complained, "we had to feel our way very gingerly on foot over heaps of ordure and amid indescribable filth.") In the place of the mud walls of the old city and the medieval *souk,* we have here one level bulging with every conceivable foodstuff, soft drink, condiment, vegetable, meat, fowl and frozen dessert and, at the top of a very long escalator, a virtual Wal-Mart of sundries. Up here, they sell shoes, toys, sporting goods, power tools and a selection of T-shirts, peaked caps and umbrellas in the national colours of red, green, black and white, all stamped with the motto FREE KUWAIT, which now has passed from a defiant command chanted by Kent State students and James Baker into a declarative clause reflecting the national mood, if not the Sultan Center's sky-high prices.

Gliding down the moving stairs, I meet the manager of the operation, a young, well-dressed Jordanian. He says that, yes, it is true that he had to bribe the occasional Iraqi general to remain in business during the seven-month annexation, but this was a modest price to pay to escape the general pillage and, besides, who knew if the United States really would go to war to liberate a kingdom full of Arabs. The huge store, he says, had been forced to close for only five days last August, as the Iraqis rolled in, and for two days in January, when the first attacks on Baghdad led many people here to expect that the Americans might try to free Kuwait by bombing it back to the pearl-diving age.

But the manager's success in avoiding his store's obliteration has come with a price; Kuwaiti customers are accusing him of collaborating with the enemy, and this is no frivolous gibe. Already, reports suggest that dozens, maybe hundreds, of non-Kuwaitis have been lynched for their complaisance—or merely their indifference—during the half year of Iraqi usurpation. In a compact state whose prewar population was more than half nonnative—Palestinian clerks and mechanics; Filipina housemaids; South Indians imported to muck about in the oil fields and now, to sweep the ashes from the Meridien Hotel—the sorting out is getting ugly. It is the story we mean to cover, after the oil fires.

"They are harassing me," the Jordanian manager says. "They say, 'Why did you pay the Iraqis?' It's getting worse. I'm a little afraid. Now my car is missing. It's a 1990 Caprice."

Leaning against his own Chevy of Nixonian vintage, Rochester watches us go about our filming of customers bustling in and, heavily laden, out of the Sultan Center. There is a lovely moment: two Kuwaiti army officers in khaki and braid deposit some sacks of groceries in the boot of a Mercedes, climb in and whisper away. And there are a number of United Nations peacekeepers, newly arrived in country, loading up on pop and chips. These are Kenyans, Austrians, a brace of Canadians, and two Russians who stand near the row of cash registers, mesmerized by the abundance, yet seemingly afraid to actually begin shopping, like young kids at the lip of a chilly swimming pool.

The only items we purchase, among all the bounty of the Sultan Center, are a couple of cases of Emirates brand spring water and a copy of the broadsheet, light-green *Arab Times*, printed in Saudi Arabia and trucked up from Dhahran, along with virtually everything else on sale these days in Kuwait. The paper is excellent in most respects—it includes everything from Stanley Cup playoff results to insightful analysis of the Indian parliamentary election campaign, state by state. Only on one subject does the *Arab Times* go a bit snaky: an article about the rough treatment of jailed Palestinian women in the West Bank, even as they are giving birth, is headlined, Israel Sets New Record for Genocide.

The *Arab Times* reports that Peter Arnett, the CNN man whose network was allowed to remain in Baghdad after all other correspondents were ordered to leave—and who refused to let Brian Denike, or anyone else, file reports, or simply reassure a frantic home office, on their network's private telephone line—is in Copenhagen to receive an award.

Another article notes that the superb Polish journalist, Ryszard Kapuscinski, has written his memoirs, harrowing tales, the newspaper says, of "more than fifteen wars and insurrections," not counting numerous other riots, disasters, assassinations, overthrows and close shaves.

It is, indeed, an estimable total, far more death and misery than any one pair of eyes should have to endure. But foreign correspondents have been measured, ever since William Howard Russell sat down calmly on a hilltop to monitor the Charge of the Light Brigade—probably, since Homer—by their proximity to the red glare.

This is not always glorious. The BBC's John Simpson, congratulated on his return to London for his coverage of a fierce battle during the Iran-Iraq war, wrote of his embarrassment, "remembering how I had grovelled fearfully in the mud of Faw while the bombing was going on." It was the cameraman, Nick Reed, who had stood his ground and kept "shooting."

Another man widely respected for his fortitude was the Australian cameraman Neil Davis, whose dedication and courage in Vietnam and Cambodia became the subject of a documentary film that was nominated for an Academy Award. During my years as a resident correspondent in

China, the foreign press corps often was reporting little more than stories of disco dancing, "rich" peasants and the gala opening of Maxim's de Pékin; my personal nadir was a profile of a Shanghai surgeon who specialized in the reconstruction of penises for men who had sliced their willies off in industrial accidents and suicide attempts or who, in one unlucky instance, had it bitten off by a pig. We would sit around and bemoan the trivialities of our beat and voice admiration for real men like the valorous Neil Davis.

Then, in September, 1984, during a brief and unsuccessful attempt at a military coup d'état in Thailand, Neil Davis and his sound man went out to do their jobs and a stray bullet hit Davis who, his camera still rolling, fell dead. In Beijing, we swallowed hard and went back to our innocent features.

Since then, blessed by outrageously good fortune, I have been kept out of the line of fire. In the Amazon, warriors who a few years earlier had massacred a group of white interlopers in their jungle fastness wanted only to sell feather headdresses when I dropped in. In Panama City, a military officer was airlifted out of prison by co-conspirators and, before he surrendered, several insurgents were shot in a downtown street; but, when Brian Denike and I showed up, ten minutes later, it was over. In Kurdistan, when I scaled the mountain, there were blankets, tents, water, food.

On Friday evening, June 2, 1989, I flew from Beijing to Hong Kong, my crew and I—and a dozen other journalists—believing that the stalemate at Tian'anmen Square, now three weeks old, would hold through the weekend. It didn't, but by the time we managed to make our way back on Sunday morning, the massacre had been done.

In Sri Lanka, in the Punjab, in riot-torn cities of India and Korea, even in Bangladesh, after a devastating cyclone in May, 1985, that killed tens of thousands, erasing their lives and dwellings from the fragile sandbars of the Bay of Bengal, I have been too late, sometimes too timid to bear witness to the very worst of times. Or perhaps just too fortunate.

Maybe not. Finishing the newspaper just as we arrive back at the Kuwait International Hotel, I thank Rochester for his safe conduct, help the crew hump the gear upstairs, stroll down the hallway to 522 and find that instead of installing a new knob and lock, now they've taken my door.

3 MAY
Kuwait City

One way to contract a fixer in a strange place—a process producer Denike continues to labor at this morning, so far without success—is to use a little ingenuity. In Brazil, when it came time for my crew and me to fly in two small chartered planes into the very heart of the Amazonian darkness to visit the endangered Kayapo Indians, the translator we had been using throughout the shoot—an American expatriate living in Rio de Janeiro—announced on the very eve of lift-off that he was refusing to go.

Some people have the attitude "Never say die"; this man's was "Never say live." We were flying into a restricted area without formal government approval, he protested—that was true enough. (But the Indians had invited us.) He said, "I can't be caught doing anything like that. I'm a foreigner. I'll get in a lot of trouble."

We suggested, then, that his wife, a Brazilian woman, accompany us instead, while he would stay behind and luxuriate in the delights of the frontier city of Maraba, which weren't many. He rejected this idea also. He said, "She can't be caught doing anything like that. She's a Brazilian. She'll get in a lot of trouble."

"Is there anyone else in Maraba who speaks English?" I asked our helpmate.

"Not a chance," he replied, pleased with himself.

I got up and went to the front desk of our hotel. In my excellent Portuguese, I asked the clerk if there was a college in Maraba, or even a high school. He nodded. I told the clerk, "Call the high school and tell them we want to meet the English teacher."

Within the hour, a small, bookish man—in spectacles, the mark of the anglophone, worldwide—walked into the lobby. He announced himself as the local instructor in the world tongue. We marched him into the restaurant for a brief interrogation.

The little man said, "I have translated the works of Poe."

My producer cocked an eyebrow.

"'Once upon a midnight dreary,'" I tried.

"'While I pondered, weak and weary,'" the professor replied.

"'Over many a quaint and curious volume'?" I posed.

"'Of forgotten lore'!" he closed.

"You're hired," we, in unison, deposed.

It was a major mistake. The next morning, before dawn, the bard arrived to join our convoy to the rain forest. We were hauling hammocks, food, rainwear, hiking boots, special antiinsect jackets with mosquito netting to cover the head and face, and all the usual television gear, plus a staggering load of gifts that the Kayapo chiefs had demanded in recognition of their hospitality: fishhooks, flashlight batteries, hunting knives and thick ropes of pungent chewing tobacco for every man in the village.

The Professor showed up with a greenish complexion and a briefcase.

We took off, the planes crammed with the equipment, the gifts and, after a brief halt at the town of Redençao, a half-dozen Kayapo elders in loincloths and beaded necklaces with feathers in their hair. They had been visiting the outside. We were taking them home, winging over the verdant majesty toward a tiny settlement imperiled by deforestation and development.

The Prof turned even greener. When, at last, the Kayapo settlement hove into sight—a cleared circle of thatched dwellings, cut from the giant trees; a red-clay landing strip; tiny, dark figures running out of the houses, coming to greet the planes—he began to shudder and groan.

We dropped toward the runway, stall-warning buzzers screaming from both motors as our pilot, wiping away cataracts of sweat with a handkerchief, marshaled all his skill and scraped the overloaded aircraft to a safe halt on the russet soil. I looked over at the professor. He was saying, "No, no, no." He wouldn't get out. Small boys with blue-black face paint were climbing on the wings now, peering through the windows at us.

When the planes took off, leaving us in the circle of primeval huts, the English teacher still was aboard. I saw him waving from the porthole. From then on, I let the producer find a fixer.

There was a sequel to the episode with the schoolteacher from Maraba. Shortly after our return from the Kayapo village, the little man ventured into the hotel to collect his pay. Not only did he expect compensation for his morning of *mal d'air*, he wanted money for the two succeeding days he would have spent with us if he hadn't been feeling so punk.

This resulted in a rather unseemly dialogue that revealed even more of the teacher's English vocabulary. Moving aside, I let the producer, Harry Phillips, handle the affair. With Harry, the scholar was lucky if he got bus fare home.

"What a jerk," Harry spat as the poet stormed away. "He said if I didn't pay him for three full days, he'd tell the police we were in an Indian area without permission."

We shrugged it off and headed for Manaus on the Upper Amazon. A few days later, talking to Toronto and our researcher, Daniel Schwartz, Harry blanched.

"Schwartz says he's just spoken to a contact in Brasilia," Harry reported. "And this guy tells him that the police are searching for a Canadian film crew, somewhere on the Upper Amazon."

At the Kuwait International Hotel on the sixty-fourth day after Liberation, breakfast, like dinner and lunch, is an epicurean extravaganza of fresh fruits, omelets, flapjacks, delicious Middle-Eastern *foul* beans with diced onions, croissants, cereals and a selection of tortes, tarts, honeycakes and custards that renders all of us willing casualties of Operation Dessert Storm. The dining room clientele is an interesting mix of British, French and Saudi officers, Arab and Western businessmen hoping to reap lucrative reconstruction contracts and a few journalists mopping up. I sit with cronies from my China years—a man from the *New York Times*, another from the *Daily Telegraph* with whom I'd last crossed paths a year ago this week, on May Day in Havana—swapping stories and rumors and memories, basking in the easy fellowship at a lull in the world's tragic race.

The foreign press corps has been greatly reduced from what must have been a fractious, frenzied legion of sleepless reporters in the first days after Bob McKeown, and then the Marines, arrived. (Linda reports on the phone that she has seen McKeown and Arthur Kent on the Phil Donahue show. I wonder if Bob mentioned the night he and I went to the topless cabaret show at the MGM Grand in Las Vegas as a highlight of his formative years.) Though CNN still is holding an entire restaurant just off the main lobby as its production facility and studio—No Admittance Without CNN Escort, a sign on the door proscribes—NBC's exhausted producer expects his network to finally pull out in a week or so, and most of the American newsmen and women here are waiting for the last U.S. troops to be withdrawn from the Kuwait-Iraq border so that they, too, can go home.

My enthusiasm, by comparison, makes me look like Anne of Green Gables in a den of half-alive opium fiends. All the elements we are so assiduously pursuing—the fire fighters, the Palestinian dilemma, the mess in the streets—they have been reporting for weeks and months, chained to this assignment and this groaning buffet. (They are also, many of them, quite savagely hung over. How?) But I am used to this. I remember arriving in Dhaka six days after the cyclone of '85—it was the fastest available connection from Beijing to Bangladesh—and breezing into the elegant Sonargaon Hotel just as a friend was paying his bill and checking out, singing, "Hi, Al—story's over!"

These are some of the things the other reporters tell me. Some of them might even be true.

—A week after the war began, knowing they'd be routed, Iraqi troops in Kuwait began taking the rims of bicycle wheels and packing them with plastic explosives, set to ninety-nine-day fuses. Tomorrow is the ninety-ninth day!

—Red Adair's famous fire-fighting team from Texas, pissed off with the Kuwaiti government, has packed up and left the country.

—A herd of wild horses has been seen roaming the blazing oil fields.

—A Filipino laborer engaged in cleanup work picked up a pair of gloves in an abandoned Iraqi bunker and both his hands were blown off by a booby-trap.

—There will be hot water in our hotel, beginning tonight.

—And one U.S. newspaper has reported, quoting local residents, that the emir himself, the dour Sheikh Jaber al-Ahmad al-Jaber al-Sabah, has resumed his custom of selecting young virgins, marrying them as "temporary wives," plucking their delicate flowers, then divorcing them in the Islamic manner, a short time later, by reciting a few sentences in Arabic. The offspring of such assignations, the newspaper says, is at least thirty-seven children and possibly as many as 120. The reporter involved has been hauled in to the Ministry of Information for chastisement, or disembowelment.

It is a much brighter day. With the smoke blowing more toward the south and east and out over open water, Kuwait City reveals itself, from my balcony, under the warm blue desert sky, the balls of the Kuwait Towers reflecting blindly in the glare. Below me, in the grounds of the U.S. Embassy, I see a slide and a swing in a children's play area, a satellite dish, a swimming pool. The glimmering gulf, the beach, the palm trees, the low-rise pastel-painted residential neighborhoods spreading from a concentrated urban core—it much resembles, on this dry, pleasant day, St. Petersburg, Florida. But beyond this city is a sandy haze, and behind the haze, Iraq.

In the lazy midafternoon, Brian comes to my room—there being no door, he needn't knock—and invited me down to the lobby to meet the man he has hired to work with us, a young, good-looking Lebanese named Aboud. Though he has lived most of his twenty-six years in the realm of Kuwait's reputedly amorous emir, Aboud is not a Kuwaiti citizen, and never will be. (The privilege is reserved for male descendents of native Arab families resident in Kuwait before 1920.) But he hardly sounds bitter. Jovial, hip, a little playboyish, Aboud is a mirror of the emirate's modern history, part of the large expatriate managerial class his social standing midway between the white-robed oil tycoons and the dark-skinned laborers) that has prospered here and had been well accepted, until the Iraqis came.

When that happened, Aboud, and many like him, neither hailed the invasion as the first hammer blow toward the liberation of Palestine, nor joined the Kuwaiti resistance, sniping at occupying troops from rooftops and windows. He got by; he changed the license plates on his silver Audi to the new ones that said Kuwait, Iraq; he drove all the way to Baghdad to try to phone worried relatives in California and England; he recalls being stopped at a military checkpoint near the Sultan Center and an Iraqi officer laughing and saying, "So, where is George Bush?" When George Bush answered, Aboud lined up for a new "foreigner's" identity card and changed his license plates again.

Brian has found him through another young man who is working here for NBC. Unmarried and unhurried, Aboud is eager for the good life to resume. (One of his few complaints is that during the Iraqi occupation, there were no fresh bananas.) Aboud is no journalist, no Kamran Farzal; educated in Britain, he cannot even read Arabic, though he speaks it, of course. He has never translated a single line of Poe.

We hope he will lead us to beleaguered Palestinians hiding from vigilante mobs, a symptom of lingering anger and displacement in a society our audience might be thinking of as liberated and free; a problem solved. We hope he can help us contact the incipient democracy movement, the growing opposition to the hereditary oligarchy. Most of all, I hope he will be another Mihai.

The morning after the gun battle we blundered into in the streets of Timişoara, at the height of the Romanian revolution of December, 1989, we made our way across the nervous city and found the hotel where the body of the world's press had taken refuge. The young Hungarian translator, barely out of high school, who had come with us from Budapest had not expected the rumbling through the hostile night in a flimsy, unprotected Lada, following an iron-clad armored vehicle; the rifle fire that trapped us in a narrow alley at midnight; the sanctuary of a bare lobby floor. Now, the morning after, she made it clear that she wanted to go home.

So did I, but we were duty-bound to travel on to Bucharest, at the other end of the bloodied country, hundreds of miles to the east. I set about to find a translator who might talk us through the barricades and navigate the roadways. In the breakfast hall of the Hotel Continental, I stumbled onto Mihai Carp.

He was an American of Romanian extraction, a student at the London School of Economics, whose father had been a radio broadcaster. He was fluent in Romanian, thanks to his parents, but had never been in the country before. He had come over to visit an aunt in Bucharest, for Christmas, in Ceauşescu's tortured state. Now he was trapped in Timişoara. I offered him passage if he'd become our interpreter.

Like most outsiders to our bizarre, intrusive enterprise of sound bites and pieces-to-camera, Mihai knew even less than I did about how a monumental event like the downfall of a dictator gets transformed into "news" reports on somebody's little screen back home. In the next few days, we'd both learn a lot in a hurry.

We made it across the country without incident—again, my arrival had caused the guns to be put away—and in the ensuing week we explored the legacy of a tyrant's rule. Through Mihai's aunt and her circle of contacts, we met a writer who, days earlier, was living in internal exile for having criticized the Genius of the Carpathians; now, suddenly, he was minister of Culture. In a full-scale Manitoban snowstorm, we interviewed an architect who had been compelled to help design a megalomaniacal president's palace for the Ceauşescu dynasty. And we found the former home of the gymnast Nadia Comaneci, once a national adornment, then an officially vilified traitoress who had defected to America, and now simply a confused young woman who had left hundreds of teddy bears and china dolls behind.

On New Year's Eve, the first rumors began to reach us of the existence of vast, secret orphanages where thousands of unwanted children—their lives a product of the dictator's prohibition of birth control—allegedly were being raised as automatons to be put to the service of the one-party state, or to be sold to foreigners. We asked Mihai to help us locate one of these places. He found someone who knew where one was.

In the melting mush of late afternoon we pulled up at the gates of what once had been a Christian school; a small, sad church stood at the heart of the complex. We started to unload our camera, recorder and tripod, but two officials of the orphanage spotted us and dashed out to intervene. They told Mihai they were not yet ready to let the world see the world within the fence. They were afraid, they said; the revolution might yet be lost; the Securitate might return.

Mihai asked if he might leave his name and telephone number in case the officials changed their mind. They assented, but when our translator handed them a small piece of paper, the men began to gasp.

"Carp?" one said. "Are you related to Carp of Radio Free Europe?"

"He is my father," Mihai replied.

"Oh, God! The son of Carp!" the men cried, and Mihai interpreted their exultation. "He kept our hopes alive, for so many years. He was our voice of truth. And you are his son...."

The gates of the orphanage swung open. Behind them were infants in bare metal cages; perhaps the pictures that we and others took helped open for a few of them the door to a life of love. It was a pretty good showing for a first-time fixer. Maybe we'll get lucky with Aboud.

4 MAY
Al-Ahmadi

Aboud doesn't drive like Rochester. He drives faster. We are on the al-Safr Motorway heading southward out of Kuwait City to meet our fire fighters, Aboud is pushing the Audi up to a nice round 150 km/h and when I, in the back seat, venture politely that maybe he could slow it down a little—say, by half—the young Lebanese turns around and giggles.

"Am I scaring you?" he asks.

"No," I reply. "*I'm* scaring me."

While this is going on, Aboud continues to rocket down the freeway, passing the airport, a soccer stadium, the surprisingly seedy residential district where many Palestinians live, dozens more burned-out, abandoned cars and, finally, sailing right past our intended exit, which, like Baghdad Street, has been painted over so that the blue sign shows only a splash of white stain.

The town to which we are destined—after Aboud finds a way to get off this highway and turn around—is al-Ahmadi, named for a Kuwaiti monarch of the first half of this century, Sheikh Ahmad al-Jaber al-Sabah, a link in the unbroken line of the al-Sabah family that has ruled Kuwait since the seventeen-fifties. (There now are more than twelve hundred al-Sabahs in Kuwait, each distantly related—and consanguineously beholden—to the current emir, the result of centuries of "temporary" marriages to the daughters of aspiring clans.)

It was Sheikh Ahmad who, in 1934, signed the first agreements under which British and American companies began to drill for petroleum in the Kuwaiti desert. In 1946, Sheikh Ahmad turned a silver handle aboard the British tanker *Grenadier* and began the exportation of oil, making himself, with the stroke of a pen and a flick of the wrist, the proprietor of one of the world's richest patches of sand. The meticulously planned community nearest the drilling zone, headquarters for the Kuwait Oil Company, took the name of the emir who sanctioned its enterprise, but when the Iraqis arrived in August, 1990, they changed this to al-Nida—"the summons" or "the beckoning"—as if they had been invited, and erected new exit signs along the thruway.

This was followed, of course, by Desert Storm, and when the war began to go badly for Iraq—after about half an hour—Saddam Hussein made ready to destroy the Kuwaiti oil industry and the wealth of the al-Sabahs. The latter is probably impossible—the money, some eighty billion dollars, is too well and widely invested—but the sabotage of the wellheads has been a brilliant success. Hundreds and hundreds of fires are uncontrollably raging, al-Ahmadi, as we finally approach it, is sheathed in a black, toxic fog, nearly all the men who worked in the oil patch have fled, and, so far, the Kuwaitis' principal act of reconstruction has been to throw paint at the al-Nida signs.

The exit ramp from the motorway leads us to a military checkpoint set at the end of a slalom run made of the charred shells of dead cars. An Iraqi artillery piece sits blankly on the curb. A half-dozen Kuwaiti soldiers, most of them snoozing unconcernedly in lawn chairs, are posted just outside the town limits, guarding against vandalism and enemy attack, though, in this regard, they're a little late. This hardly matters. Behind them, the curtain of darkness that obscures the western sky is warning enough that this is the turnstile to Hell.

The road divides here, separating into one-way crescents as it circles the abandoned town hall, then rejoins as we enter the deserted, ghostly, company town. On our left is the headquarters complex itself—large, hangarlike structures that contain offices and pumping machinery. These have been looted, blown up, burned and, from two precise wounds in the roof of one building, apparently "smart-bombed" in an attempt to stanch the flow of oil into the blue gulf waters that began when the Iraqis opened all the valves and, laughing, ran away.

To the right is part of the housing area, long streets lined with bungalows for KOC executives and less handsome garden apartment blocks for laborers, nearly all of them—engineers, pencil-pushers, roughnecks—lured to Kuwait from somewhere else to take up residence in this neat, shaded, trim little town that, again, feels so much like Florida. My map shows parks, a kindergarten, boys' and girls' schools, a riding club, playing fields, cinemas—a nineteen-fifties vision of Americana dropped onto Thesiger's "bitter, desiccated land which knows nothing of gentleness and ease." Oil had changed this—al-Ahmadi even had a country club—but the fount of prosperity had been put to the torch, and three months later, the gentleness has not returned.

In unison, nervously, the five of us take a last, dramatic draft of air just as the Audi moves under the canopy of smoke. Here, it is not the high ceiling that, two days ago in Kuwait City, created beneath it a cool, comfortable shade; in al-Ahmadi, the smoke billows and boils, sometimes just a gray haze, then a coal-black tornado barely, it seems, out of reach. It is as if Denike, the tallest of our team, should duck out of the poison's way.

And now, for the first time, we *hear* the fires—though we cannot see them from the center of the town—a dull roaring from the south and west like a jet flying overhead, circling and circling without cease.

We are trying to find Ahmadi House, the KOC guest quarters that is serving as dormitory and cafeteria for the men who are battling with the Iraqis' blazing bequest. Looping around a succession of traffic circles—there is absolutely no traffic—we come to it in midmorning, a compound of motel-type residences and a central meeting and eating building with a long, shaded porch. From the smoke and the noise and the drawling voices of the men emerging from the breakfast hall, it could be the Sodom and Gomorrah campus of some Oklahoma bible school.

The men are employees of the three U.S. companies that have been hired by the royal family to put the golden egg together again. Most are in uniform: crimson, for Red Adair's unit, which has quite obviously not quit and gone home (although the celebrated Adair, now past seventy, has been standing well back from the smoke and heat; he's in Houston); yellow, for another Texas outfit called Wild Well Control; and nut brown, the team color of the Boots and Coots varsity, though, in each case, the men's coveralls are so filthy, so utterly soaked in oil, tar and grease, it is nearly impossible to tell the Harvards from the Yales. The faces are sunburnt, basted and barbecued; the hands are bear paws, the hair lathered in petroleum shampoo. Blue eyes burst from worn leather sockets and torn lips emit black-speckled spit and spectacular profanity as the veterans of one of the world's dirtiest, daringest and highest-paying outdoor jobs sprawl on the veranda for a few moments' ease, picking their teeth with pocket knives.

We are a motley assortment in our own right, in our jeans and clean shirts and running shoes, about as apt for the fire and filth of Kuwait as the Professor was for exploring Amazonia in dress pants and a suit jacket. Already, standing in front of Ahmadi House, we are noticing little black dots on our forearms and the backs of our necks. Picking at one with a fingernail bursts the globule of tar and a little stream of grime runs out, then quickly hardens and dries. And, as the desert wind ebbs and gusts and blusters, the smell of smoke blows in from the nearest fires, which are not more than a half mile away. Some sparrows flit through low bushes. When they alight, on the eaves of the mess hall, I see that they are blackened, like miniature crows.

The Canadian employees of an Alberta company called Safety Boss, fourth of the firms under contract to the KOC and the ruling emir, the grandson of Sheikh Ahmad, do not appear to be about. As with the Kuwaiti visas and the rooms at the International Hotel, we are advised that Toronto has arranged with the owner-president of Safety Boss, Mike Miller, for access to his crewmen while they essay their hazardous task. Unable to telephone Ahmadi House from Kuwait City—this twenty-mile linkup remains severed while intercontinental satellite calls fly about with perfect clarity—we have come to appeal in person to Miller for permission to spend a few days with Canada's blowout boys.

The yard where Safety Boss has stockpiled its equipment is a few blocks away, part of a huge storage and engineering area that, like the KOC headquarters complex, has been pillaged and wrecked by the villainous foe. The sight has already become a commonplace—the carcasses of pickup trucks and tractor-trailers; the big holding tanks, crushed like soda cans. We are at the edge of the town when we enter the Canadians' fenced compound. The roar of the fires works through the windows of the Audi. The sky has disappeared.

In the Safety Boss yard, men in overalls and gauze masks are building a shed for some of the company's tools. The workers—they are Pakistanis and Egyptians—shake their heads; the Canadians have all gone out into the fields. We look around. There are two full-sized house trailers being used as management offices, two dark red fire engines labeled Smokey I and Smokey IV—perhaps II and III are in-country also, but out at the job site—and big freight containers scattered around the sandy quadrangle like cabanas on some tropical beach. I have had no idea of the amount of hardware involved. I thought they just cleared off all the melted metal and stuff and went at the wellhead with a fire hose.

Filled with courage, swaggering and drawling like the heroic Houstonians we saw at Ahmadi House, we decide to take the silver Audi out into the oil fields to shoot some wallpaper and look for Team Canada. We are out of al-Ahmadi, following a sticky two-lane blacktop toward the blazing orange fountains when I remember an item in one of the Toronto faxes and I realize: this is how those British journalists got themselves killed.

I don't remember many of the details; it was part of that thick pile of background articles I read while we were in Frankfurt, lounging on the sofa on Sunday morning while listening to Aerosmith warble "Love in an Elevator" on the satellite TV. What I do recall is that two correspondents from the *Financial Times* were driving, unescorted, down one of these long, straight oil-patch access roads when they lost their way in the impenetrable smoke, slid off the pavement and were engulfed in the horrible flames. Maybe this is the road. If Aboud wants to motor like Parnelli Jones around here, I promise to myself, I will get out and walk home. I'm scaring myself again.

In this mood, we enter the inferno.

Now the landscape we had seen from the descending jumbo spreads out before us, as flat as some satanic Kansas, the limb of the horizon broken by dozens of vertical orange jets, as if a crust of sand had fallen over an ocean of flame that, here and there, had managed to burn its way to freedom, leaping out from narrow vents. Hypnotized—we all are—I get out of the car and stare at the closest fire. It is about a hundred yards away, screaming like the engine of a Boeing on a taxiway, captivating yet terrifying, as if the whole surface of the earth might blow apart at any moment. Maurice is set up and shooting, his big body hunched over the viewfinder, twisting the focus ring, then, satisfied with the framing, turning to me and saying, "It's unbelievable, what they did."

No one else is in sight; from here, it doesn't appear that anyone is trying to put the fires out. Then, behind us, a pickup truck zips by. It's some American soldiers. Leaning from the windows, they snap some souvenir photos, turn around and drive away.

We continue ahead, a little farther into the alien world. There are fires on both sides of the road, not big ones—it is easy to tell that some of the gushers are more powerful than others—but even more menacing, because one of the burning wells sits in the center of a pool of leaked oil and all around the perimeter of this jet-black lake are little wispy flits of dancing flames, as if the ground itself is burning away. We are so close now that even with the windows rolled up and Aboud's air conditioner set at its maximum, the ferocious heat first warms my cheek, then pinches it with pain.

Outside, a little distance away, it is hot but not uncomfortable, even when the billows of smoke abate for an instant and the full Kuwaiti sun falls through. A stiff wind is blowing from the northwest—from Baghdad—and when I face it, I can watch more of the tiny black specks accumulate on the lenses of my glasses.

A mile or so south of the Safety Boss trailers, with us still unable to see anyone at work anywhere in the fields, the road curves slightly and around this bend is a wall of the blackest smoke we have yet encountered, an opaque cone of ebony rising, narrowly at first, from a fire just a few feet from the pavement, then expanding to completely cover the roadway, blown horizontal by the whipping winds. I, for one, am not going to try to punch through this wall in anybody's car, certainly not Aboud's Audi—but there appears to be a detour around it, a pair of wheel tracks leading onto the sands, bright white marks in the blackened soil. We're about to test it.

"Would anybody know a land mine if he saw it?" I ask, and hearing this, Aboud wheels his baby around and we head back to al-Ahmadi, Kuwait.

We're plunked in purple leather sofas on the porch of Ahmadi House as the Hellfighters begin to come in for lunch. A convoy of four-by-fours, small buses and oil-splattered pickup trucks rumbles into the small parking lot. I call out, "This van must be the Canadians—they're wearing their seat belts and using the turn signal!"

In moments, the cafeteria is transformed from a quiet, orderly commissary, the trays neatly stacked and cutlery stowed and steam tables of shepherd's pie, beans, rice and vegetable soup ready to be served, into the freshman dining hall at Redneck State University. Cussin' and slurpin' and suckin' back the grub and oglin' the Filipina waitresses, the five of us fit right in. Half the Texans have cleaned off one plate, two plates, risen and bolted before the first of the Canadians come in.

The Canadians have stopped to wash their hands.

On the breast pocket of each of their light brown work suits, a tongue of flame leaps from a fallen derrick and this is the insignia of Safety

Boss Ltd. of Calgary. We introduce ourselves to a few of the workers—
the chatter is about the hockey playoffs, mostly, the Edmonton Oilers
carrying Alberta's hopes against an upstart Minnesota team—and then
Mike Miller appears. He is about my age, but big armed, heavy chested,
of medium height with receding blond hair and a drooping, flamboyant
foxtail of a mustache that must add half a pound to his weight. Yet his
voice and manner do not match his build or his occupation. He is soft-
spoken, patiently explanatory, like a grade-school teacher or a good
youth hockey coach. He welcomes our enterprise. With him, I expect
we'll survive it.

Miller provides a fifth ingredient to my kitchen-tested recipe for
journalism: curiosity, compassion, serendipity, local help and, sometimes
most important, access. An hour ago, we were strangers in the fire zone,
unable to crank out anything but some scenics from the side of the road,
like those American soldiers collecting happy-snaps from their truck.
Now, we hold the promise of joining Mike Miller's team, and of him
joining ours. After this, the work becomes "easy," just as, a reviewer
once wrote, it was "easy" for us to produce a sixty-minute documentary
on criminal justice in the Soviet Union, once the Soviets agreed to open
the door of the courthouse and the labor camp. Perhaps the reviewer was
correct; CNN, with its live cameras in the Iranian wilderness, is making
it seem too quick and automatic.

From here on, then, the burden of our effort falls almost entirely on Maurice Chabot and Lucille, his forty-thousand-dollar Sony CCD (Control
Camera Digital) color television camera. The hardware is far less important than the person who wields it. In China after Tian'anmen, in East
Berlin before the wall fell, in a dissident's flat in Havana, "Journal"
shooters have crafted first-rate scenes using ordinary home-video cam-
corders hidden in briefcases and satchels. What matters is the soul of the
mechanic. As my cameraman in the Amazon, David Donnelly, said, not
immodestly, waving off the dubious morsels offered by women of the
Kayapo tribe, "If you guys get sick, that's OK. I'm the only one we can't
live without."

The bond between the cameraman and his hardware is tight and
sacred. A couple of years ago, Maurice was filming in midtown Man-
hattan, working on a story about a Canadian fashion designer who had
hit it big in Gotham. Maurice was suffering with a heavy cold. After

completing a sequence, he gently placed Lucille on the sidewalk and reached for a handkerchief to blow his nose, the only part of his facial anatomy not covered by his Amazonia of beard and hair.

As he pulled the cloth from his pocket, a few five-dollar bills fluttered to the ground. He reached to grab them.

When he looked down again, Lucille was gone.

The big cameraman commenced to panic. He realized that the money wasn't his; it had been a distraction, a setup. Then he noticed a man leaning on a delivery truck, who was beckoning to him.

"They're in the brown car across the street," the man whispered.

What happened next, Maurice recalls in a blur of fear and foolish energy. He vaulted over a knot of snarled traffic, climbing onto trunks and hoods. He went to the brown car, reached in the driver's window, yanked the man's head out of joint, grabbed the keys from the ignition, opened the trunk and rescued his woman.

"They could have killed me," Maurice says of the affair. "They could have shoved me in the trunk and drove off. But you react at the moment, eh? She is your tool of work."

We are in Mike Miller's office in one of the house trailers at the Safety Boss camp in al-Ahmadi town. He is going to take me and the crew deep into the oil field in his high-clearance four-wheel-drive truck. (Brian will go back to Kuwait City with Aboud in the Audi and try, somehow, to get us a suitable vehicle for our own trips through the desert. He also is trying to find a helicopter pilot who will take the crew up for an overview of the destruction.)

Miller allots us each a pair of protective plastic goggles, heavy work gloves, and knee-high boots of a thin, rubbery material that the Iraqis left behind in the trenches, part of the bodysuits designed to protect against the chemical weapons Saddam brandished, but never dared deploy. He is rummaging through his desk for some gauze masks when he comes across a pair of business cards.

They are the two men of the *Financial Times*.

"They were with us just before they were killed," Miller says. "And the three Egyptian truck drivers who also were killed that day were working at one of our job sites."

The Egyptians, too, had gone off the road, confused by the blowing smoke.

"Some of our guys drove right past their car, a couple of minutes after it happened. There are so many burned-out vehicles out there, they didn't realize what it was."

"Where did it happen?" I ask, recalling our tentative probing this morning.

"About a mile south of here," Miller replies. "There's a little curve in the road where a really big fire is throwing a lot of smoke right across the highway. That's were they went off the road, right into the burning oil."

Maurice Chabot and Chris Davies climb into Miller's four-by-four and I get into another vehicle with Ken Rose, a Safety Boss engineer who, if this is possible, is even more gentlemanly than Miller. Rose, a father of three, soft faced, shy, aw-shucksy, is looking forward to the end of his first tour of duty here. Miller's men are working twenty-eight days in Kuwait without a break, then being sprung for twenty-eight unpaid days off—with a plane ticket home if they choose to go that far. Ken Rose, as we drive out of the equipment yard, tells me that he is looking forward not to four weeks of alcoholic debauch, as I'd expect, but to visiting his aging mother in Orillia, Ontario.

Our truck follows Miller's, down the paved road we had taken this morning in the Audi, to the lake of oil where the burned-out skeletons of a small car and two big water-tanker trucks rest, half submerged, in the lifeless sea. This is where the two British journalists and three Egyptian teamsters lost their way, left the road and died. It is exactly the spot where, with my jest about land mines, I convinced Aboud to turn around.

The lake of pure crude oil, as we stand by its shore, stretches a couple of hundred yards eastward from the paved road. Miller says that it is only about five feet deep, a mere puddle compared to the black oceans that lie farther into the desert. The surface is calm, flat, reflecting the flames and smoke that arc through the furious sky. Beyond it are more of the giant squashed soda cans, a storage-tank farm the Iraqis torched. A bewildered swallow flits and darts over the oil and the wreckage, as if this was some prairie pond and these were boulders, not twisted metal tombs.

The bodies have been removed and a bulldozer has created a dam of sand along the shore of the oil pond, to keep it from running onto the pavement. No one will ever know what really happened. One theory is that the heat of the engines ignited the oil into which the vehicles sank. It may have been a sudden conflagration. Or the men may have had time to try to escape, frantically jamming the gears as the honey-thick oil ensnared them and the flames began to rise. With so much other work to be done, the wreckage has been left where it is, a reminder, as the fire fighters drive past each evening, that they have made it through another day; a hint, each morning, of what may lie around the next bend in the road.

The smoke today is as thick and impenetrable as it must have been the day the five men died. The fire from which it erupts is not a simple jet of flames surging from a severed pipe, as some are, but a miniature volcano of sand and rock and the molten metal fragments of one of the nine hundred wellheads the Iraqis blew up, or tried to. Dousing and capping the cleanly cut wells will be simple, a walk in the park, Miller says. But a fire like this one, seething through a small mountain of glass and coke from a pipeline that might have been sheared away twenty feet underground, will require months of labor. It will be several years, he predicts, before all the treachery is undone, the oil flows, the skies clear and expatriate executives once again loll on the porch of Ahmadi House, sipping Shirley Temples and foamless Islamic beer.

The detour around the roadblock of smoke leads us right onto the desert sand. The trail has been well blazed; we rock and roll deep in white-yellow ruts that have been carved into the black-crusted soil. After just a few hours here, our arms, necks and hands are polka-dotted with little spots, and my favorite baseball cap, bright green, with the insignia of the Estellas Orientales (the Eastern Stars) of San Pedro de Macoris in the Dominican Republic, has been ruinously blotched. But after three months of unceasing carbon rain, the fragile earth itself shows the most awful evidence of torture. All around us, the ground is thickly coated with a layer of fallen tar. Grasses and low bushes, specialized for this dry ecosystem, are matted and soaked. Yet uncountable thousands of anthills have been pushed up through the crust, forming bright little circles on the dark lunar tableau.

Just to our right is a half cylinder of beige plastic, about four feet long, lying on the ground. There is some English lettering stenciled on it, but I can't make it out as we bump and grind along.

"What's that?" I ask Ken Rose.

"Cluster-bomb casing," he replies, yawning.

He points out a couple of unexploded American bomblets that are embedded in the sand a few yards from the trail. Only the little tail fins are visible, poking up a few inches out of the ground, like minor irritants from the lower worlds of a Super Mario Bros. video game. Their success rate must have been rather low, I venture.

Maybe not—a moment later, Mike Miller halts so that the crew can shoot the remains of a camel that, unwisely, stepped on one.

Parts of the beast are scatted for dozens of yards—a leg bone has been planted vertically in the sand, but I think some twisted Kilroy must have put it there on purpose—and not far away is a low bump on the flat landscape that turns out to be an Iraqi bunker.

We are just about to climb down into it when I remember the Filipino who had his hands blown off and the ninety-nine-day fuses on the bicycle wheels that are set to go off at any moment.

"Is it safe?" I ask, then swallow the words, trying to sound as cool as possible, manfully bedecked in my ball cap, gloves, goggles, face mask and chemical-warfare leggings. This is a curious tug-of-war, the fear of being blown to shreds vying against the lust for souvenirs.

Lust wins. In the underground chamber, we find ammo boxes, helmets, booklets in Arabic that appear to be the owner's manuals for a late-model Soviet tank, empty ration tins, khaki canvas shoulder bags and an empty package of Oreos that proves either the Iraqis ate better than we think or some other scavenger got here first.

Miller and Rose cluck for a moment about the sad state of the Iraqi conscripts who must have been stuck here for months. Their orders were plain: stay here until you starve to death or the Americans come and kill you. The Canadians have been combing through the Iraqi redoubts every day, after work. The spoils include uniforms, rifles, foot-long live artillery shells that will make great Christmas gifts in Calgary and, once, a collection of snapshots left behind when a young man either retreated, surrendered or stepped on a cluster bomb.

Mike Miller keeps the photos in the glove compartment of his truck. Most are out of focus. One of them shows a soldier shaking hands with a thickly set man in a dark suit who might be Saddam Hussein. Another picture is of two young men in uniform standing beside a mounted heavy gun. In my head, staring at the photo, I hear Pejman the driver at the Cemetery of Martyrs in Tehran: "My brother. My brother." Shamed, I drop the things I've collected and climb back into Ken Rose's Dodge.

In their first few weeks in Kuwait, Miller and his team have reached two conclusions. First, that they must work on the wells at the western edge of the field first, even though these are the farthest from al-Ahmadi, because out there, the prevailing wind will keep them from having to breathe as many of the unknown by-products of combusted Kuwaiti crude. And second, that despite the apocalyptic fire and smoke and the predictions of global atmospheric calamity, they should begin by concentrating on sabotaged wells that are spouting oil, but *not* burning. The lakes of oil, already covering hundreds of square miles of desert—each one containing more oil than the notorious *Exxon Valdez* spilled into a pristine Alaskan bay—are the greater catastrophe. Their portent is triply evil: they could overflow into the Persian Gulf; they could soak deep into the soil, poisoning the water table and killing the desert environment forever, or, as the heat of the Arabian summer increases—it is still only about 110°F in the shade, though there is no shade—the standing crude could somehow ignite into a science-fiction holocaust that no amount of equipment, nor of courage, could quell.

To attack these gushers, Miller has about forty Canadian men—more will be coming in later—a couple of planeloads of heavy equipment, a number of Arab and Asian drivers, mechanics and construction workers, a sublime confidence, twenty years of experience in a company his father started in the Alberta oil patch, a million dollars a month in fees from the Kuwaiti Oil Ministry and a proud corporate track record, on jobs from Iran to Indonesia, of never having had one of his men killed on the job. The deaths of the two reporters and three drivers have hurt Miller, but they have hardly broken him. In a safety huddle with his men—we're now out at the extremity of the field, at a nonburning well spouting furious bursts of reddish-brown crude fifty feet into the clear blue sky—he tells his crew, "This is the job of a lifetime, guys. You'll never see anything like this again."

The problem, of course, is that neither Miller, nor Red Adair, nor Boots nor even Coots—these are the stars of the hell-fighting galaxy—has ever seen anything like this *before*, either.

"The fact is, in an average year, there might be two or three blowouts in Canada, maybe fifteen or twenty worldwide," Miller says. During the Iran-Iraq war, Safety Boss was called in to work on eight wells in the Islamic Republic that had been hit by Saddam's bombers. In 1917, at Baku in Azerbaijan, a skirmish of the Russian Revolution left an entire field of perhaps thirty wells ablaze, but that was before Miller's time, or even the immortal Adair's. The fires of Kuwait cannot be conquered by reference to history. The men are on their own.

"There's no instruction manual," Miller says. "We're not even covered under the Occupational Health and Safety Act. What we do is kind of peculiar."

What Safety Boss is trying to do at this particular well is to "sting" it—to insert a long, thin tube into the broken pipe from above, and then, using an undamaged valve still attached to the wellhead, to force in a thick clayey chemical soup called "mud" that, being heavier than the gushing oil, will reverse its flow and force it back below the ground. Then the stinger can be lifted out, the valves closed and the well declared officially capped.

The procedure would be simple except for the fact that oil is exploding from the wellhead at a velocity of approximately eight hundred miles an hour. The pressure would take a man's hand off, or his head.

It has taken several days of preparatory earth-moving, grading and careful probing for buried mines and cluster bombs to get to this stage. A full-sized yellow construction crane is holding the thirty-foot-long stinger tube high over the spewing wellhead. Two workers in thick, padded fire suits are kneeling in the sand, holding hoses connected to high-pressure water pumps, in case the oil somehow ignites. (The water has been brought in by truck from the gulf. And a couple of men are standing right at the well, wearing orange slickers over their coveralls, with metal handles sewn into the waistbands of their suits so that, should things go wrong and they fall, helpless, into the frothing oil, a rescuer might be able to find a handhold and pull them from their certain deaths.)

The area is alive with roaring machinery, shouted commands and the rush of the oil itself as Maurice and Chris take their places just behind the men with the fire hoses. There is no smoke at all here, though by climbing a berm of earth that has been bulldozed around the well I can see more than fifty fires to the east, plumes of black and, sometimes, white smoke rising, joining, merging into a roiling fog, blowing toward the coast. I look up into the brilliant sunshine. At just this hour, the plane from Cairo should be coming in. I imagine someone at my right-side window seat, looking down at the desert, the orange flames and, just before crossing the edge of darkness, seeing us and our trucks and our big yellow crane, pecking away at the great disaster.

The crane operator is a Filipino named Ogi; the Canucks call him, fondly, Augie Doggie. Slim and studious, his hard hat plastered with souvenir stickers of various engineering and wildcatting firms, Augie

Doggie works his levers and toggles, gingerly positioning the stinger over the erupting well. Ropes hang down from the tube and are grabbed by the men at the wellhead. As they yank at the tethers, trying to swing the pipe so that it is exactly over the center of the spray, it flicks in and out of the oil flow and splatters the men, like a child who places his thumb over the spout of a schoolyard water fountain to splash the others waiting in line.

Thirty feet from the wellhead, Maurice has no way of knowing what will happen next, whether to zoom in for close-ups of the workers being showered with oil or to stay with a wide shot of the entire operation. We don't have an instruction manual, either. Denike isn't here and I'm fighting the urge to run down from my little hill and play Cecil B. DeMille.

A cameraman edits in his head as he works; he thinks, I've got the wide shot. Now come the close-ups of the men doing the work. Then I'll turn around for the faces of the others, watching. He sets up, repositions, unlatches the camera from the big German tripod and moves a few feet closer, towing the sound man with his heavy recorder in its blue canvas case like a rubber raft behind a motorboat. In the midst of melee and confusion, the two men exchange a clipped repartee: "Cut. Roll. End of tape. Battery. What the hell does Abel want?"

What I want, usually, is obvious: faces, people, emotion. I run down to where the boys are working, tap at Maurice's shoulder—he's magnetized by his filming, Monet at the lily pond—and tell him, "I've picked out the guy I want to interview." He pivots and growls at me, "We'll do dat later." Chastised, I turn to walk away and, tripping over the fire hose, nearly do a face-plant in the sand.

The stinging goes well for all concerned. After two or three passes across the powerful spray, Augie Doggie gets the vertical pipe right in the middle of the jet stream and the three men on the ground pull it down into position with their ropes. A wheel is turned, the fountain is shut off, and Maurice has got it—he says that we will be able to see the oil cease coming out of the top of the stinging tube.

Now I can do my interview. I want one of the men who was at the wellhead, shouting orders to Augie Doggie, controlling the action while being liberally slathered with thick, clinging, red-brown goop. He is a squat, roly-poly man named George Connon, seventeen years in the oil patch out of Red Deer, Alta. On the knuckles of his left hand are tattooed the letters *L O V* and *E*.

"What did you do before you went into the oil industry?" I ask him as Chris tries to position his boom microphone so that he can hear our voices and not just the droning motors of the pumpers and the crane.

"I was in the penitentiary," he replies, winking.

"As a guest?" I tease him.

"No, I worked there, as a prison guard."

"Why'd you switch?"

"This is less dangerous."

The tape deck begins rolling. We chat about his first month in this madness—he is going home, on leave, tomorrow—about danger, about the brilliantly crafted vandalism that will keep George Connon and the rest of these men busy and well paid for years. When I mention the name of Saddam Hussein, Connon says, "I'd like to get him, yeah. I hate him."

"Is this beyond the power of man to control?" I ask.

"Oh," Connon answers, wiping his face with a rag, "we can do it but it's going to take time. They're going to have to have the patience for it."

"Have you got the patience for it?"

"Oh yeah. You've got to have patience because if you start rushing into things, you're going to die."

The interview concludes; that was the clip I was aiming for. The crew shuts downs, coils the cable, folds the tripod and heads to Mike Miller's vehicle to continue our tour. Walking away, I ask George Connon what his plans are for his home leave. I wonder if, like Ken Rose, he's going to visit his mother.

"When I get home," the hell-fighter replies, "I'm going to stick my face in the beer and not come up till I pass out."

Miller and Rose have angled their trucks so that I can get a little shelter from the wind as I try to do a stand-up with a nice big fire behind me.

"Go for it, cowboy," Maurice says, as always.

"You don't see many Kuwaitis out here in boots and coveralls," I begin, "fighting to save their nation's economy, and their environment...."

It is a transcendent moment—the brave reporter, in prescription sunglasses and an oil-spattered shirt, standing unconcernedly with his back to one of the paramount disasters of the age. The wind is blowing, the sun is beginning to retreat toward the clear western horizon, the two senior men from Safety Boss nod in agreement as I pontificate knowledgeably after six whole hours in the field, and producer Denike is not around to inveigh against me, after I've finished a take or two, with his half laugh, "You can't say *that*."

We are still parked along this remote stretch of desert road when another pickup truck hauls alongside and its driver, a Safety Boss worker named Randy, hops out to say hello. Randy is an avid collector of Iraqi war souvenirs; he is trying to figure out if there is any way he can mail home a T-72 tank. He invites us around to check out part of his trove, leaps up on to the bed of his truck and, rummaging through a cornucopia of guns, ammo, grenades, casings, mortars, shells and bombs, jumps back to the ground again, shouldering a green cast-iron antitank weapon into which he is loading a bright red, winged rocket.

"Do we want to film this?" Maurice inquires.

"I guess we do," I command firmly.

"This is going to make a little bit of noise," Randy announces, "but just for a second."

In the distance, about a mile away, a man-made hillock breaks the monotony of the desert.

"See the pillbox on top of the hill?" Randy chortles. "Watch!"

Suddenly, before any of us are ready, there is a thunderclap, Chris— he hasn't had time to turn his microphone down—is tearing off his head-set, crying, "My ears! My ears!" and, about halfway up the hillside, there is a little puff of brownish dust.

"Shit! Missed it," Randy says, reloading.

We have come so far from al-Ahmadi and the zone of fire, the desert here is green. The sand beneath our wheels is pure and golden, the view infinite, the sun's heat dry and pure. I had no idea there would be so much plant life, so many birds. A flutter of small green parrots parallels our travels; swallows dart behind us as our tires churn up the soil. In the small details of this resilient natural community, the vast destruction looming back to the east seems even more venal and obscene.

"I think we'd all like to get our hands on Saddam," Ken Rose says as we turn back toward the smoke and the fires. I'm not expecting this from a man who is eager to visit his mom.

"Even though he's given you the biggest payday of your life?" I ask.

"I think any of us would trade all the money for this thing to never have happened."

Every few hundred yards, heading back toward the oil field known since the thirties as al-Burgan ("the Volcano," an apt, if innocently given, appellation), we pass a well either on fire, gushing oil or, occasionally, wired to explode but still intact, either through equipment failure or the premature departure of the troops assigned to blow it. We can see the sandbags piled around the well-head—the dynamite was packed down in a hole dug around the pipeline—and from there, a thin wire leads across the sand to one of the abandoned bunkers. (There never were towering derricks or nodding pumps here, as in North American oil fields. The Arabian reserves are so rich, the oil under such high pressure deep underground, it vaults out of its epochal confinement as soon as a pipe is sunk, the world's easiest exploitation of fossil fuel.)

The destruction of the Kuwaiti oil wells was not a decision hastily taken. In the war of kept promises—George Bush vowing that "this aggression will not stand"; Tariq Aziz calmly assuring the world from Geneva that Israel would certainly be attacked—Saddam Hussein declared that he would have his innings with the al-Sabahs, and in that game he has been victorious. The sandbags, the wires, the pillage at al-Ahmadi speak of studious planning and malevolent genius—a Professor Moriarty, a Lex Luthor—wreaking terror on a grand, cartoon scale, and though the men in these meager little fortifications were merely the instruments of evil, it was they, not their commandant, who huddled here, in the bomb-sights of the enemy's computerized killing machines, until the order came to light the fuses and flee. The fact that the man who gave the order still sits unharmed in Baghdad makes Ken Rose sicker than the smoke.

But the pollution, as we dive back into it, has Rose concerned as well. He says he sometimes feels a tightness in his chest, "like I had when I used to smoke," and that other men have been complaining about difficulty in breathing. One morning early in the work—before Miller decided to move to the edge of the field—they were trying to cap a gusher just outside al-Ahmadi town, the smoke was so thick they couldn't see ten feet in any direction, and everyone, Rose says, felt edgy and lethargic. He puts it down to "lack of oxygen." It might have just been fear.

We are in the heart of the fire zone again, parked, it seems, at the edge of a great body of water. The tracks in the sand run toward the sea, enter it and vanish. But this is not the Persian Gulf. It is the giant of all the oceans of oil, so huge I can't see the opposite shore; how deep it is, no one has waded in to find out. It must be more than a mile on each side. It will take months, at least, to drain. And there are dozens more.

As Maurice pans across the unbroken smoothness of the oil, capturing the reflection of the burning wells that mark its perimeter, Mike Miller says he's heard that some of the Texans plan to go sailboarding on this petroleum pond, and then send the tape of their exploits to "America's Funniest Home Videos."

The idea is so loopy, today's whole adventure so ridiculous—the package of Oreos in the Iraqi bunker, the Canadian aiming his rocket-launcher at the distant hill, the scattered smithereens of camel—I decide to mention that back at the International Hotel, the other reporters told me there is even a herd of wild horses roaming this Kurt Vonnegut range.

"Yes," Miller says. "I've seen them."

He has seen them, but they do not run free. In the center of the al-Burgan field, there is an oasis. At this oasis the al-Sabah family has built a small palace, a holiday retreat. At this kingly cottage on the Arabian sands, the monarch has kept his thoroughbreds, feeding them on the finest grass.

Now the oil field is a raging tempest, but the country palace still stands. We approach it, carefully, cautiously, threading our way toward the distant walls and towers in a little-trodden landscape of cluster bomblets and shallow lakes of oil that splash the door-frames and splatter the windshield as we slowly motor through them, hubcap deep. Ken Rose navigates a little nervously in the wake of Mike Miller's truck. We are just about to tiptoe through another swamp of oil when we notice that Miller's tail pipe is on fire.

It's too late—there's nothing we can do. The lead vehicle is already in the black lagoon, but the oil does not ignite. The fire in the pipe goes out. I start to breathe again.

Miller has been out here once before—he saw some horses nibbling at oil-sodden trees beyond the yellow-brick palace walls—but the falling tar has covered his tire prints. Bouncing and bumping on the unbroken sand, passing in and out of blinding smoke, the heat of the fires burning my face though the window—looking around, I count seventy-nine burning wells within my range of vision—we circumnavigate the palace enclosure, searching in the darkness for the gate.

Along the southern wall of the compound, an ornamental door

stands open. Beyond it, I see palm trees, hanging heavy with shiny oil; a driveway lined with ornamental bushes, some of them with bright pink blossoms erupting from blackened mats of leaves; garbage, wreckage, some small outbuildings and garages trashed and burned, a smashed and overturned Jeep. The main building of the palace—about the size of a modest Rosedale mansion—has been violated and sacked. And at the end of the garden pathway, a gray-haired man in a stained blue shirt who is holding a little green bird.

The wind roars. The sky turns orange, white, black, purple, impossible colors in an impossible place. Two parallel rows of towers in a side garden look like light standards, but they are dovecotes; a single pigeon, last of the emir's racing flock, perches on the ledge of its nesting hole, glistening, soaked in gum. The Iraqis ate the others.

We climb down from our trucks.

"The set for David Lynch's next movie," Chris says.

The man who is holding the bird stares at us through the swirling smoke. The disbelief is mutual. While Maurice hurries to film the pigeon houses, the sodden trees, the wild, windy sky, I introduce myself to the man in the blue shirt. He is a Bostonian, John Walsh, representative of the World Society for the Protection of Animals. He has come to rescue the horses.

Walsh has been in Kuwait since the first week of March. He is weary, exhausted, a little confused. His first priority had been the Kuwait City zoo. The Iraqis had shot some of the animals, fed others to the lions for sport and dined on the deer and the antelope themselves.

"I took fifty-six animals out of al-Ahmadi when I first got here," Walsh says. "This is April...May...this is May...back in, early in March, we took out cattle, sheep, goats, donkeys."

This is May 4. I suddenly realize: today's the Kentucky Derby.

When he arrived in the emirate, Walsh didn't know that any of the emir's thoroughbreds had survived the war. A photographer had been here and had seen them, oil soaked and shrunken, muzzling the blackened arbor for edible morsels of green. The photographer had told John Walsh.

A water pipe had been laid years earlier, from the coast to the monarch's pleasure garden. The horses had found the outlet. The water had kept them alive.

Four horses survive. Walsh has moved them into a stable behind the main house. Fodder has been flown in from Canada, not only for these helpless victims of sabotage and ruin, but for the few remaining livestock animals—about fifteen hundred out of twenty thousand—in the country. Tomorrow, Walsh will bring a truck down here, through the lakes of oil, the cluster bombs and the swirling blackness, and try to get the four horses out.

We set up for a quick interview, the setting sun painting our faces briefly golden as it searches for a passage through the smoke, then, the sun defeated, everything goes gray.

"Can you describe the extent of the devastation?" I ask John Walsh.

"It's affected everything," he answers, speaking very rapidly; as with all on-camera interviews, I'm measuring his words, editing in my head, listening for useable clips, in-points and out-points, the antithesis of normal human conversation. Even here, we are focused on lighting, battery life, sound bites.

I ask Maurice for a close-up of the bird in Walsh's hand. It is a bee eater, robin sized, iridescent green, but its beak is clotted with tar and it is barely alive, not fighting to break free, slowly blinking. It has come from Africa, bound, possibly, for Iran.

Walsh says, "The birds that are migrating through are dying. I'm seeing large numbers of them here in the trees that are unable to fly. I think everything migrating through that's going to be lightly oiled will continue on its migration, will have cleaned itself, preened, ingested the oil and will die later on during its migration."

The Bostonian leads us around the palace to the stable behind it. We pass heaps of wrecked furniture; lawn chairs; a basketball. The former residents of this Xanadu draw no sympathy from Walsh; he is horrified that the government, which is the al-Sabah family, has shown no concern for all the animals of Kuwait.

"The government says they have other priorities," Walsh says.

He is reluctant to put on a pony show for the sake of the CBC. The interior of the stable, a low stucco building, is far too dark for Maurice to enter and shoot. We prevail upon Walsh to bring one of the horses out into the weakening daylight. There is a little exercise yard, a walking ring where Walsh has piled up some hay.

The animal that slowly steps out of the building is a chestnut mare, smallish, subdued, with darker patches of matted oil along her flanks and twisted clots of tar in her tail and mane. She stands stock-still, makes no sound.

What is she thinking, I wonder, of this world of men?

There isn't much daylight left. We retrace our tracks through the epicenter of the firestorm, past the shallow lakes, the little unexploded bombs with their tiny fins.

"If we ran over one of them," I ask Ken Rose. "Would we be killed?"

"It depends," he says. "If it went off under the engine, there might be enough metal in there to absorb most of the impact. If it went off right under the passenger compartment, I think we'd be blown through the roof."

We're heading north on a paved road the men from Safety Boss don't recognize when Miller, in the lead car, slows down to inspect an object off on the shoulder. It's an Iraqi antiaircraft gun, still aimed at some long-gone Phantom in the sky. We hop out while Miller inspects his prize. There already is one ack-ack gun in the Safety Boss yard, back in al-Ahmadi. As soon as he can get a trailer down here, Miller will tow this one back and then he'll have a nice set of bookends.

Miller walks over to the gun. It's a two-seater, with some cloth still matted over the metal bum-rests for padding during raids. He is just wiping an icing of grime off the calibration lines on the gunsight when a large bird pops out of the undercarriage of the weapon and limps away.

It's a heron, I think, about two and a half feet tall with a long, pointed bill and a body that might once have been white but now is brown-black with oil. It cannot fly. It staggers off the pavement, walks out into the desert, is caught in a gust of wind and falls over.

We stand back as Maurice films the pitiable sight and Chris records the howling, heated gale. The bird is walking out into the sand of destruction, far from home, as are we all.

The image is compelling, the scale of horror reduced to the faltering struggle of one helpless, smothered bird. When Maurice has got the shots he wants, Mike Miller walks out onto the sand, picks up the bird and, with three quick twists, wrings the creature's neck.

5 MAY
Al-Ahmadi

Update: they have brought back my door. It has been painted with a fresh coat of dark green. The brass numbers 522 have been polished up. There is still no lock and no doorknob. There is still a two-inch hole.

Producer Denike has, finally, found us a suitable vehicle. It's a four-wheel-drive Jeep Wagoneer with a hatchback and just enough room for the four of us to squeeze in. He's paying an emir's ransom to some loan shark Aboud tracked down. The van has been hidden under some packing materials in the corner of a warehouse all through the Iraqi occupation. It is covered in so much dust, it looks as if it's been dredged in Shake'n Bake. Denike says, "The guy wanted three thousand dollars for four weeks. I told him we only needed it for one week. He said, 'Okay. We compromise. Three thousand dollars for *one* week.'"

Fixer Aboud has found us the protective clothing we'll need when we return to work in the oil fields. He has bought four sets of matching powder-blue coveralls at the Sultan Center. We try them on. We look like baggage handlers for Bad-ass-man Airlines.

Laundry service has begun in the hotel. Cold-water washing only.

A cyclone in Bangladesh has killed thousands. Whole villages have been swept into the Bay of Bengal. There are reports that parents tied small children to trees to keep them from being carried away by the storm.

The Aga Khan will give a press conference later today at the hotel. Dick Cheney, U.S. secretary of Defense, will be in town Tuesday. An independent commission of Kuwaiti and American physicians is touring local hospitals, checking on rumors of secret wards where Palestinian victims of vigilante attacks are being hidden. Three satellite technicians from CBS who disappeared in Southern Iraq have been released in Baghdad.

The Hash House Harriers are looking for new members. All joggers invited.

With producer Denike at the wheel, we load up our Jeep and head down to al-Ahmadi. (Aboud isn't needed when we work with Canadian-speaking fire fighters. He stays behind in Kuwait City, arranging interviews for our second documentary on politics and society.) For the third day in a row, the sky over the capital is clear, hot and blue. We motor along the deserted freeway through the southern suburbs, pleasant communities of stone and stucco houses, few trees, small gardens. On the roof of each house is a steel water tank and a television antenna that, almost always, is in the shape of the Eiffel Tower. We are in rather good spirits; yesterday's pictures of the flames and the oil lakes and the horses will make riveting TV.

The car radio is turned to FM 107, the voice of the U.S. Armed Forces. A catchy jingle caps the station ID: "the Desert Net-*work*!" Randy Travis, Reba, Hank Jr., Vince Gill, AP "Network News," Paul Harvey's "the Rest of the Story." There are no commercials. Thirty-second propaganda spots attempt to enlighten the troops.

"Remember that local customs in the country you're stationed in can be very different from our own," a typical announcement advises. "In dealing with local people, remember: you may be the first American that person has ever met."

"Yes," Chris chimes in. "And if you *kill* him, you can be the *last* American that person will ever meet."

At the exit ramp to al-Ahmadi, we pause to shoot the soldiers at their lawn-chair barricade with the morning sun on their white gauze masks and the black wall of smoke behind them. The gentle rain of tar begins again. I remember the Virginian at Cairo airport: "If you can see it, breathe it." But so far, none of us has complained about respiratory problems. Chris and I are the picture of health, Maurice's asthma has been quiescent, and Denike is sucking at so many Benson & Hedges, his lungs must be thankful when he snuffs one out and takes in nothing but oil smoke for a while.

As we are dressed like caddies in our baby-blue jump suits, we head first for the Ahmadi Country Club to see what the Iraqis did to the golf course. Safety Boss is making a crew change today, so we are devoting our time to a tour of al-Ahmadi, or what little is left of it.

The course is at the north end of the tidy company town, with a small clubhouse, locker rooms and a restaurant on a rise above what must be the eighteenth green. But green is not the word—there is not a blade of grass anywhere, and as we walk the fairway, which is bare brown earth, we notice some unusual hazards: washing machines, refrigerators, domestic garbage, abandoned cars and Iraqi sandbags are heaped in piles from tee to green. At a slight dogleg in the tenth fairway, I notice what might have been a dog's leg. A couple of grimy cats root among the ruins.

The clubhouse, where visiting engineers and their Kuwaiti hosts once passed their nonalcoholic cocktail hours, has been thoroughly and painstakingly trashed. Fueled by what?—jealousy of the oilmen's wealth? Xenophobic hatred of the foreign game? The Iraqis here had indulged in a graduate-level course in vandalism. Every glass in the kitchen has been smashed, every locker emptied and overturned, every piece of rattan furniture thrashed with mashies and niblicks stolen from the members' bags. On the floor of the lounge, I call Maurice's attention to a copy of the *Arab Times*, dated August 1, 1990. It was the eve of destruction; the next morning, the invaders were here.

Brian and Chris, the golfers among us, pick up scorecards, pencils, bits of the flotsam of the storm. I find a name tag that once would have been attached to a bag of clubs; it belonged to a Mr. al-Faruq. I envision a well-fed Kuwaiti in a flowing *dishdasha* in the locker room, changing into tweed plus-fours. And here is a three-iron, snapped off about a foot from the clubhead.

I hand the relic to Denike, who strides up to the tenth tee—par 4,363 yards—and drives an imaginary ball straight down the middle, then hooking, hooking.... In hushed, reverential tones, I deliver the commentary.

"Oh, bad luck," I whisper. "He's put it in a bunker...."

Someone has found a heavy black iron triangle and has placed it near the tee. Painted in white is a subtle understatement. It says, Course Closed.

At lunchtime, we chow down with the good ol' boys at the feed trough in Ahmadi House. I haven't seen the rooms here but the board is first-rate: tender steaks, macaroni, Southern fried chicken (southern Luzon style;

all the cooks are from the Philippines), apple pie and even a soft-serve ice cream machine. The plates are cleared by the cute Filipinas and the room is swept by a pencil-thin janitor from tortured Bangladesh. I think of the news from Chittagong and *Cox's Bazaar*, the churning waters, the death toll that the Desert Network says may reach a quarter-million.

It was Ramadan, the holy month of fasting, when I went to Bangladesh in 1985. Dhaka seethed, overloaded and frantic, but by night the pace slowed, men slept on their shop floors, rickshaw peddlers took their siesta in the shade of their gaudily decorated chairs. But at night—at the hour when, a mullah decreed, it was so dark that one could not discern a black thread from a white one—we feasted, and women browsed through the bazaars, under the colored lights.

A hundred miles south of the capital was the zone of watery death. It was May, the month of cyclones. Most of the foreign journalists had already gone home. Television crews were packing their metal cases and hurrying to Europe. There had been a riot at a soccer game in Belgium and more than fifty white people were dead.

In Bangladesh, the government said the storm had taken fifty thousand of a darker race. The dying was done—we turned to the living. I went to the airport and lied and said that my name was on the priority list for media seats on a relief helicopter. The ruse worked. It was a Soviet-built Ilyushin chopper that rattled, trembled, shook. We flew south, over the lushness, to the lowlands where the sea had laid claim to the land. We brought water, medicines, rice.

Bangladesh. The Philippines. Later that summer of '85, I went to an island called Negros. It was a fertile land of great sugar plantations worked by landless peons. But the world price of sugar had fallen below the margin of profit demanded by the owners of the estates. They abandoned their crop and left the cane workers penniless. I saw their children in the starvation ward of the hospital in Bacolod City. A five-year-old boy weighed fifteen pounds. His name was Nino. Through the window of the hospital, you could see Shakey's Pizza across the street.

The world spins. I'm in a noisy dining hall full of Texans in the Kuwaiti desert, alone with all these strangers. But my ghosts go with me, everywhere.

Too bloated after lunch to move, we crash into the purple leather furniture on the porch of the Ahmadi House. We are joined by a few of the

American wildcatters and about three hundred flies. Maurice stretches out on a sofa and begins to snore like an Ilyushin whirlybird. His pastel jumpsuit is about four sizes too small. A fly is crawling into his mouth.

Denike has gone off to try to rouse the helicopter pilot. We have been denied official permission to fly over the fire zone. The man in charge says, "That's a privilege I haven't granted to *anyone,* not even CNN." So Brian is trying to swing a private deal. We need these pictures.

The pilot resides in one of the dormitory buildings adjacent to Ahmadi House. Just as Brian is about to arrive at his room, the door opens and out pop two little Filipinas. The airman follows. A time is arranged for the flight.

"He said, 'They were just giving me a haircut,'" Brian reports to us on the porch.

Chris says, "Yeah. With their *teeth.*"

The tour of al-Ahmadi town resumes. In a city park at the center of the symmetrically ordered community, a man in a red-checkered head scarf is tending a small flock of sheep. The animals mow through the greensward—the vegetation here is darkened, but not smothered, by fallen tar—and Chris sticks the microphone right in their snoots; chomp, chomp, chomp.

All the sheep are black, but not by nature. Their wool is matted, clotted, tangled with soot and oil. Hungrily, they devour the black-dappled lawn. The fallout is on them, and in them. I remember the sign outside Paveh, Iran: Saddam Is Wolf. Here, then, his lambs.

We drive around to the headquarters of the Kuwaiti Oil Company, the big hangar that was, we believe from the holes in the roof, smart-bombed in an attempt to demolish the pumps that were sending crude oil in disastrous cascades into the Persian Gulf, five miles to the east. At the time, it was reported that Allied air raids had halted the flow at its source, which must have been right here. This attack might have been part of one of those videos the briefers played for the hamstrung press corps in Riyadh, miles and miles from the front, a camera in the nose cone recording the missile's approach until the instant of impact, and then the screen going to hash.

Across the street from the KOC complex is an unadorned mosque of yellowish stucco that the Iraqis, manifesting their devoutness, did not so much as scratch. In the center of this brutalized town, the interior, under its high, plain dome, feels cool and peaceable. Water still flows from the taps in the courtyard where the prayerful would perform their ritual cleansing, when this was a living city. Drinking glasses are stacked on top of an electric water cooler. Carpets, prayer books, pairs of sandals in the shoe rack—all unscathed.

A narrow spiral staircase leads to the top of the minaret, a difficult sixty-foot climb. Professing a fear of heights, I volunteer not to carry any of the gear up the steps. The fear of heights is genuine. So is the fear of hernia. When the others descend, glaring at me, we move on.

Whatever primal passions they restrained at the holy mosque, the Iraqis unleashed at the helpless schools. Following my map, progressing slowly—amid all the windblown garbage—past a group of shabby, low-rent dwellings where several families are still living despite the dangers of the polluted air and soil, we come to the al-Ahmadi kindergarten.

It is hard to conceive of the pleasure a grown man might derive from tearing apart a play-nest of five-year-olds. The enmity that propelled the troops in their orgy at the golf course could not easily have been reignited here. But the kindergarten, a U-shaped structure surrounding a central, partially roofed courtyard, has met the same fate as the rich men's fairways. Every classroom has been ripped up, desks heaved about, papers shredded, children's drawings shat upon with graffiti and bayonet cuts.

Maurice sets up a scene of me walking along a corridor, stopping here and there to open the doors of offices and classrooms to inspect the damage within. And each is the same—papers strewn everywhere, files scattered, furniture in ruins. On the floor we find medicines from the school dispensary, folding cots, bandages; Chris and I gather up a few heavy steel helmets and heave them in the van for souvenirs. We kick one back and forth like a soccer ball. Then I remember the tale of the booby-trapped gloves that blew a scavenger's hands off. Game over.

After making us wait for only an hour and a half—maybe this time he was having a manicure—the helicopter pilot shows up to take the boys, a little surreptitiously, into the belly of the firestorm. (If anyone asks, they've gone for "fuel.") Once again, as at the minaret, I decline to ride along, even though the aircraft is new and safe and commodious enough for the four of us, the helmsman, and Lucille the camera. I'm not afraid of flying, far from it. But I figure that I've already seen the fires from the jumbo jet on landing, I've been all the way to the other end of the burning field in a truck, and it is so windy and choppy and smokey, I might be in some danger of tossing my steak and my soft-serve ice cream.

So the chopper lifts off while I sit in our van and sing along with the oldies on the Desert Network, chawing on a strawberry Roll-Up. I see them disappear to the northwest, then circle around so that Maurice, squinting through his viewfinder with the camera perched in an open window, can make grand, sweeping passes over the fountains of flame. It's another victory for the intrepid Denike. I would have given up when the official said that not even CNN could fly.

Forty minutes later, after heaven knows how many loops of the fields, the helicopter returns to base, the engine is shut down, the big blade slows and finally stops and out of the cockpit comes Maurice, staggering on sailor's legs and, with his too-small coveralls and his rather green complexion, looking like Lou Ferrigno in full makeup, an Incredibly nauseated Hulk. A passenger can fix his eyes on the horizon, but to a cameraman focused on features on the ground, a bucking wind-tossed chopper is an open invitation to look at lunch again.

(Only a bobbing boat is worse. I once had to do a stand-up in a small fishing dory off the coast of Inchon, Korea. The cameraman was on another boat, riding the heaving swells, trying to hold his tripod steady while zooming in on my face. He became dreadfully sick, but it might just have been my Egyptian good looks.)

"Oh, God, I feel awful," Maurice says, collapsing in the back seat. So does Brian—the flight was so bumpy, he doubts that Maurice was able to record any of the smooth, majestic, moving panoramas of the devastation that we'll need for our title shots and as general wallpaper of the fires of Kuwait.

"We might have to do it again tomorrow," Denike says.

"Oh, God, Brian," Maurice groans. "I got the shots. I swear I got them."

"Come on, cowboy," says Davies, the indestructible sound man. He has traded the Australian accent for a deep Tulsa drawl. "Let's go up again anyway, just for the damn fun of it."

"It was sickening, just absolutely revolting," says the uncannily named Larry Flack. He is not talking about a helicopter ride. Larry Flack is the coordinator of all the fire fighting and fire fighters. He is talking about his first view, back in March, of what Saddam's saboteurs had wrought.

Larry Flack is a Houstonian hired by the Kuwait Oil Company to hire people to fix this country so that petrodollars will once again course like blood through the national veins. We are interviewing him outside his office behind Ahmadi House, with a big black plume of ugliness positioned nicely behind us. (This huge fire, the nearest to the town itself, has been christened Old Smokey. Left alone, we are told, it would burn for twenty-five or thirty years.)

A stocky man in glasses, a cocksure "A" student with a pen holder in his shirt pocket, he is the kind of guy who, back at my college, Unfathomable Tech, we would have called a "tool." Part of his job is not to tell the media what they are not supposed to know. To Larry Flack, this is almost everything.

"Certainly, it can be put back together," he tells me, helpfully. "It's just time and money. Time and money. How much money, how much time, I'm not prepared to tell you."

(He wasn't prepared to let us have one of his helicopters either, but there's more than one way to get a haircut around here.)

"Give a thought to the men who blew this place up," I posit.

"They were like little children with a toy taken away from them," Flack says. "They had to destroy the toy rather than give it up to some other child."

"What about Saddam? Still sitting up there, I guess, pleased with his handiwork."

"Yes, he's pretty much done what he's intended to do and still lives in his little comfort. I wish somebody'd put a gun to his head and blow his brains out. And I got a lot of volunteers."

The four (proverbial) bedfellows who ride back to Kuwait City, trading the pall of al-Ahmadi for blue-orange sunset off to the freeway's left, have been together almost without pause for exactly twenty-one days. (Come to think of it, during the two nights in the green tent at Do Ab, we *were* bedfellows.) There has been little dissonance, but this could change at any time.

Alliances form and re-form: the three nonsmokers against Denike and his two packs a day; the three men lugging the equipment up the spiral staircase against the jerk in the courtyard of the mosque. There is an almost palpable attempt to stay cool, not bicker, keep driving toward the finish line, still a week or more away. The heat and the dirt don't make it any easier. At the end of each day there's an ice-cold shower and dinner with the same three guys.

Maurice's back is beginning to bother him; for a cameraman, this is unto death. Walking all day with a forty-pound weight on one shoulder is not a prescription for a well-tuned spine. And Chris complains more often now about the ballast he has to haul around; he calls the recorder, simply, "the tumor." I waltz around with my knapsack full of fig bars, making awful jokes.

I lasted five weeks with Denike last fall in Germany, though there were days when I could have strangled him over the cigarettes and he could have throttled me on general principle. Two months later, we were in Panama City together, speeding toward the scene of that pissant little insurrection in which quite a few people got shot. They could have been us.

In Toronto, this is the night of a close friend's wedding; Linda will be going alone. "Al's in Kuwait," she will tell her inquirers, and what they think of this life with its long separations and its mandatory fellowship, I have no idea. On the twenty-first day, as on the first, I'd rather be home. But at home, I'd die to be here.

6 MAY
Al-Ahmadi

When Sheikh Abdallah al-Salem al-Sabah decreed, in the nineteen-fifties, that medical care should be made available free of charge, to everyone in Kuwait, citizen or not, he may not have expected that the ranks of future patients would include many young men sent here to blow his kingdom to bits.

The national health-care system took some setting up. When Sheikh Abdallah acceded to the throne in 1950, Kuwait had one hundred thousand people and four doctors. This was not enough. In 1932, four thousand people had perished in an untreated epidemic of smallpox. But that was in the pearl-diving era, when Kuwait's main export commodity was sand, for the construction industry.

By the time of the Iraqi invasion in August, 1990, Kuwait's bottomless oil wealth had created an excellent network of hospitals and physicians, supplied with state-of-the-art equipment that the visiting army happily disassembled and shipped north to Baghdad. There were even reports that Iraqi soldiers had raped nurses and tipped premature infants out of their incubators to perish on the cold stone floor, but after Liberation the anecdotes about the babies, though not the rapes, were discredited.

Certainly, the physical structure of the Kuwait Oil Company hospital at al-Ahmadi, our first stop this morning, has been treated with respect. There is not a sign of damage anywhere. No one challenges me as I walk along the straight, color-coded hallways past Radiology and Pediatric. In my light blue bib and tucker I look as if I've come to fix the air conditioning, or escaped from the psycho ward.

When al-Ahmadi town housed thirty thousand people, this hospital must have been quite a busy place. It is quieter today, but not deserted, like the mosque, or trashed, like the kindergarten. A few patients are lined up at the admitting office in the lobby, and a brace of British soldiers turns up to visit a comrade who has been admitted, not with a wound suffered in the heroic heat of battle, but with a case of the shits. Through the window of the director's office, there is a perfect view of Old Smokey, a mere three hundred yards away.

The invasion of the oil patch replaced the contented suburbanites of this sultry Little America with the spear carriers of Saddam Hussein's front line. These were not the professionals of the Republican Guard—those men were not to be sent to be slaughtered until absolutely necessary, when Iraq itself was in peril—but a haggard assortment of too-young and too-old "volunteers" ordered to wire the wellheads for demolition when the time came and, meanwhile, to hunker in the bunker and wait.

When the waiting dragged into the fall and winter, the vanguard of the great jihad began falling ill. A doctor who is showing me around remembers the Iraqis as being "undernourished, anemic and depressed." A deal had been stuck with the Iraqi commanders: the staff would remain and treat these pitiful warriors if the hospital was declared neutral territory and all guns were left at the door.

"According to medical ethics, you have to treat any patient who comes to you," says Dr. Mohammed-Walid Daoud. "Whether we did so willingly, or whether we enjoyed treating them, this is a different question."

Dr. Daoud agrees to an interview in a small laboratory where machines are humming and test tubes are bubbling in an attempt to find out what is in the air we all are eating. He is a stern looking Arab, hawk nosed, with a thick, pointed beard and flinty, challenging eyes that make me suspect he has figured out that I am not Egyptian man. When I ask him how long he thinks it will be before it is safe to live in al-Ahmadi again, he cuts me to the quick, without anesthetic, and says, "I didn't say it is unsafe to live here now."

In fact, Dr. Daoud says, he has kept his own family in al-Ahmadi and he hasn't recommended that anyone panic and flee, except perhaps for asthmatics, one of whom is operating the camera that is recording the interview. Yet even Maurice has not needed to use his bronchodilator, even in the blackest zones. This is not the grim prognostication we had expected, perhaps even hoped, to hear—"nuclear winter" is a much sexier scenario—but Dr. Daoud says that so far levels of pollutants and known carcinogens in the smoke have been "far below maximum allowable concentration," and I guess we'll have to make some room in our story for facts.

(This analysis would cheer Larry Flack, who maintains that the climate of al-Ahmadi is invigorating. Flack is the Ernie Banks of the blowout business, always ready to play a doubleheader. He thinks the tightness in the fire fighters' chests is merely psychological. He says, "We have these black days when the sun doesn't shine. There's a hell of a lot of depression from that. They see this; they think all is lost. There's no hope left.")

A minute later, Dr. Daoud changes horses and says he thinks that Bhopal and Chernobyl were "minor disasters" compared to the fires of Kuwait. To anyone who lived there, or here, this is an odious argument that statistics alone cannot win. Dr. Daoud was in al-Ahmadi the night the Iraqis set the world ablaze. He tells this story:

"We were staying in the hospital at night and we heard explosions. We were used to explosions when the allied forces were bombarding the Iraqi troops, so we were not surprised, because many bombs, even cluster bombs, were thrown on Ahmadi and a few people have been killed. But then it went on and the noise of the explosions was coming closer, closer, closer to us.

"So we went out and saw these huge fires occurring. This well which is close to the hospital, about three hundred meters from the hospital fence, is one of the highest-pressure wells. The earth was shaking, it was like an earthquake, the windows continued to rattle for weeks afterward.

"For weeks, we were like living in an earthquake. We were scared of having burning oil—lava if you want—like a volcano, running through Ahmadi and burning everything in its way. The burning oil would have come through the domestic area, the living area of Ahmadi, and that would have created a greater disaster.

"We sent an ambassador to investigate. He came back with a report that everything is burning as far as the eye can see. And we knew that the threats that had been served on Kuwait in this matter have been committed. We saw the fires surrounding us from three directions, then from the fourth direction when they burned the north pier. We were middle of hell."

Ahmadi House. On the porch. Mike Miller of Safety Boss. Waiting for the new crew. Hot day.

Van arrives. Another television team. Camera. Reporter. Handsome. Dark haired. No nonsense.

"Mike?"

"Yes."

"Gene Randall, CNN."

"Gene, nice to see you."

"Working on the fires?"

"Yes. Today a new crew's coming in."

"How many wells you capped?"

"Eight."

"Eight?"

"Eight."

"Small ones, right?"

"Well, we've been concentrating on..."

"Where're you based, Mike? Still in, um..."

"Calgary."

"Right. Calgary. Thanks."

"You're welcome."

Van backs out. Hot day. On the porch. Ahmadi House.

The first Hiace bus that rolls up to the barracks unloads a mountain of suitcases and blue duffel bags, and the second one, blue and white and disgustingly clean for this prefecture of filth, disgorges Mike Miller's new Team Canada. Miller has put on a spotless crimson jumpsuit for the occasion and most of the men descending from their Airport Shuttle also are in crisp, virgin red. (The same bus has brought in some new hands for the Texas outfit, Wild Well Control. They are in bright yellow uniforms. When the two teams stand next to the pile of blue carryalls, it looks like the Romanian flag.)

Some of the men arriving at the finish line of an interhemispheric marathon—Calgary to Toronto to Amsterdam to Dubai to Kuwait—are greeted by Miller as old, trusted mates. "The tourists! The Middle East tourists!" he cries, shaking hands, tousling hair. But from the blank stares that fall to the ground as other men disembark, it seems as though some of these death-defying mercenaries are total strangers to their commander, and he to them.

In fact, they are. In an industry that might be called upon to snuff a blowout two or three times a year, there is no reason for Miller to maintain a large permanent roster. But this job is the Dieppe of oil-well fire fighting; an entire battalion has been raised to venture where no sane man would go.

Our program, "The Journal," has played its part in the recruitment. A few weeks ago, while I was in Oklahoma with the baseball Hall of Famer Ferguson Jenkins, Mike Miller was interviewed on the show prior to his departure for Kuwait. He let slip that he was going to have to hire more hell-fighters. He got five thousand applications.

(Interestingly, to me and to Miller, none was from a woman. Though al-Ahmadi is manifestly a man's world, except for the culinary and tonsorial services of the young Filipinas, Miller certainly would have hired a qualified woman, had any applied. "I wonder how the Kuwaitis would have reacted," he says. That's a difficult question to answer; out in the burning oil field, we've not seen a Kuwaiti to ask.)

The first point Miller wanted to make when we met him was that he doesn't need any more help. The minions he already has under contract are a varied and amusing breed. Most have at least some experience in the Alberta oil world, though not as fire fighters. But one slim, young man in spectacles—he must speak English!—says that it was Miller's appearance on our very own "Journal" that incited him, untypically, to manly action.

"I called Mike and said, 'I must come with you,'" the young man explains, with a serious smile.

"What were you doing at the time?" I inquire.

"I was a graduate student in philosophy."

"Philosophy?"

"Yes. I had to come. For me, to combat the evil of Saddam is a deeply philosophical act."

For most of the other men, it's the money. Salaries are on a sliding scale according to the hazards of each man's assigned task. The novitiates at the rear of the wellhead formation—the men who bring out lunch from the commissary or drive the water trucks or tend the first-aid kit—might earn three hundred dollars for each of their twenty-eight straight days on the job. The men who dance with death at the crucible can make as much as two grand.

Two thousand dollars a day times twenty-eight days times a year, maybe more, at the front: the product is a fortune to a hard-boiled roughneck, if not to an Arabian emir. Some of the men are thinking of buying condos in Dubai, villas in Spain, declaring themselves nonresidents of Canada and enjoying a tax holiday.

("This is a lottery in which every ticket's a winner," I announce in one of my thundering stand-ups. Then I deepen my voice, or at least try to. "But it's a game in which some of the players can end up dead." The challenge of television is to distil human wisdom into inanities like this.)

We propose to shoot the new men as they enter the fire zone for the first time. It's been forty-eight hours since we made our own initial sortie in Aboud's sleek, snazzy Audi up to the pool of burning oil where five men had died. Already, on this third day, we have become sagacious elders of the desert; the flames, the wall of darkness at the al-Ahmadi checkpoint, the lifeless lakes, the wreckage and the constant, overhanging fear have become part of What We Do. We scan the latecomers and snicker.

Close to al-Ahmadi town, on the southbound highway that leads to the looted little palace where we saw the horses on Derby Day, Miller halts his truck and the rookies tumble out of their bus to look at the king of all the five hundred fires. This is the Mustache, the Texas Longhorn, Yosemite Sam—a double plume of flame shooting horizontally at first, then arcing up into a red-orange, boiling, roaring letter U, the noise as phenomenal as the heat and flame as we stand and confront it, mere insects against its titanic fury. The new men seem to visibly shrink. Now they know.

"This one's unassigned to any of the teams, guys," Miller says. "But I sure hope we get it. It would be a real feather in our caps."

The Mustache is Iraqi demolition at its finest; here, the explosives must have ripped the pipeline far below the ground so that oil, and now flame, rockets out in opposite directions from the same open wound. When it is conquered—and the fire fighters will not rest until it and all the others have been snuffed—it probably will be doused by a technique that someone will invent about five minutes before he tries it. In an industry without a training school or textbooks, invention is the child of defeat. If everything else fails—water, dry chemicals, explosives, metal caps—the Texans will stand in a row and piss on it, and the Canadians will throw philosophy books.

The next burning well the new men are taken to doesn't even merit a name. On the topographical chart of the area that hangs in Mike Miller's trailer, it is designated simply as number 94, a mediocre little hell-fountain that is shooting only about fifteen thousand barrels of combusted petroleum per day into the sky. It is at this well at the western extremity of the huge field, under smoke-free skies (unless the wind shifts), that Safety Boss has been practising its own favored techniques.

This involves five steps. One, a backhoe builds up a wall of sand around the blazing well, like a lunar crater. Two, water is sprayed into the crater—at first, it boils on contact—until the ground is sufficiently cool. Three, dry chemicals, similar to those in a home fire extinguisher, are used to put out the flames. Four, more water is pumped in to keep the fire from reigniting. Five, the remaining gusher is "stung" and capped.

Now, gathering his farm team around him at number 94, Miller explains how each of the five steps can go completely wrong. Safety Boss put this fire out last week, he says. Then why is it still burning?

One, the Egyptian backhoe operator couldn't shift into reverse gear quickly enough; when flames started to lick his equipment, he jumped and ran and the earth-mover went up in smoke. (Its charred vertebrae have been dragged to the side.) Two, the water couldn't get the ground any cooler than eighteen hundred degrees. Three, the dry chemicals managed to get the fire out. But, four, after they poured water on the well-head *for eight hours*, number 94 burst into flames again.

Five, they'll have to do it all over again, tomorrow.

At the next stop, we pull aside one of the men who has just flown in from the True North. This is Joe Chudleigh of Sandy Bay, Vancouver Island, British Columbia. Joe is a big man, a little soft from inactivity, I think, with a wife and five children waiting for him to bring home the biggest paycheck of his life. Joe has a kind face and a droopy handlebar mustache that, if he cultivates it for fifteen or twenty years, might grow to be as thick as Miller's sagebrush. He saw Mike on "The Journal."

"I can't believe it. It's unbelievable. Never seen anything like it. Never will, hopefully," Joe says. His uniform is as pristine as a prom dress; his shiny steel helmet looks as if it was minted an hour ago.

We have the following conversation:

"Joe, how much have you been around oil fires before?"

"Fires? Never. Gas blowouts. We did gas blowouts, but never fires."

"You've never been around oil-well fires before."

"Not fires. No."

"Now you've got five or six hundred of them here. Are you frightened? Nervous? Scared?"

"I was a little nervous driving through that pool of oil with that well on fire beside it. And I imagine you guys were too, eh? Just a little bit?"

(I love this kind of snappy repartee. Last year, I did a story in a small town in Florida where everyone claims to be a spirit medium, a psychic or a new-age Merlin. The only sane person in town was the waitress in the local hotel. I asked her, "Are these people around here a little strange?" She answered, "No. But you are.")

Joe Chudleigh is a technical guy; his brief is to devise plugs and clamps to secure the wellheads after they are tamed. Behind him, as we talk, is just such a challenge, another gusher, similar to the one we filmed being stung on Saturday, that is spewing and spouting irate globs of chocolaty goo.

This well—I don't know what number it is—looks all right from the outside, but it has suffered massive internal injuries and is bleeding from every pore. Three men are right at the source, turning valves and pounding with mallets, trying to shut the gusher down. This succeeds, but now the oil, instead of shooting skyward, just oozes out through all the manifolds and gaskets like ink from a cheap fountain pen.

Off to the side, other men are rummaging through a barrel of rags and old clothes like ladies at a Hadassah Bazaar, then stuffing wads of cloth and even old inner tubes into a pipe that leads to a hose that leads to the wellhead. This is called "trash"—it is supposed to be sucked into the pipeline and to clog it up—and if it works, the well is defeated and if it doesn't, Safety Boss has at least contrived a clever new form of recycling.

But it does work. Maurice and Chris are right behind the firemen as they move up, hoses cocked and armed, to rinse some of the soy sauce off the men who were right up front. The men line up like soccer players defending against a free kick—heads down, eyes closed, hands over their private parts.

I want to interview one of these oil-soaked heroes while the euphoria of victory is still fresh. Maurice wants us to climb part-way up the bulldozed lip of the crater so that there is a panorama of dozens of far-off fires in the background. Chris wants to move as far away as possible to minimize the whine of the machinery. I just want to do it. Now.

For the first time on this twenty-thousand mile roller coaster of a shoot, the bedfellowship breaks down. Chris is livid: "This is the worst fucking place on earth to do a fucking interview." He yanks off his headset, makes as if to fire it down on the ground, sees the oil-soaked sand—

we are in it up past the ankles of our Iraqi chemical-warfare boots—and hangs on.

Now we're all screaming at once, trying to be heard over the bedlam of the pumps that are pushing more cloth and rubber down the hole. Maurice wins—we've got to do it here. He grabs our subject—a lean, fit young athlete named Ron McMahan—and fairly picks him up and plants him where he wants him, with the vanquished well over one shoulder and the fires on the horizon.

"Can you hear him?" I shout at Chris, who is pawing the sand like a Pamplona bull.

"Just fucking do it," he shoots back.

McMahan is yelping and giggling. He's so pumped up, our in-fighting doesn't even register.

"What's it like right now?" I ask. (That's one of the Three TV Questions.)

"It's a high greater than any...I don't know...it's awesome...when you work that hard and it finally happens, it's really an exhilarating feeling."

"And you think—we killed it, we nailed that sucker?"

"Yeah. Oh, yeah. It's kind of like Moby Dick. Man against nature...."

We are just walking back to the truck, apologizing to each other, when on the shimmering sands, about a mile to the north, we see a line of blindingly white minivans, moving toward the fire at number 94.

It's the minister for International Trade.

The caravan, which carries the minister's personal retinue and a coterie of Canadian business executives and embassy personnel, creeps across the featureless desert like one of Wilfred Thesiger's camel trains of old, "a cluster of tiny dots moving imperceptibly across Arabia." The vehicles spread out and slow down to avoid the dust-devils kicked up by the flailing wheels of their forerunners.

The minister is on a rather tight schedule—his plane is due to leave half an hour ago. He has come all this way from Kuwait City, apparently, for two reasons. He expects Mike Miller's men to put out an oil-well fire, or at least try to, in his presence, and he thinks we are going to interview him in the middle of this hellacious *mise-en-scène*.

Unfortunately, he is wrong on both counts.

First of all, there is the trouble with the fire at 94, the one that Safety Boss extinguished at the cost of one backhoe, only to see it spring back to life eight hours later. In preparation for tomorrow's renewed assault on this recalcitrant blaze, two enormous bladders have been laid on the sand and filled with seawater from tanker trucks. They are side by side, each about forty feet long, grayish white and looking like giant garden slugs or queen ants.

At the exact *second* the minister for International Trade pulls up in his minivan, one of the bladders decides to spring a leak and issues forth a Niagara of burbling water.

The contents emitted from the rapidly collapsing tank create the largest body of water between the Persian Gulf and the Red Sea, a milky-white oasis in the parched heart of Arabia, and we would like to dive in, despite our chem-boots and overalls, were it not for the arrival of the minister and the fact that from the depths of this unlikely lagoon, two enormous black cockroaches have just swum to the surface, paddling furiously with all six legs.

And secondly, Brian Denike has already left a telephone message at the Canadian Embassy advising that the proposed interview with CBC Newsworld—our fledgling twenty-four-hour all-information service—cannot be achieved because we have no way to talk to Canada out here on the borders of hell. Larry Flack won't let us use his satellite phone.

This is unfortunate, because Newsworld, this very day, is inaugurating a new breakfast-hour package—it is dawn in Calgary about now—and a live interview from number 94 would have been a timely fillip to draw viewers from, as the reworded Woody Guthrie song goes, Bonavista to Vancouver Island, or at least Joe Chudleigh's wife and five kids in Sandy Bay.

Struck by this double whammy, the member of cabinet, Michael Wilson of Toronto, until recently Canada's minister of Finance, architect of the Goods and Services Tax, one of the most unpopular legislative actions in the history of the Western Hemisphere (which may be why he's traveling in the Eastern), unfolds himself from his van. He is a tall man, square jawed, handsome and understandably going gray. He stands in a little huddle of his handlers and peeps about at the flames and the smoke and the sky.

I step in to introduce myself—as if the minister couldn't recognize me from the jumpsuit, the work gloves, the knee-high boots, the goggles and the Dominican baseball cap. The Hon. Mr. Wilson is wearing a white dress shirt and striped necktie—it is 115°F—and on top of that, they have wrapped him, and many of his attendants, in thin protective suits of white parachute cloth that make it appear that Kuwait has been re-invaded, not by the Iraqi army, but by Bim, the Michelin man.

To top all this off, after the minister, uninterviewed, departs some-what sheepishly for the airport, we motor about fifteen yards toward al-Ahmadi and our van gets bogged down in loose, powdery sand. Denike, who does all the driving, bucks and rocks, shifts gears, spins the wheels and does everything else you do at home when you're caught in a snow-drift, none of which ever works. But, since none of the four of us is speaking to any other one of the four of us, no complaints are heard.

Eventually, one of the larger Safety Boss trucks rescues us and we are nudged out onto the main track again, to continue the half-hour jour-ney. But the truck driver ahead of us—it's Ron McMahan, the sky-high athlete from the good ship *Pequod* we interviewed earlier—suggests a shortcut.

So, we follow him, up another sandy track, onto a paved road we've not traveled before. But the pavement points us toward a fire that can't be more than twenty feet from the road. The smoke we enter is the black-est yet, a total eclipse. Ron McMahan leans out of his cab and yells, "Follow my taillights!"

It's too late—we can't see them. We can't see anything. "Oh, God," someone says. (It might be me.) It is suddenly cooler, much cooler, in this man-made midnight. I am thinking, One wheel off the asphalt, and we die.

It is one of those instants—like when a plane takes a sudden dip in a storm cloud—that is over before it begins, yet seems to last for hours. We bust back into the sunlight. The heat feels wonderful.

After dinner, on a patch of lawn that lies between the rows of motel rooms at Ahmadi House, the fire fighters sit in folding chairs and take their rest, chatting, relaxing, thinking, as in the James Taylor song of the young range-riding cowboy, about women and glasses of beer.

The spirit is soft. An orange glow overhangs the moody gathering, the fires lighting the sky, the earth illuminating heaven. The roaring of the wild wells continues, but, after a while, one ceases to notice it. Some of the men are already asleep.

Bone-tired, our hair matted from the grime, our clothes—even under the coveralls—oil stained and stinking, we set up to do our formal interviews with the Canadian blowout boys. Two lawn chairs are arranged, far enough from the main body of men that they will not whistle and heckle and boo. I sit with my back to Maurice's camera. He has run some extension cords out of one of the rooms. He switches on his portable lights. Every flying insect in the Arab world flutters in to join us.

We begin with Ron McMahan. As soon as he opened his mouth this afternoon I thought, He can't be a Canadian. He's too glib, too self-assured. I was right. He's a Californian. A year ago, he was working as a primary-school teacher and counselor of children with special needs. He spent most of his time, he says, "in sandals and short pants." Then he met the oldest of Mike Miller's three daughters, a student at Long Beach state. Now he's the boss's son-in-law, a thin-faced, blond, well-muscled volleyball player at work on the world's largest beach. He was no better schooled for the fires of Kuwait than Joe Chudleigh was, or I was.

"I think pretty much we all walked into it unprepared," McMahan says.

I didn't expect this. I thought they'd all be seasoned desert rats, practiced actors playing John Wayne playing Red Adair in *Blowout*. The experience has chastened the Californian beachboy, frightened him, left him changed.

"You get to a different emotional and physical state," he says. "It's a primal thing that you're doing. It's almost like you're trying to force something back into the earth that's trying to force its way out. I remember, I did think about it one time—What if this blew up right now?"

McMahan has done a lot of thinking about a lot of things. He says he feels sorry for the ordinary Iraqi soldiers who were commanded, on pain of death if they disobeyed, to blow this country apart. He says, "I don't think that all these people were mindless barbarians."

"You're no soldier," I say to him.

"I'm probably the farthest thing," McMahan replies.

At nine-thirty, the interviews concluded, too weary to be friends or enemies, we wind up the extension cords, remove the sheets of white gauze paper that soften the harsh portable lights, close the black louvers, take down the lamps, fold the tripods, pack the big black lighting kit, unscrew the cable that connects the recorder to the camera and load everything into the hatchback of our four-wheel-drive ship of fools.

There is still one more task—night shots of the fires. After that, we can go again through the empty town, up the freeway and into the hotel with the cold, cold showers and the doors with no locks. Tomorrow morning, we will be back here before six-thirty to watch the men go after number 94.

I am in the left rear seat of the cramped little van, picking the tar off my hands. We are on a paved road leading northwest out of al-Ahmadi—toward Old Smokey—when we see barricades blocking the way ahead and a sign that says Road Closed. A detour seems to lead off to the right, into the sort of deep, soft sand we got stuck in this afternoon.

Brian rolls onto it, shifts to four-wheel low, and the traction holds. We are bouncing north now, mesmerized by the brilliance of the flames that leap from the punctured landscape to light the dark side of the world.

For a moment, we each walk separately a short distance from the mother ship, to be alone with this indelible sight. Then Brian gathers the crew and I hear them talking: how will this register on camera? Can the microphone capture the baying of the wind? Will the colors, the radiant anger play?

I walk a little farther away, until their voices disappear. I think, when Armageddon comes, I'll sleep in. I've already seen the last picture show.

7 MAY
Al-Ahmadi

"God, I love a nice breakfast," Maurice says dreamily. "Coffee, orange juice, maybe some French toast or oatmeal. Take my time, relax, have some more coffee."

We're in the van, it's a quarter to six in the morning and I'm handing him a Fruit Roll-Up. (The hotel buffet opens at six-thirty.) We are leaving at this insane preprandial hour because Denike, who eats cigarettes for breakfast, wants us to be at al-Ahmadi for the morning safety meeting at the Canadian equipment yard. After twenty-three days, when the producer says jump, we curse, argue, protest, refuse, blaspheme, conspire and, eventually, yes, boss, we jump. But not far.

It is another beautiful morning in Kuwait City, the sun, already risen, glistening reflectively in the still waters of the famous gulf, which looks warm and inviting. A small navy ship putters slowly offshore, trolling for mines. An American soldier, crew cut and muscular, jogs along the corniche in sateen briefs, his gray T-shirt stained darkly with honest sweat.

If the pollution won't come to us, we'll go to it. Each morning, it hangs like a grim aurora over the exit ramp to al-Ahmadi town. I can see why Larry Flack judges the smoke's effects to be mostly in men's minds, why, on the worst days, you think, All is lost. There's no hope. This time, when we enter the cloud, Maurice, the asthmatic, puts on a white gauze mask to cover his mouth, his nose and his nerves.

The six-thirty safety meeting convenes at a quarter to eight. Mike Miller, bright-eyed and bushy lipped, is in his clean red suit again. He goes over the day's assignment—the dousing, once and hopefully for all, of fire number 94. This is the blaze, far away at the western edge of the oil field, that the Canadians put out a few days ago, only to see it reignite eight hours later, sparked by the radiant heat of the encircling sands.

Today's battle is to be our climax, our denouement. So far, we have shot birds, horses, lakes of oil, men coated in syrupy crude, old clothes being stuffed into pipes, buses arriving, antitank weapons being fired and hell-fighters waxing philosophical at their bivouac at the close of the day, but we do not have a single frame of tape of anyone trying to put out even one of these five hundred fires. And putting out fires is what our senior editors—who hold even more meetings than Safety Boss—might reasonably be expecting us to film.

Miller's crewmen sit on benches ringed around a captured ack-ack gun, fiddling with buttons and zippers, picking at their fingernails, their attention level inversely proportional to the length of time they've been in country. Yesterday's fresh-faced arrivals hang on every phrase; the old hands, nearing the end of their four-week sentence, just want to get on with it and move one day closer to their home leave, their honey and their hooch. Scanning their faces, I try to guess who will return to Kuwait for another tour of duty and who will swallow one month's money and go back on the unemployment.

When we arrive at number 94, which now seems as familiar and constant as the desert sun itself—a fiery Old Faithful—the first thing the men commit to is yet another meeting. Already, an advance guard has detected some problems. We are out in the scorching sun, shooting this powwow, when one of the senior foremen, Jarvis Jackson, strides over with even more bad news.

"The fucking manifold sprung a fucking leak and we'll have to plug the cunt," Jackson says, right into Chris Davies's boom microphone.

There is a slight pause.

"Is this an X-rated documentary?" another of the foremen asks.

"There'll be a lot of fucking bleeps if I'm in it," Jarvis Jackson says, walking away.

This is the problem: the water bladder that sprung a leak yesterday afternoon, just as the minister for International Trade washed up, has only lost half its contents. A creamy, foaming lake continues to fill a depression on the desert floor. But the manifold to which a hose must be connected to drain the remaining seawater from the tank is somewhere at the bottom of this accidental ocean. Volunteers are appointed to submerge themselves in the hope of locating the troublesome valve. Despite the heat, a morning swim here is less appealing than it might appear. Those two big insects I saw yesterday, doing the roach-paddle, have been joined by their families and friends.

But before you can say "surf's up," the Californian, Ron McMahan, and the British Columbian, Joe Chudleigh, have stripped to their jockey shorts and are standing, shoulder deep, in the soup. Alternately, they duck down below the surface and feel for the outlet from the half-collapsed tank. The sun is merciless; I hope they've used a wide-spectrum sunscreen with a high SPF rating. (I have.) A pair of swallows dip and dive above the oasis. This is fire fighting as directed by Wolfman Jack: "First you got to take off all of your clothes...."

It is going to be an hour, at least, before they get the hoses hooked up to the water bladders and move the trucks into place to begin cooling the sand around the wellhead, and the spraying will require at least another hour after that. Brian has tried to park our van so that it has its tail to the sun, but this is fruitless; even the air-conditioning is no match for an early-summer morning in Kuwait. We can roast in the truck, or we can broil outside it.

I get out and walk into a part of the desert where the bushes are living and green, but then I remember the mines and the cluster bombs and I retreat to the groomed and beachcombed zone. The wind is unrelenting, whipping light, fine sand into my face, but yet, when I put my gauze mask on, the breeze makes it bearable to be outside. The temperature is certainly 115 again, but it is an Arizona heat with all the moisture boiled out of it. The only shade in sight is a solitary tree about two miles to the south. The men call it "the tree."

As fires go, number 94 is no Mustache, no Old Smokey. Because the flame is shooting straight up into the air before the wind catches it and a thick exhaust-plume of jet-black smoke bellows off to the southeast, there has probably not been too much damage to the pipeline underneath. Yet, as I pace around the work site, killing time, the searing heat from this comparative pipsqueak begins to make my face uncomfortably hot at fifty yards—upwind—and when I try to move any closer, squinting, holding my gloved hands in front of my face, the laser heat drives right through my sunglasses and my eyelids, and I feel that my pupils themselves will melt. The noise is Cape Canaveral at lift-off.

When, finally, the hoses are connected and the trucks are in place, the Canadians begin to put on their protective clothing for their combat with

number 94. For the front-liners—the men who will earn up to two thousand United States dollars today—this means flameproof long underwear
and a close-fitting hood, then a thick, quilted, insulated suit, a steel fire-
man's helmet with a broad brim to deflect spray and a plastic visor to
cover the face. There will be three men with water hoses right at the rim
of the crater that has been bulldozed around the wellhead. Ken Rose and
Ron McMahan will be two of them. Their fire suits are khaki-tan with
reflective yellow stripes around the waist, arms and calves and metal handles sewn into their waistbands, for lifesaving, if it comes to that.

Just before beginning, Miller gathers all his men in a tight circle,
points out the designated medics and announces that in case of explosion
or other mishap, we are all to scramble immediately to the leeward side
of the equipment truck, Smokey I, for a head count and instructions.
Jarvis Jackson numbers off each worker—the total comes to thirteen fire
fighters, plus four bozos in baby blue.

"Did you count the CBC?" Miller asks.

"Yeah," Jackson answers. "I guess I had to."

Two men are assigned to the big red truck—Smokey III—whose
cargo bed holds a cylindrical tank of dry chemicals, mostly carbon diox-
ide, that will be used to actually extinguish the fire. Others will wield the
water hoses, two crews pouring water on the sand around the wellhead
and one maintaining a constant, cooling rain on the men at the very front.
Another hose has been mounted on the roof of a pickup truck. Joe
Chudleigh, twenty-four hours off the plane, has been designated to drive.
His last words to me as he climbs into the cab are, "So far, no scorpions!"

Now we're ready. The men pick up their hoses and, stiff in their
padded beachwear, walk steadily toward the fire. Maurice and Chris, in
their thin blue coveralls, take a position just behind the kneeling hose
teams, about fifty feet from the well. Brian goes with them to act as eyes
and ears, attentive to sudden trouble as they concentrate on their work. I
sit on a pile of sand, well back from the action, and think, If the wind
shifts, they're toast.

No one has given Maurice a script of the battle—this isn't
"E.N.G."—so he works through the most indispensable shots first,
making sure he has a "wide" of the entire operation, then choosing his
close-ups of the men with the hoses, Joe at the wheel of the pickup, Ron
and Ken in the life-giving rain with the mist above them and the flames
behind. In Toronto, weeks from now, an editor will screen these tapes,

oblivious to the scorching, screaming extremity in which they were made, and care only that Big Mo got the cutaways, and curse him if he failed.

For this, we have come from Canada to Asia to Europe to Africa, then back to Asia again, propelled by our avarice for this spectacular story and by Canadian taxpayers' money. At most, this intense drama at number 94 will be edited down to three minutes of late-night television, part of a twenty-minute piece. If Maurice weaves his usual artistry, the fire will look even more enormous than it is, the kneeling men even closer to it, the earth hotter, the crew braver, the danger more imminent. Yet it will all be true, proved by the pictures.

After about a half-hour of waterworks, Mike Miller, standing in overall command about seventy-five feet from the wellhead, waves his right hand in small circles above his head like Arsenio Hall firing up his audience, and this is the signal for James (Mac) McIntyre, who went to high school with my brother-in-law in Kingston, Ontario, to turn on the CO_2. Two other men now climb *inside* the sand crater with a hose that will direct the chemicals at the flames, which cannot be more than ten feet in front of them.

But something's wrong. Nothing is coming out of the hose. Another try. Still nothing. And, on the bed of the truck with the chemical tank, McIntyre has fairly disappeared into a wispy white cloud. Some connecting gasket must be busted—the chemicals are escaping into the air. Quickly, orders are shouted, signals waved. The men inside the crater are called back. The water hoses are shut down. Number 94, giggling, rages on.

The men retire to the meager shade of one of the big tanker trucks, peel off their suffocating clothing, drain one-liter bottles of Emirates spring water in a couple of long, hungry gulps. One man—he also arrived just yesterday—pulls down his trousers to reveal a lobster-red patch of skin below his left knee. He has been kneeling on the berm and the heat of the baking sand has burned him, right through his "fireproof" suit.

Brian and I retire to the barely air-conditioned Jeep to share a fag— first he smokes it, then I inhale it. With a suspension of gentility that surprises even myself, I say, though it hardly needs announcing, "If they don't put this fire out, we're fucked." Maurice opens the hatchback and lets all the coolish air out. His back is getting worse.

The gloom is dispelled. The men are rising, getting dressed in their unseasonable ski wear, to have another go. The process is repeated—the head count; the half-hour spray of water from the rapidly shrinking bladders; the command to start the chemicals flowing down a long, thick tube.

This time, a few puffs of vapor emerge from the nozzle, but nothing more. If this is a joke, it isn't funny. The proud, committed men of Safety Boss are trying to take the Alamo with a popgun.

When the men of Safety Boss finally do extinguish fire number 94—in early afternoon, on their third try of the day, with a ten-second burst of bright white spray from the refitted chemical truck—there is a brief whoop of exultation from Ron McMahan, the excitable Californian, but the others are too beaten to bleat. Maurice, sunburned, aching and feeling tightness in his lungs, is not sure if he captured the exact instant of the dousing, or not. It was so quick—a whitish burst from the chemical hose, a lot of smoke and then the orange fire segueing into a brown-black fountain of liquid oil—he doesn't remember if he was focused on the wellhead, on the men with the water hoses or just on his own exhaustion. If he missed it, we can come back tomorrow, and the next day. The death of number 94 leaves about 460 wells still burning.

A fire goes out when it is deprived of oxygen. One way to do this is with a smothering mix of chemicals; as practiced by Safety Boss, this is swift, neat and effective, at least on smaller blazes. Another way to cut off the supply of air to a fire is to introduce something that sucks in even more oxygen; say, some high explosives. This is a tactic being pursued by some of the American wildcatters. They set off a charge above the wellhead, then rush in to sting the gusher before it relights.

The bright idea I had in the airplane flying in from Cairo—to waterbomb the sons of bitches like a forest fire—is exceedingly stupid. The water would just boil away. And another brainstorm—to use a giant crane to lower a concrete or cast-iron housing over the wellhead—is equally futile. The oil has been trapped for millions of years at a depth of about four thousand feet. When one route to the surface is blocked, it is going to burst through somewhere else along the damaged pipeline.

My suspicion that the Canadians have been assigned a rather secondary role out here is not refuted by the indubitable Larry Flack— "They're not a real large well contractor," he says—and even Mike Miller himself allows that the Texans see him and his company as "the junior participants" in all this.

We are leaning on Miller's four-by-four on a highway down in al-Burgan with an extremely large fire in the background. Maurice is filming our chat, which lasts nearly a half-hour with all the cutaways and reverses of me in my jumpsuit, and when it ends I realize that I am unable to move. The soles of my boots have gotten stuck to the half-melted tar on the surface of the road.

Ron McMahan describes his father-in-law as "a very intelligent, worldly, sensitive, caring, brave, very brave man." A John Wayne for the nineties, Miller will be a big, big winner if Safety Boss can hang in for the duration. Getting more men to replace those who, after a month or two in this murderous heat, decide not to reenlist will not be a problem; he can always go on "The Journal" again and solicit another five thousand applications.

In our interview, I wonder if the boss himself can last that long.

"On a day like this," I ask him, "don't you ever think of giving this up and opening a flower shop or something back home?"

"I suppose that sometime in my life, that may come," Miller replies. "Though this is all I ever really wanted to do since I was ten years old and my father started this company. I dreamed of fire trucks I'd build, I dreamed of them twenty years ago, and years later, I built them."

We chat for a while about duty and danger and the deaths of the two reporters and the three tanker-truck drivers who, leaving one of Miller's work sites, lost their way in the smoke and went off the road into a seething lake of oil. I remember McMahan yesterday, entering the heart of darkness—"follow my taillights!"—and how, any day, he could be next.

Mike Miller is prepared to commute through this nightmare, week after week, until Old Smokey and the Mustache prove willing to expire. He'll be back in Canada every other month or so, of course, and each time he will be asked, not only for a head count of the fires his team has snuffed, but for some explanation of how the capacity for such willful destruction could lie in the hearts of men.

"I'm still floored by the devastation," he says. "I guess, maybe in Canada we're so isolated from what's happened here—the vandalism, the devastation...it was all done by conscious act, it wasn't a natural catastrophe. People have literally gone around and caused all of this damage.

"I'm just not aware of people with that kind of mentality, growing up in Canada. We've seen one building after another with every window broken and every stick of furniture broken and every light bulb broken. And then of course, the oil wells themselves. It's just a devastating thing to do, when there's no benefit to anybody...."

He starts to laugh.

"Except me!"

Two hours later, with the sun about to collapse from heat prostration over the western horizon, Miller and his number two, Jarvis Jackson, set off into the uncharted desert, looking for souvenirs. Jackson, who came in yesterday with the change of crews, is a tall, loose jointed, loquacious quipster who, at normal times back home, is one of the men who sit around Calgary for months at a stretch, praying that somewhere on this mortal coil, an oil well will blow up and they'll have some work to do.

After twenty minutes or so of reconnoitering in a part of the country that they, and we, have not previously explored, Jackson spots a teeny object far out among the scrub, and after a jouncing zigzag among the cluster bombs that does no good at all for Maurice's back, this turns out to be an Iraqi tank.

I am half hoping and half dreading that there may be bodies inside the monstrous war machine, which would make for incredible pictures and me incredibly sick. But there aren't. All the Safety Bosses find when they open the entry ports and climb down inside are leather helmets, gas masks, shell casings, operations manuals, ration kits and a couple of dozen cartons of live hand grenades.

Also, scattered about the area as if fallen from Fibber McGee's closet, three hair brushes, a five-foot-long two-man hand saw, a couple of paperback books in Arabic and a soup ladle.

It's getting late. Maurice grabs some very quick shots of Miller on the tank, Miller in the drifting sands, Miller in the setting sun. It is all very heroic, the commander of Operation Desert Snuff amid the spoils of war.

On the ride back to al-Ahmadi, Jarvis Jackson is quiet, unusually so. He looks out his window at the shimmering sunset, the leaping fires, the gathering wall of gloom. Then he looks up.

"I've been thinking," the fire fighter says. "How the bleep could people live in this bleeping desert and not drink bleeping beer?"

8 MAY
Kuwait City

$\mathbf{A}$ book could be written about the Kuwait International Hotel, but this isn't it. Physically, the complex consists of two towers whose lobbies are connected by a long, marbled corridor lined with what may once have been shops and small meeting rooms but that now have been taken over, respectively, by government information officers, the American telephone service, the French army, a group of young entrepreneurs selling FREE KUWAIT caps and T-shirts and a passionate environmentalist named Rick from Hamilton, New Zealand, who tells me that since the Kuwaiti authorities are engaging in a massive cover-up of the extent of the degradation of the Persian Gulf from sabotaged oil pipelines, he is going to have to go out tomorrow morning in a rubber raft and lay floating booms around the intake valves of the desalinization plants, all by himself. Then, after lunch, he's flying back to New Zealand.

The tower where I'm staying, the older phase of the hotel, is fifteen stories high but the buttons in the elevator stop at eight. This is because when the Iraqis checked out of their so-called "nineteenth province" they set fire to the International Hotel, and floors nine through penthouse are a shell that I expect to collapse any minute now. A wide, sweeping stairway leads down from the main lobby into an equally ash-strewn, ravaged basement. Another set of stairs descends past the billiard lounge to the bowling alley and a small video arcade where, prowling around last night in my Chinese slippers, I found a Kuwaiti soldier in full camouflage battle dress playing Fighter Attack, a real-life warrior frenetically engaged in a deadly dogfight in an imitation war.

The housekeeper on the fifth floor of my tower is a Filipina whom everyone calls Dory but whose Christian name, on her hotel identity card, is sacred and sexy at the same time: Adoracion. In the long, desperate months before the hotel's in-house laundry service resumed, Adoracion was earning a few extra "goo-goos" by washing guests' clothing herself, at night, at home.

Now, she sobs, they have ordered her to desist. Free-lance washerwomanizing has been banned. Between large Imelda tears, Adoracion tells me that this prohibition will be a serious blow to her income, since the Kuwait International "only gives us twenty," which may be weekly, monthly, yearly, I don't know, U.S. dollars or the newly reissued local currency—the Kuwaiti dinar, K.D., or, as Chris Davies calls them, appropriately, "langs." The "kathy dawn" has been valued, perhaps over-valued, at its prewar level of nearly four times the American Washington, which produces quite a jolt when the bill for breakfast comes and the total is "six" but it really means twenty-two bucks.

Adoracion says she stayed in Kuwait City throughout the occupation. When I ask her, "How did the soldiers treat you?" she quickly says, "No problem, no problem," and hurries away.

Periodically, notices from Hermann Simon, the careworn hotel manager who, with his bituminous eyes and sallow complexion, looks like a tortured POW, or the father of a newborn baby, are slipped under my unlockable door. One missive reminds us not to drink the tap water. Another, attempting to address the hotel's spectacular overbooking problems, suggests that we "reconfirm our departure date" at the front desk.

This is a polite way of saying that if we are still on the premises at ten past noon on the day we had promised to vacate, Manager Simon will personally come to our rooms, heave us out, change the locks (ha!) and donate all our belongings to Baggages Meester.

(But even this sword of Damocles is rendered pointless when another letter informs us that sometime in June, the entire hotel is going to have to close down for massive renovations, and then *everybody* will be thrown out.)

I don't know how it would be possible to tell the people behind the front desk when you planned to check out anyway, because every time I try to get near it to ask a reasonable question—such as, where the hell is the laundry I gave to the "official" washing service four days ago?— my way is blocked by entire battle groups of tormented room seekers, elbowing each other in especially sensitive regions as they scramble to attain the attention of the beautiful, olive-skinned, multilingual young woman behind the counter. I personally have heard this woman tell devastated supplicants that no beds are available in English, Arabic, French, Spanish and German, but whenever I ask her about my laundry, she falls mute and looks at the floor until, defeated, I shrink away.

But there is a singular reward that comes from bunking at the International—the food. A week ago today, when we blew in from Cairo, I laughed when I saw the buffet. It seemed like a mirage, as unearthly as the fires we'd just flown over.

A week later, if I went down to dinner (or lunch, the spread is identical) and *didn't* find a roast leg of lamb or sirloin of beef, a huge, round tray of saffron rice baked with raisins, pine nuts and chunks of meat, a choice of soups, enormous platters of chicken, fish, vegetables, houmous, tabbouleh, olives, tomatoes, cucumbers, dinner rolls, whole-grain breads, fresh apples, kiwi, peaches, berries, watermelon and cantaloupe, twenty to thirty different pastries and puddings, not to mention baklava, pistachio nuts and coconut-custard pie, I'd be very upset.

My intense interest in the provender of the hotel kitchens is no secret—ten minutes before the wrought-iron gates to the dining room open, I'm out there, pacing the floor, counting down the seconds on my one-dollar watch. This seems to amuse my friend from the *New York Times*, Edward A. Gargan, whose personal style, as we meet for breakfast this morning, is to collapse into a chair and to murmur as the life force slowly drains out of him, "Coffee...coffee...coffee...."

"Why is it," Gargan asks me, when he has been revived, "that every time I see you, you're eating?"

"Because," I tell my friend, "every time you don't see me, I'm not."

From today on, the men of Safety Boss will just have to put out the oil-well fires without us. Brian has screened a portion of the twenty-five tapes Maurice filled with scenes of the blazes and the blowout boys; when the burst of chemical succeeds in extinguishing number 94, our producer reports, Maurice is right there, and right in focus. The twenty-five tapes—about five hundred minutes in total—will be edited down to a tight eighteen or twenty, and the other ninety-six percent of Maurice's painstaking labor will be "bulk-erased," never to be seen again. But the crucial instant has been captured, and when Jarvis Jackson takes his head count this morning, there will be four fewer heads.

We are off, then, to begin our second Kuwait documentary, the third item of a twenty-four-day shoot. (A hard-news team might already have shot and satellited twenty-four stories, but they'd be brief, two minutes or less.) This project has been growing in the womb of our fixer, Aboud, the jaunty Lebanese I last saw on our initial sortie into the fire fields, when I fully expected him to floor the accelerator on an oil-slick byway and accelerate us all to kingdom come.

But Aboud, charged with arranging a survey of Kuwait in the aftermath of Desert Storm, has done well. To start off, he has scheduled appointments at the National Museum and at the nation's largest BMW dealership—both of which were looted, trashed and thoroughly burned by the peevish Iraqis—and tonight we are supposed to be meeting what passes in Kuwait for a "youth gang," some break-dancing teens who cruise menacingly on their motorcycles through what little remains of the commercial core.

By now, I'd estimate that we've used up fifty percent of our two-week Kuwaiti visa and eighty percent of our energy. It is hot; by the time we arrive at the National Museum, sometime after ten, the sun is directly overhead, and opening the car doors and standing in the concrete parking lot is like entering a Sudbury smelter that takes your breath away, and keeps it. Our four-man coalition is barely holding; the temperature is melting the glue. It is far hotter here, in the center of the city, than it was on the windblown, baking sands at number 94.

Dividing into two vehicles eases the tension a bit. Maurice and Chris ride in Aboud's clean, lean Audi. That leaves me with Brian in the four-wheel-drive, which, after four full days at al-Ahmadi, is coated on the outside with indelible splotches of congealed crude and on the inside is even dirtier, with globs of sandy tar and tarry sand all over the seats, the paneling, the carpets and the dash. The three Iraqi battle helmets Chris and I picked up at al-Ahmadi kindergarten rattle around the floorboards.

Denike's legs are beginning to bother him. It started in al-Ahmadi, he says, a pain that was more than simple cramping but less, so far, than the intense agony of dengue fever, the mosquito-borne case of "break-bone" he contracted last December in Panama. (The other crew members laughed when I used insect repellent on the Panama trip. They laughed even louder when I made a conspicuous show of applying it in our tent in the Sirvan Valley, then woke up with two big red bites on my wrist while the rest of them went unprotected and unmunched.)

In this case, I diagnose constricted venous circulation caused by cigarette smoking, but the patient rejects my prescription, which is to jettison all the Benson & Hedges out the truck window, and then back up and run them over. So we cruise on, both of us aggrieved, down Arabian Gulf Street with the flat blue water to our right and the baking, barren avenues of the central business district to our left, until we come to the National Museum of Kuwait, or rather its cremated remains.

The museum, founded in 1983 by a niece of the emir, is part of a complex that included, in happier times, an exhibition of Islamic art, a craft center that offered courses in traditional spinning and weaving, and Badr House, a restored nineteenth-century waterfront mansion, surrounded by adobe walls, one of the few buildings still standing in Kuwait that predated the oil boom. A curator of the Metropolitan Museum of Art in New York City once called it "the largest comprehensive collection in the Islamic world."

That there were people here long before the al-Sabahs consolidated their rule in the eighteenth century—indeed, long before Islam—was not known conclusively until the nineteen-fifties, when a Danish archaeological survey digging on Failaka Island just off the Kuwaiti coast found, among other relics, pottery fragments from the Dilmun civilization of the third millennium B.C., the ruins of a Greek temple, and a coin that bore the head of King Antiochus III of Syria, circa 200 B.C.

That was just about the time that the first mention was made of the strange, thick, heretofore useless black liquid that oozed out of the sands of Arabia.

"Asphaltus," wrote Eratosthenes of Cyrene, quoted by the Roman Strabo, quoted by the British writer Peter Mansfield in *Kuwait—Vanguard of the Gulf*, a primer on the country fortuitously, or haplessly, published in the spring of 1990, a few weeks before Saddam's tanks rolled in, "is found in great abundance...it is of a singular nature. When it is brought near the fire, the fire catches it, and if a body smeared over with it is brought near the fire, it burns with a flame, which is impossible to extinguish, except with a large quantity of water."

In February, when the Iraqis put the asphaltus to the Kuwaiti National Museum, the result was the mess we now see before us, a tall, square exhibition hall blackened by smoke on its exterior latticework and inside, as we step through the frame of what once was a glass door, ankle deep in broken display windows, fallen light fixtures and soft ashes that puff into the air with each step we take, creating miniature toxic clouds.

"Its fate," observes the glossy magazine *New Arabia*, published in London by Kuwaiti interests, "prompts comparison with the sack of Rome by Attila the Hun."

The Iraqis were vengeful, but not stupid. Before withdrawing—in fact, just after arriving—they sent experts down from Baghdad to carefully pack up all the precious contents of the museum and bring them north. (For "protection," the Iraqi Department of Antiquities explained.) While negotiations begin in an attempt to have these treasures returned— their removal, notes *New Arabia* rather punctiliously, was a violation of Article 4 of the 1954 Hague Convention—I walk around the charcoaled main hall with a museum employee named Ahmed al-Tattan, a pleasant young man who, when I ask him if he can forgive the ordinary soldiers who were ordered to do this dirty deed, replies, "You can't imagine how I hate them."

"Because they destroyed your museum?" I say.

"Not because of the museum. Not because of the museum. They killed, they raped, they steal, they burn. That's why I hate them."

"How do you get revenge on the people who destroyed this museum?"

"Myself, I can't revenge," the young man says. We are walking among the wreckage and Maurice is shooting close-ups of Ahmed's sandals and my tar-encrusted Bass deck shoes. "I can't. I have nothing in my hand to revenge with. All I can do is to hate them."

(But the Kuwaiti National Museum did gain one small victory over the latter-day Huns. Parts of the displays of Failaka Island pottery and Greek temple columns the Iraqis pilfered were forgeries. The actual pieces were kept in a secret storage room, and survived.)

At the National Museum, breathing ash with every overheated gulp, we are not hearing a lot of talk about healing and reconciliation and pan-Arab brotherhood. When we set up to interview one of the associate curators, a pretty, long-haired woman named Gazza al-Dawoud who looks like the folk singer Joan Baez, she fairly seethes with enmity for the Iraqi army, and the Iraqi nation. She calls them "savage barbarians." When I ask her if she could imagine doing the same to them and their ancient artifacts, she replies, "No, never. Because we are civilized."

When the Iraqis came, Gazza, like nearly half of all Kuwaiti citizens, was abroad; she was at a seminar at Oxford. She came home in March to this fractured little state. For our interview, she is wearing a long, raspberry-colored skirt and a multihued pullover, at the collar of which is pinned a black-and-green button that says, We are FREE—thank you Desert Storm. But Kuwait is not free; it is still, I am seeing, bound by its collective agony, even in educated, equable people like Gazza.

"It's over," she says. "Politically, it's over. They withdrew from Kuwait, they left Kuwait, and we want to thank everybody who helped to liberate Kuwait. But what about the feeling of the people, we still feel anger inside. I can't forgive them for what happened to my country. It takes hundreds of years. Hundreds of years to forget them."

The interviews at the National Museum are interrupted by a taut little tiff between myself and my producer that begins when he asks me to jot down someone's name—I am, after all, the reporter—and I reply that my notebook and pens are in my red knapsack and would he please tote this for me while I am on-camera doing my "reaction shots," those patently phony nods and head wiggles that we use in cutting long quotations into manageable sound bites. (Otherwise, you would see the subject's head suddenly jump, at the point where the trim was made, like the video-cyborg Max Headroom.) The spat escalates as we drive back to the hotel for lunch until, finally, I abandon all restraint and ask:

"Brian, is there anything I can do besides commit suicide that would make you happy?"

Denike gives me his little demilaugh and his look that says, despite all this bickering, he really does enjoy taking me out on the road for a month and being my wife and mother.

"I'm under a lot of pressure, Allen," he replies.

I cool down; I don't want to ask what he's hearing from the office, from the crew, from home.

The other men also have kept unshared secrets to themselves. Maurice's only report from Quebec is that his sixteen-year-old daughter—her mother and Maurice are divorced—has begun driving and he is scared for her, seven thousand miles away. From Chris, there has been not a single mention of wife or home. And I won't ask.

From Linda, I have heard nothing but good cheer in our chats these three weeks and more, though sometimes, as soon as she answers, I can hear pleurisy in her breathing or an empty tiredness in her voice, the lupus talking. We speak about the oil fires and my brave days at the front, the wedding she went to, alone, the other day and the people she met there who saw me in Iran in "Valley of Despair" and marveled at the fractured, fascinating life we lead. For seventeen years, we have kidded ourselves that the separations are a blessing, that they reinforce our hours together and make them doubly precious, and from Kuwait, every other night, we have maintained the charade. I'd guess that we've been apart, in sum, about three years of the seventeen.

But now the romance of this excursion has been broken—after the fire fighting, anything else must be anticlimax—and when we all get back to the Kuwait International, Maurice's back is in such bad shape he has to lie flat on the floor with his legs elevated on a packing case to get any relief. This surprises the hell out of Adoracion, the housekeeper, when she enters his room and finds him there, eyes closed, rhythmically breathing like a Hindu ascetic, this hairy bear of a yogi.

"I'm not paying full price for this room," he says, when I come to tell him that my laundry has finally been brought back, after five days, minus one of my favorite Banana Republic all-cotton "foreign correspondent" shirts. "There's no hot water. They've lost half my clothes. I don't have a key to my own room. I'm not going to pay."

It is a far cry from the exuberant hulk who pretended to find a cache of lager in a fundamentalist Iranian fridge, or from the colleague, sincere and committed, who told me, as I awaited our take-off from Toronto in distraught apprehension, that I had the "heart" for this shoot.

In this state, not even the Grandma Gretzky story seems to cheer him up, and usually this is a code word that sets both of us to peals of laughter while everyone around us blankly gawks. In the fall of 1988, while working on our documentary commemorating the 150th anniversary of the invention of the photograph, I used my status as an old friend of the Gretzky family—next to Gordie Howe, I was Wayne's childhood idol—to arrange a shoot during which the star's paternal grandmother would leaf through the album of yellowed photos that recorded her girlhood in Poland, her migration to Canada, the ascent of her famous grandson.

Maurice was the cameraman. We had Wayne's sister Kim join the homely scene, as if asking to see her grandma's pictures. They came to a page that included a lovely portrait of the immigrant woman with her husband, Andy Gretzky, now deceased. Sensing the moment, Maurice zoomed in, very tight.

"When you see that photograph of your husband, when you see his face, Maria, what do you feel?"

The old woman opened her mouth to speak. All was silent.

"He's dead," she snapped. "What's to feel?"

But this time, when I walk into his room and in my best Polish accent, look at Big Mo lying on the carpet, and say "Hiss ded, vat's to fil," the cameraman merely grimaces. This is a bad sign.

The thought of going to interview a man whose auto dealership was looted and set afire seems to energize Aboud. Cars are everything to him—his Audi, his brother's BMW—and, although he is not Kuwaiti, through him I am getting some sense of what life must have been like here, for the better off, before August 2, 1990.

I haven't heard him say of the Iraqis, like the young guide at the National Museum, "You can't imagine how I hate them." On the contrary, to Aboud the Lebanese fixer, the former occupiers are objects of ridicule, not contempt. He doesn't see them as "barbarians," like Gazza al-Dawoud, but as mere riff raff, the unwashed.

"When I drove up to Baghdad to use the telephone," he says, as we load up the Audi and the little truck for the afternoon's filming, "nobody hassled me. There were checkpoints but that was not a problem. But the roads were *terrible*. It took me seven or eight hours—I couldn't go over ninety.

"And when I had to stop to eat—well, you know that in Iraq you have to order two kebabs. One for you, and one for the flies."

The exclusive BMW dealer for the State of Kuwait is a round, friendly gentleman, about fifty years old, with a salt-and-pepper mustache and thick eyebrows, who looks almost exactly like the old character actor Akim Tamiroff, but in *dishdasha* and *ghuta* head-dress of rich white-on-white cotton. How anyone can stand this costume, buttoned tightly at the collar, in this heat, I have no idea, but my own knit shirts—I bought a few in Frankfurt, dark colors that wouldn't show oil spots too badly—are magnets for the sun and I feel that my skin is baking underneath my clothing, like fish wrapped in waxed paper in a microwave oven. Maybe the men who have lived here since the days of Antiochus III know what they're doing.

Ali al-Ghanim walks us around his showroom, which is a cinder, and his service area, in which nine expensive German cars still remain, but in various states of undress. Unable to find the keys or, in one case, to figure out how to lower a bright red, two-door sports coupe from its elevated position on a hydraulic lift, the rather finicky barbarians simply stole whatever they could remove: tires, wheel covers, door handles (in some cases, the doors, too), gearshift knobs, brake pedals, radios, taillights and gas caps. But this was a minor inconvenience. At Ali al-Ghanim's storage yard, they took 409 new cars worth fifteen million dollars and another seven million dollars in spare parts.

And that is just what Ali al-Ghanim lost from his BMW business. He is adding up his total losses for me as we stand in the charnel house of his parts department. Fifteen million from the auto dealership, thirty million from a telecommunications products center, thirty million from his steel mill...

"And then we have the hotel," he says. It's the Continental, the one just off the al-Istiqlal Expressway with the Welcoming Back to Business sign.

"So we have a total loss here, I would say, about 130 to 140 million dollars," al-Ghanim reports. "And we are still counting."

"But you're laughing, you're smiling about it," I notice.

I think, Maybe this is an Arab reflex, like the way the Chinese giggle when they nearly get hit by a car.

"There is a saying in Arabic," al-Ghanim replies. "When things are so sad, you have to laugh."

The al-Ghanims have been this hysterically rich for less than seventy years. In 1925, Ahmed al-Ghanim, a sea captain plying the trade routes from Bombay to Basra at the tip of the Fertile Crescent, lost his wooden dhow in a storm and thus, in a sense, washed up, had to look around for another line of work. He and his sons branched out—into timber contracting, quarrying, the oil fields and, after the Second World War, received from the emir as a token of friendship, the exclusive importing license for General Motors products, a family sideline that, when the Iraqis arrived in August, 1990, resulted in one of Ali's uncles being unwillingly divested of more than four thousand brand-new Chevys, Pontiacs and GMC Trucks.

"They have put on fire everything," Ali says. "Go around the corner and see. The Toyota people the same thing. The Nissan people the same thing. Chrysler, Mitsubishi and so on, exactly the same situation."

Ali al-Ghanim plans to sue Saddam Hussein if his insurance company can't or won't cover his hundred-million-dollar loss. (I can just hear Saddam receiving the writ and growling, like Harold Ballard when threatened with a slander suit, "Join the crowd, pal.") He says that the reason he hasn't cleared the ashes and twisted metal from his showroom is that he fears he will be unable to prove how much damage was done when the adjusters come around. It's a novel idea—that any move toward sweeping Kuwait clean could be construed as destruction of evidence.

More commonly, the excuse is a shortage of Third World janitors. In addition to the Tamils we filmed hauling the ash and shattered glass out of the Meridien lobby, we've seen one dark-skinned man picking up litter on the al-Safr Motorway and two more sweeping the sidewalk a block from the BMW dealership. These are men who remained in Kuwait through the invasion. The *Arab Times* reports that out of sixty-two thousand laborers who fled from home to India, exactly one has so far come back to Kuwait.

But we have not come to visit Ali al-Ghanim to hear only of his material losses, substantial though they may be. (Certainly a debit of $130 million would not make *me* burst out laughing.) In fact, he is adamant that what he seeks is more than financial compensation. He wants a new Kuwait.

"Money, money, money," he says. "Money is not the solution. Money can come and go. But freedom and democracy has to stay. And I think the people of Kuwait, they are demanding democracy. Whatever money you pay them is not going to stop them calling for democracy."

"But the emir has promised democracy," I say. "He's promised elections sometime in 1992. What if that promise is broken?"

"Well, this depends on the Kuwaiti people," al-Ghanim says. "I mean, the Kuwaiti people have kept their promise to the emir. During the invasion, not a single Kuwaiti cooperated with the Iraqis because we stood one hundred percent behind our promise in the constitution to support the emir. I think it's the duty now of the emir of Kuwait to keep his promise, and I have a feeling he might keep that promise."

"He *might* keep it," I say.

"He might, yes. But frankly speaking, if this promise is not kept, the Kuwaitis have to fight for their freedom."

Ali al-Ghanim, wealthy and well fed, seems an odd sort of duck to be calling the masses to the barricades. But opposition, at least to the al-Sabahs, runs in his family. In 1938, his progenitor, the beached sea captain, and other merchants, petitioned Sheikh Ahmad for the creation of a legislative council that, when granted, immediately began writing laws, appointing ministers, lowering tariffs and indicting corrupt police and

Customs officials and opening schools, including, for the first time, one for girls. Six months after it was inaugurated, the parliament was abolished by the whim of the emir, who also tried to quiet the family by marrying an al-Ghanim. The al-Sabahs do not play games with their oily, sandy little kingdom.

Half a century later, the al-Ghanims are trying again. (Aboud says that they were quietly bankrolling certain prodemocracy groups, even before the Iraqi occupation.) With a latter-day legislative assembly suspended since 1986, with the crown prince, who is the emir's second cousin, not his son, still serving as prime minister, and with thousands of captured Iraqi guns hidden away in closets and under beds, Ali seems to be predicting a rather messy confrontation. But his brand of democracy would grant suffrage, just as before, only to male Kuwaitis whose families have been resident here for generations. It would not include women, the Palestinians and Tamils and Egyptians, or even Aboud, the twenty-six-year-old son of a Lebanese man who has been here for thirty years. But I suspect that Aboud will not complain of this, as long as the highways are free of potholes and there are no flies on his kebab.

When the interview is finished, Ali al-Ghanim bids one of his employees bring us some cold water to drink. This the man does, in tall, clear bottles on a tray. Brian takes a slug, and I've just had a couple of sips, when I notice that the caps on the bottles are not sealed. Remembering the admonition from the management of the Kuwait International not to drink the tap water, I ask the bearer whether this water has come from the faucet and he says, yes, it has.

Meanwhile, Brian has gone out and handed two bottles of the dubious stuff to Maurice and Chris, who are out shooting exteriors in the murderous heat. The boys have already drained the water and are begging for more when I burst out of the building and ask if Denike had informed them that it was possibly unsafe. This results in a stream of invective directed toward the producer, not to mention my own certainty that I am about the become the first person ever to contract amoebic dysentery at a BMW showroom.

I walk around the corner and scribble in my notebook: "We are four men in a lifeboat, all rowing for home in different directions."

What I need now is something on paper that guarantees that, someday, this shoot will end. Denike doesn't agree. We have a million more things to do before we can leave the country—visuals of the city and harbor, interviews with frightened Palestinians and the families of Kuwaitis still missing in Iraq, a long drive to a war-refugee camp at the Iraqi frontier. But sometime, obviously, we are going to have to buy our air tickets out of Kuwait, and that time, by a vote of three to one, is now.

When we get to the ticket office of Kuwait Airways—"Meeting the challenge and flying high"—in a lightly damaged downtown tower, half an hour before it opens for the evening shift at four o'clock, the queue already drifts from the office door, down some steps, around a corner, into a courtyard and halfway around the building. Again, the producer and I have it out: he doesn't want to waste our time in this lineup; I insist that we'll have to do it sooner or later; there is no other route of escape. Then I have a brainstorm—I ask the security guard at the door if First Class passengers must lower themselves to stand and wait, like rabble.

I don't think anyone broached this before. (Or, more likely, before the war, everyone in Kuwait flew First Class.) Whatever the truth is, rising on this patrician note of privilege has us immediately ushered into a private side office while the three or four hundred other supplicants slug it out in the line.

One thing we do not want to do is go back to Cairo and wage war on Egyptian Customs again. This leaves Bahrain and Dubai as potential targets as Kuwait Airways, although "determined," according to its full-page advertisement in *New Arabia*, "to keep the flag of Kuwait flying throughout the world as it does in all our hearts," is still serving only a very limited route network. With the Kuwait City airport only fractionally functional, with all its computers stolen and with Iraq having swiped fifteen of its planes—seven of them, including two Boeing 767s and two Airbus 300s, were reportedly destroyed in Allied bombing of Iraqi airfields—Kuwait Airways actually is doing quite well. And when Brian allows that, yes, we can go home via Dubai and its renowned duty-free shops, peace is once again restored. Chris Davies can taste the bargains already.

"Yes! Yes!" he chirrups, flaunting the ticket envelope and pretending to fire his microphone boom, like a rifle, into the overheated sky. "Dubai! Ladies and gentlemen, that's spelled dee owe bee you why—Do Buy!"

We are leaving Sunday morning at nine-thirty. Today is Wednesday. That gives us three full shooting days to go to the border, get the "scenics," meet the Palestinians and plumb the soul of a complex, shattered, alien society. "I'm under a lot of pressure," Denike had said, this morning. Now we all are.

At sunset, in a block-square lot of barren, blowing sand, five men squat with their instruments—two drums, two tambourines, and a stringed box that, mournfully twanging, sounds like a sitar or a crying girl. In front of the musicians, in neat semicircles of wooden chairs, or sitting on rattan mats spread on the bare dirt, are about a hundred children. The music begins, and first one girl, then several—but no boys—rise and begin to dance. I watch their leader, a ten-year-old houri in a green-striped dress, spinning and whirling, her right hand at her navel, her left curled expressively over her head as her long dark hair whips around.

Now the music stops and two men in dun-colored *galabiyahs* emerge from a tent at the side of the arena. They are carrying long cudgels—it is an exhibition of Egyptian stick-fighting—and, as they enter the flood-lighted area and begin to swing their weapons in wide, practiced arcs, I see that one of the fighters is an old gray man and the other is a boy. But they are merely toying, and though the clatter of the poles sounds deadly, neither youth nor experience prevails.

We are at a carnival arranged to entertain the children of men whom the war has swallowed and lost. Some were Kuwaiti soldiers, others were civilians snatched up as hostages as the routed invaders fled, or simply murdered and their bodies never found amid the city's ashen residue. A society formed by some of these men's families and friends estimates that 5,300 Kuwaitis are still missing, in the tenth week after peace was declared.

I am walking around the ring of seated mothers, trying to find an English-speaker, when I meet a woman in full black costume, her scarf drawn tightly, not a hair showing to betray her Islamic purity. She is holding a year-old, big-eyed boy and watching two daughters as they sit in the sandy proscenium and watch the show. She has soft eyes and her English is excellent; she is, of course, wearing glasses just like mine.

"Kuwait is not free," the woman tells me, but not on camera—Maurice and Chris are shooting the musicians and the whirling little girls. "It will not be free until my husband returns."

"Where is he?" I ask.

"Allah knows," she replies evenly. I think of the father in rural Illinois whose daughter had gone off to battle leaving her infant behind;

"This is like a cancer, eating away at me." But his daughter had come home. Now, here, after all the scenes of jubilation and release—the rifles fired heavenward, the portraits of Saddam doused with petrol and set afire—families still are living with the worst of war's agonies, a nightmare unrelieved.

But the woman in the glasses will not go on camera, and as it was with the Christians in the refugee camp in Iran, I am not about to plead with her, for in the same circumstance I would see no benefit in sharing my own grief with some impure stranger. She gets up and carries her son to the candy stand and buys him a bag of chips, collects the two girls and goes away, into the gathering night.

We are scouring the festival for another potential subject when I see a familiar face—it's one of the newspaper reporters with whom I've been breakfasting, Tracy Wilkinson of the *Los Angeles Times*. As she is the first North American female any of us has spoken to in nearly four weeks, and since she is very good-looking, very friendly, and not dressed in a robe and veil, Ms. Wilkinson has become, in our minds, the very embodiment of Woman and now carries every dreamy attribute thereunto presupposing. So, when she asks to borrow our fixer so that she can talk to some of the wives of the Kuwaiti missing, we are hardly about to say no.

Tracy and Aboud stand and talk for about fifteen minutes to a very dark-skinned woman who is wearing a black *ghisura* over a blue-and-white-striped sweatshirt, a Koranic adaptation of California style. Then they break up, Tracy smiles her thanks, I collapse in a heap, and when I recover, I remember how simple it was when I was writing for the *Globe*: you take note of the scene, do your interviews and go. Tonight, we will spend three hours here and get one minute of television, maximum, and even that will be difficult because the light keeps changing and the music stops and starts.

When Tracy leaves, we abandon the hunt and for the first time on the shoot, set up to do an interview with a non-English-speaker, with Aboud translating. This always is a tough choice to make, because, while a subject may speak only fractured English, it can be more effective to hear him say, in English, like the doctor at Ahmadi Hospital, "we are middle of hell," than to hear a more eloquent disquisition recited by an actor as voice-over studio translation. But here, since we have found no one who speaks English at all, we ask the woman whom Tracy has just finished interviewing if she would mind going over the same ground, for us.

She agrees. Her husband, she says, is an officer in Kuwait's tiny navy who has not been heard from since early September, a month after the invasion. Since then, she has heard that he is in Basra, he is in Baghdad, he is in Mosul, he is dead. She tells this in clipped, guttural Arabic, her large teeth flashing in the lights. She is the mother of seven; they cluster around her and a baby boy writhes and wriggles in her arms.

"What do you tell your children when they ask about their father?"

"To the little ones, I say that he is traveling," she replies, according to Aboud, who is standing directly behind me, so her eye-line is aimed toward the source of the questions. "But to the older ones, I try to elevate their morals. I tell them, 'If your father died defending his country, thank Allah. Allah loves him. It is a big honor for you.'"

"How do you feel about the Iraqis who destroyed your country and took your husband?"

"I cannot describe my feelings; only that if I see who did harm to my husband, I will kill them. We hate them more than before. They invaded our country, they were mad, insane, uncivilized. No one would act in the way they did. They were even worse than the Jews."

After an elegant dinner of *shawarma* and 7Up at a dirty street-corner stall—*shawarma* is shaved lamb, spit roasted, then rolled in pita bread with tomatoes and spices—we press on with this endless day of shooting, one of those rare occasions when what I do actually begins to seem like work. (For the crew, of course, every day is labor day.)

The brick-oven afternoon has become a humid tropical night and we are in the commercial neighborhood near the Sultan Center, which has come alive with bustling businesses, cruising cars, flashing neon and thousands upon thousands of strolling pedestrians out for their evening *paseo*, traversing the uneven, busted-up sidewalks and popping in and out of the clothing and electronics stores as if nothing at all had happened here, in Kuwait City. Pizza Hut is open, Hardee's is open, the Nintendo outlet is packed, men are selling, from the backs of trucks, T-shirts that say See You in Free Kuwait and Thank You Desert Storm, and crowded into a tiny Kentucky Fried Chicken outlet—Hamburger cook to order 4.5 minutes, a sign says, precisely—are about twenty-five American and French soldiers in fatigues and spit-polished boots, making faces for the camera.

This is where we are supposed to rendezvous with Aboud's promised "youth gang," but this alleged menace disassembles into a couple of rather tame-looking hoodlums on a bright red Yamaha outside a music store who, when Aboud implores them, lazily condescend to mount their machine and, suddenly, tires screaming, go tearing down Salmiya Street, nearly killing an elderly Hindu couple trying to cross the road.

We are able to corral two other teens on the sidewalk to ask them about life in postwar Kuwait. One of them is tall and clean-shaven, and the other, with a scraggly mustache and an overbite, looks just like my college roommate.

"What do you guys do for fun?" I ask them.

"For fun," the first one says, "we come to shops."

"Is not Iraqis around," the second one inserts. "That is *big* fun."

"What happened to you during the occupation?" I continue. One of the boys is Egyptian and the other is Palestinian.

"Two days, the Iraqis arrest us," the one with the facial hair replies. "They hang us upside-down, hit us with sticks. Then they say, okay, now we can go home."

In the middle of all this, I am leaning on a pillar outside Kentucky Fried Chicken, the crew is off doing some traffic shots and Denike is chatting with Aboud about tomorrow's program, when unexpectedly I hear a tiny voice say to me, "Hello, you are CNN?" It is a small boy, dark haired, in a polo shirt that is divided down the middle, gold on one side, blue on the other, speaking impeccable English, and wearing glasses. It breaks my heart to tell him that CNN we are not.

The boy is Kuwaiti. He is ten years old. I wave for Maurice and we set up, me squatting like Carlton Fisk and firing questions like Robert Fisk, the preeminent British journalist and expert on the Middle East.

"My father in Ahmadi Hospital," the little boy says.

"Why?" I say anxiously. "What happened to him?"

"He works. He is doctor in hospital," the boy says.

"What happened to your family during the war?"

"Everybody left Kuwait in the war but all the war we waited in Kuwait. Our car, it stole. We woke up, my father found his car stolen."

"When you see buildings destroyed, buildings burned, what are you thinking?"

"I think that everybody leaves Kuwait. I cried in my eyes. And also I went very sad. Why did they burn them?"

"Are you sad or happy?" I ask.

"I'm a bit happy," the little boy replies.

9 MAY
Kuwait City

On Thursday morning, with Sunday breathing down our necks, we are taken by Aboud the fixer to a place he knows well, from personal experience—a school building in the neighborhood called Hawalli where non-Kuwaiti citizens, like him, must register periodically for "foreigners" identity cards. Since non-Kuwaitis, even if they were born here, cannot vote in the emirate's intermittent elections, are generally forbidden from owning land, houses or other real property and cannot control more than forty-nine percent of a business—though this, often, is enough to make them very rich—the system might be called, for want of a better word, apartheid.

Until last August, the machine worked smoothly: manual laborers from the illimitable ranks of Third World remittance men and Filipina housemaids at the bottom; millionaire Kuwaitis at the top, and in the middle, the Palestinian, Egyptian, Pakistani, Lebanese and other expatriate technicians, shopkeepers, mechanics and tradesmen who are lined up on this blistering morning, men in one queue, women in another, inching toward the guarded entrance to the registration compound. Everyone is carrying a long brown envelope with the relevant documents enclosed, and Aboud makes a pointed reference to the fact that holding this folder over one's head creates the only available shade.

"The Kuwaitis go to another building downtown, with air conditioning," our Lebanese sniffs, and, for the first time, I detect a bit of resentment in his voice. Here, clearly, he is among his peers—he recognizes several of the men in the long line of hundreds—and when he calls me over to meet an old family friend, the sense of being among the disenfranchised increases.

The friend is an Egyptian businessman, fat and bald, a pleasant man who seems happy that we have come to record this minor public humiliation.

"How long have you lived in Kuwait?" I ask him.

"Since March seventh," he replies deliberately, and his mood darkens. "March seventh, nineteen-sixty."

Maurice gets some close-ups of the people in line. They are being required to get new cards to replace ones issued by the occupiers that indicated everyone's place of residence as "Kuwait, Iraq." Aboud recalls that when those cards were issued, it was the Kuwaitis who had to stand in the sun.

I am at the end of the queue, talking to the aggrieved Egyptian businessman, when I hear some squawking and I see that at the head of the line, Maurice is arguing with a young Kuwaiti soldier who has his right hand firmly cupping the lens of Lucille, the Sony camera.

By the time Aboud and I trot over, Mo and Chris, still connected by thick black cable, are walking toward the entrance to the schoolyard, following the young army man, and Maurice gives me the wink that indicates that he is still rolling, so at least we'll have a shot of our tormentor, from the back. Behind us, as we strut, Indian-file, through the gate, I hear a man's voice call out from the line-up, "No! Is CNN!"

We are brought up in front of a stern, good-looking officer and I show him my accreditation from the Ministry of Information, which he rejects as being a useless hen-scratching, because he reports to the minister of the Interior. He says that we are in a military area and that filming is forbidden.

"Isn't this a free country?" I poke at him. (It's exactly the sort of snide crack I was afraid I'd come out with, had I been part of our negotiations with Hatam, the man from the Ministry of Islamic Guidance, back in Tehran.) My reward is that we are all herded into a small, dim office to cool our heels and wait.

But this incarceration soon ends, and with Maurice smoothing everything over, we depart with an agreement that if we get a letter from Interior, we can come back and resume our work. Face is saved all around, we do not fear the sort of horrible potentialities that we might have suffered when we were similarly accosted at the Halabja refugee camp in Iran, and as I am the commandant pro tempore of our crew—Brian is back at the hotel, catching up on his screening of our tapes—I order everyone to return to the Kuwait International before the luncheon buffet is reduced to lamb bones and dry couscous.

"How come," I ask Edward A. Gargan of the *New York Times*, "Every time I'm in here eating, I see you?"

"Why don't you sit at the Toronto table," he ripostes, motioning toward Maurice and Chris, who are looking at me as if I have snobbishly dumped them for people who can read and write.

"Don't forget I'm from Brooklyn," I shoot back.

"I spent my summers in Brooklyn," Gargan says.

"Where in Brooklyn?"

"Albany Avenue. My grandfather lived there."

"Albany and where?"

"Avenue D."

"But that's where my father's candy store was! Albany Avenue and Avenue D!"

"That was your father's candy store?" Gargan yelps, very much unlike a man from the *New York Times*.

"Yes," I answer. "And do you remember a kid about your age behind the counter, making ice cream cones?"

"That was *you*?"

I am halfway through lunch with Gargan and the beauteous Ms. Wilkinson when Brian Denike limps in, flexing his sore leg, stands over our table and says, "I have some very bad news."

Immediately, I think, It's Linda. Something's wrong. But that can't be it. Brian wouldn't announce it like this.

Then I think, It's the hassle with the soldiers at the registration center this morning. We're being expelled. But that would be *good* news.

He sits down. Now I'm thinking, It's got to be technical. And it is. It's the worst possible.

The camera is buggered and has been for three days.

I hurriedly finish my meal and take the elevator to Denike's stadium-sized suite on the ninth floor of the newer tower of the Kuwait International Hotel. He has gone to find Baggages Meester, who has to unlock the door with a master key. When this is done, the producer pops one of our cassettes into his videotape player and shows me what has happened.

It's a color problem. One of Lucille's three primary-color "guns"—

red, blue, green—has been misfiring ever since the action scene of fire fighting at well number 94. Like a spark plug that misses every once in a while, or a fluorescent light bulb that flickers when you switch it on, everything red is dropping out of the picture, reappearing for a second or two, then vanishing again. So a shot of the Kentucky Fried Chicken shop Maurice took last night, for example, shows the famous emblem as bright red, then gray, then red, gray, red, gray, and so on. The obvious suspicion is that it must have been the heat.

My first, gasping, question is, "Do we have to reshoot the fires?"

We don't. Brian had already checked the scenes at the wellhead where Safety Boss was frustratingly engaged, right up to the instant the fire finally was put out. All of that was fine, and that's where he left off his screening, two days ago. But this morning, resuming his cataloging of the tapes, he found that the very next thing Maurice shot after the fire fight—the long interview with Mike Miller, leaning on his truck, when my boots became glued to the tarry road—periodically lost the color red, and so did everything we shot yesterday. That means the children's carnival, Ali the millionaire, the National Museum, the little boy who said "I'm a bit happy"—all are useless.

The effect of the color-drop is maddening. The little boy's blue-and-gold shirt doesn't change, but the flesh tone flickers from natural pink to alien green-gray and back again every few seconds. The pure white robes worn by Ali al-Ghanim are unaffected, but his face keeps changing color. And, worst of all, there is the loss of the crucial interview with Miller and his wonderful line, "There's no benefit to anybody...except me!"

During this chat, Miller was wearing a bright red jumpsuit that keeps alternating, on our tape, from crimson to gray. And the flaming well behind him, a fountain of orange fire, goes as yellow as lemons whenever the red drops out. A few minutes after Brian begins this depressing demonstration, the crew arrives. For a few minutes, we watch the tapes in silence. (There's no way Maurice could have known this was happening. The viewfinder that tells him what he is shooting is a tiny black-and-white monitor.) Then each of us starts to express his reaction, exactly in character.

Maurice begins cursing, stomping around, kicking walls and slamming doors.

Chris studies the technical aspects of the problem; could there be heat-related damage to the encoding chip in the camera's internal computer, or...

Brian immediately telephones Toronto, where it is five o'clock in the morning, and informs a senior editor that the Kuwait crew is having a bit of a problem.

And I start singing, "You picked a fine time to leave me, Lucille."

It's my worst camera crisis since the time the producer pointed the lens at the sun. (It wasn't Denike.) This was in the beautiful little town of Silver City, New Mexico, up on the Continental Divide. We were at a grammar school named for one of the men who had walked on the moon, talking to children about space. Later in the shoot, we would interview the astronaut himself, Harrison Schmitt, who had, you might say, risen quite far from Silver City.

There had already been a minor disruption in the shoot; namely, that our sound man was in a hospital in Deming, N.M. with severe back pain. That left the cameraman, the producer and me to do our filming in Silver City. We were just getting set up for a shot of the flag rippling in the breeze in the schoolyard. The cameraman was busying himself with something in the back of the van when the producer said, "I'll warm up the camera," flicked it on and never noticed that the lens was looking right at the unclouded orb of Old Sol.

This was disaster. Whatever it is, deep inside a television camera, that absorbs light and encodes it into an electronic signal, it burned out, overloaded, went blind, as you would have, had the producer held your eyelids open and aimed you where he aimed the camera.

A polite discussion ensued between producer and cameraman. The machine was inoperable. The shoot at Harrison Schmitt Elementary was canceled, just as the fourth-graders were being lined up for the Pledge of Allegiance. We drove down to Deming, picked up the sound man—very gingerly—laid him in the back seat and rode on to El Paso. Then we flew to Houston, rented another camera from a local station, put ours in the deep freeze in the hotel kitchen—that's what Sony advised—and, three days later, the burned-out cells had healed. That was my worst camera crisis, until now.

Our options, as we review them, are these:
1. call off the shoot and go home;
2. use the home-video camcorder we brought as a backup and carry on;
3. borrow a broadcast-quality camera from one of the U.S. networks based in our hotel;

4. have Toronto ship a replacement camera via Cairo, and wait here till Yom Kippur to get it;

5. laugh it off and go bowling.

Personally, I'm torn between (1) and (5), but even the abandonment of the secondary documentary on Kuwaiti life and society wouldn't solve one major part of the problem—the wrecked interview with Mike Miller. And, even if we get another camera and continue slugging away at the second piece, we'll either have to re-do the interviews or throw them out and start over.

This kind of thing didn't happen when I worked for a newspaper. When the typewriter broke, you used a pen.

What makes the color-drop problem so maddening is that it is not constant. In the Miller interview, for example, two or three minutes of good color are followed by thirty seconds of on-and-off flickering, then total red loss, then normal tones again. So if we just show the quotes from the good parts, and use Miller's comments from the bad-looking sections as voice-over while showing general wallpaper of the oil fields, we might get away with it. With sound and picture recorded on different tracks of the tape, this hair-splitting can be done back in Toronto, when we edit.

It's too early in the morning in Canada for Chris and Maurice to phone the CBC technicians and try to figure out how to perform open-lens surgery on Lucille. But, since we are not about to go back to the bedlam of the Kuwait Airways office and try to get on an earlier flight, it is decided that we will borrow another camera and continue the shoot. Aboud will telephone Ali al-Ghanim and ask—well, beg—him to redo our interview.

With billionaires this often is possible. I once did a talk with a Cuban expatriate in Miami who was so wealthy a street had been named for him. When we finished our work, he followed us into the parking lot, saying, "Isn't there anything else you guys need?"

The sound man suggested—sound men rarely are shy—a complimentary dinner at the magnate's favorite restaurant.

"Which one?" the baron responded. "I own seventeen."

For three days and nights, Brian and Aboud have been trying to convince a Palestinian friend of our fixer's to come on camera and discuss the plight of his people in postwar Kuwait. Before the Iraqi invasion, there were three hundred and fifty thousand Palestinians here, some of them members of families who left their homeland more than forty years ago, when the State of Israel was born. When Saddam's storm troopers came calling, professing that this was just the first blow in the destruction of the Jews, some Palestinians here hailed them. Most did not, but when Yasser Arafat embraced Saddam Hussein, he condemned a third of a million people with one bear hug.

The story of Kuwait since its Liberation has been the persecution, expulsion and, in some cases, lynching of Palestinian collaborators, actual or merely suspected. There have been calls for the purification of Kuwait through the eviction of all foreigners whose ancestral countries—even if they weren't born there—took Iraq's side. And if most Palestinians here simply changed their license plates and their identity cards and got on with life as best they could—just as Aboud, the Lebanese, had—that doesn't matter now. In the Arab world, it is said, you are what your father was, and their father was Arafat.

Aboud's friend is understandably nervous about being seen on television, even if it is only in Newfoundland, the Yukon and scattered points in between. Brian was up until one o'clock in the morning negotiating with him. Finally, it was agreed that the man would be filmed in shadow and not identified. Our policy is not to do incognito interviews—if you're going to go on camera, you should go on camera—but here, with few, if any, Palestinians willing to speak openly, we give in. I don't blame the man for being hesitant. As the Chinese proverb tells us, "The first bird out of the hole gets shot"; but how many birds live in holes?

At 8:00 p.m., well after dark, Aboud leads us to a cul-de-sac in the run-down neighborhood called Hawalli, a few blocks from the yard where we were accosted by the Kuwaiti army about twelve hours earlier. The building, as we portage the heavy lighting kits up the dimly lit stairway, is a crumbling mess of ugly concrete and scattered trash. The building is four stories high and we ascend all of it. As the "Journal" proverb tells us, "Interview in building with no elevator always on top floor."

Let us call the man Walid. He lives with his Indian wife and his chubby, computer-whiz son in three tiny rooms that are cluttered with, among other detritus, a brass candelabrum in the shape of the Kuwait Towers and a miniature of the Taj Mahal; a display of last year's Christmas cards; eleven plaster angels and a pair of porcelain hands clasped in prayer; a large library heavy on comparative religion and tactical chess,

and an oil painting, hanging over the sofa, of a dark-eyed Spanish peasant girl whose blouse has been yanked down so that you can see her nip-
ples. A tape of Zamfir, Master of the Pan Flute, is playing, and there is
no running water today.

When Chris unplugs the air conditioner—its hum is obnoxious in
what is supposed to be a dramatic scene—it is hotter in this little room
with all of our lights on than it was at wellhead number 94. The lights are
turned so that all a viewer will see is a rim of frizzy hair, haloed from
behind. The rest of Walid's face is black. The camera, it should be mentioned, has been loaned to us by CBS. Taking Bob McKeown to that topless revue at the MGM Grand has finally paid off.

"How has life changed for a Palestinian here?" I ask the man in the
shadows. His answer, as time-coded on Chris's recorder, lasts five and a
half minutes.

"What are you hearing on the street?" Three more minutes, and so it
goes. Finally, Brian waves a halt to the proceedings. He walks over and
whispers in my ear: "For Chrissake, just ask him what he's afraid of."

"What are you afraid of?" I ask Walid.

"Now I don't know the situation exactly in Kuwait about these circumstances, now it's my personal belief and many other of my brothers
or people whom I know, we don't really believe that it's the same situation, so it's better to be on the safe side, this kind of decisions come
based on advices from both my people or the Kuwaiti people in Kuwait,
if you have a proper message to give to the world, give the message, but
be careful not to involve other names in it," he replies. Well said, pal.

We pack up all the equipment, wrestle it back to the ground, and
head back to Salmiya Street to do all the nighttime shopping visuals outside Kentucky Fried Chicken all over again and try to find the "youth
gang" and their red motorbike. Aside from being arrested in the morning
and the camera breaking down and our secret interview turning out like a
filibuster in the Canadian Senate, it's been a wonderful day.

Just a thought: Why couldn't Tracy Wilkinson have lived near my
father's store, instead of Edward A. Gargan?

10 MAY
Kuwait City

Act Two with the millionaire Ali al-Ghanim goes off smoothly. He doesn't mind at all that we've dragged him out of bed on the Muslim Sabbath to answer exactly the same questions he answered two days ago. I think he would have been disappointed if we'd interviewed him only once. Ali al-Ghanim says, "Today, I come to this interview, I have nearly every day an interview, I have been interviewed by so many TVs and journalists here and abroad, we talk about this nearly every day."

Ali and I are old pals by now. When I ask him where he was last year on the second of August, he says, "I left for England August the first."

I say, "Saddam was waiting for you to get out of the country before he invaded it." He likes that.

I try to press him a bit more on what might happen if the emir reneges on his promise of democratic elections and a new parliament.

"I am very much worried," al-Ghanim says, standing in the ashes of his BMW showroom, "because there are so many weapons in the hand of everyone and it's making a lot of worries for everyone here."

"You're worried about potential violence."

"Well, exactly."

Doing the same interview a second time because of mechanical cock-up is not one of the joys of the profession. There is a tendency for your subject—Ali is an exception—to look at you throughout the repeat performance as if you are some kind of jerk. Two years ago, I did a story on racial violence in New York City. Included in it was an interview with two young black men whose neighbor had been shot and killed by a gang of white youths. A few hours after this emotional conversation, we discovered that the videotape had never been threaded through the take-up reel. It had just flapped and flapped. (It may have come unstuck at the factory in Japan.) We went back to see the two young men again.

"Shit happens," one of the young men said. And I was the living proof.

Now we're at a mosque on Mussa bin Naseer Street in Hawalli, the Palestinian neighborhood. Until the midfifties, there was a mud wall around the central core of Kuwait City. Native-born Kuwaitis lived within the pale. Foreigners, by royal decree, lived outside. The monument to that era is Hawalli: ramshackle apartment blocks, garbage everywhere, graffiti on the walls, abandoned cars, washing hanging from rusted balconies, palm trees dusted with dust. Part of this is due to the invasion, but most of it is just Hawalli. It is a slice of the worst parts of Brooklyn, a set from a Spike Lee film. But in Kuwait, before the invasion, the foreigners outnumbered the natives two to one.

I'm sitting against the back wall of the cool, clean mosque, awaiting the call to Friday prayer, when a big heavy man sits down, not next to me, not near me, but *on* me. "Good morning," I say. I'm trying my best to look Egyptian.

Brian and Aboud and the crew are setting up the tripod at the center of the great domed hall. This is where the Palestinian community, now persecuted and threatened, comes to make its daily obeisance. These days, in Hawalli, there is much to pray for.

I squirm out from under my close friend and look for another place to sit. But I needn't bother. At the center of the great domed hall, Brian and Aboud and the crew are getting the heave-ho.

"CNN outside," a man says, with anger in his eyes.

"Just set up your camera and people will flock to you," Aboud says when we are back out on the street in the midday sun. "Everyone here has a story to tell."

Maurice puts up his tripod and, surely enough, a crowd forms. But it is a crowd of eight-year-old boys. "CNN! CNN! Hallo! CNN!"

So many men come to Friday prayers, they fill the mosque and its exterior yards and spill into the parking lot, auditing the sermon on loudspeakers. The speech is furious, fulminating, terrifying, though of course I can't understand a word; it's what I thought we'd hear at the tomb of the Ayatollah Khomeini, instead of an army band. The thunder echoes around Hawalli and seems to shake even more paint and plaster from the leprous tenement walls. We wander around the corner for a soft drink, waiting out the storm.

When the service concludes, we again have the camera set up just outside the low marble walls of the mosque. Aboud is right. A few men among the thousands do come over, ask where we're from and say they'd like to talk to us, to tell the world what it is like for a Palestinian today, in Kuwait. But when we tell them that they will have to appear on camera—we're not doing any more interviews in shadow—most of the men shrink and wander away.

But one young Palestinian fellow doesn't. He is in his mid-twenties, round faced with a narrow beard and mustache, wearing light blue slacks and a navy blue shirt. He gives his name as Emad. He is a government accountant and a graduate, he says, of the University of the Sudan.

Emad climbs into Aboud's Audi, and with Brian and me following in our pigpen of a van, which awaits only a coating of chicken feathers to make it look like a full-scale Dixie lynching, he directs us to his home in a rattletrap apartment building a few blocks away. Trying to create a modicum of privacy during the interview, I suggest that we try to get out on the roof of the structure, which I'm sure delights Chris with his forty-pound recorder and Maurice with his dangerously aching back. But the crew obeys—what men these are!—and we labor up the stairs.

As we emerge, after four steep flights of steps, into the hot, hazy sunlight, I am softly singing the old Drifters tune: " 'So if this world starts getting you down....' "

I hear another voice, picking up the lyric: " '...there's room enough for two, up on the roof....' "

It's Emad. I like him already. We back him against the Hawalli sky-line and begin.

"They arrested my brother," he says. "A group of Kuwaiti soldiers broke in our house and arrested my brother. They don't say anything about what is the reason, or why, and we search for him in all the police stations in Kuwait, but they tell us in the police stations, 'Don't make trouble. Don't ask about your brother. Nobody can tell you anything about him.' Like the Iraqi soldiers did, now the Kuwaiti soldiers are doing."

"Have you seen him? Have you heard from him?"

"We went to the Ministry of Interior, they tell us he is in a government jail. Then, the next day, they call us on the telephone, they say, 'We want the passports of the whole family,' the father and the mother and me, his brother and my wife and my small brother. We ask them why. They say, 'Just come and we will tell you.'"

"What happened when you brought all the passports to the police station?"

"They tell us, 'You will leave Kuwait. Whole family will leave Kuwait.'"

"Whom do you blame for this?"

"I say the PLO. They didn't care about four hundred thousand people."

Twenty years in Kuwait City and four years on campus in Khartoum adds up to Emad's life. His father has been here thirty years. Their passports are Jordanian—they could never "become" Kuwaitis—but Emad says, "There is nothing for us in Jordan. We live here. All my live here. Spended all my life."

In the *New York Times*, Edward A. Gargan has reported, quoting Kuwaiti lawyers, that trials will soon begin of men like Emad's brother, accused of abetting the Iraqis. Ten weeks after the Liberation of Kuwait, the best that Emad is hoping for is that they can all be together again; where, he doesn't know. Emad says, "I will leave. That's the rule. What can we do? They don't want any Palestinian here in Kuwait."

A million Kurds in Iran, a million in Turkey, and now, perhaps, a few hundred thousand more of the homeless to be pushed from the tidy little emirate where they spended all their life. I walk around the roof, dizzy from the height. Across the way, a woman in black walks out of her building, stops at the base of a cinder-block wall and tips a basket full of garbage up and over the barrier, adding to a dung heap in the street.

As we're packing up the equipment, Emad the accountant takes me aside and says, "If Arafat sees this on television, he comes to kill me."

In midafternoon, when we head downtown to shoot some visuals of office buildings and the Port of Kuwait, Lucille is with us again. Maurice was up until two o'clock in the morning, talking to technical experts in Ottawa about our color-loss problem, working through a solution that involves attaching a small videocassette recorder directly onto the back of the camera. This means that as we wander around the lifeless business district, Chris has been reduced to carrying a book-sized, two-pound sound-mixing control box, while poor Mo has added about ten more pounds to his cross. He promises that the camera is working perfectly.

He is happy to be rid of the CBS loaner. Touching anything other than Lucille has made him feel easy and cheap.

On the gulf front, not far from the remains of the National Museum, our map indicates a basin called Small Dhow Harbor. A dhow is the traditional Arabian trading ship, sleek and swift, with three triangular sails; by the late forties, they were the only merchant ships on earth still powered solely by the wind. In Kuwait, which once lived on and by the sea, some smaller versions of the mighty oceangoing dhows still sailed. Then the Iraqis came.

Now the Small Dhow Harbor is a boneyard of needless desecration. Maurice is inspired—he finds the scene melancholy and haunting. On the sand, the fire-blackened ribs and keel of one ship sit like a whale's skeleton in old Nantucket, after the gutting has been done. Other craft, less completely burned, slump half-sunk in the fetid water, their masts snapped off like matchsticks, slowly bobbing against the dock while vivid blue fish sparkle and school in the shallows.

We move inland and position ourselves so that I can do a stand-up in front of the disemboweled Meridien Hotel. I stand in the median strip of al-Hilali Street and say: "Kuwait City wasn't obliterated, the way Berlin and Tokyo were in the Second World War. The buildings are still standing"—I look around, for effect—"but inside they're ravaged, looted, burned. It's the same with the people: those who fled, returning to reestablish their businesses; those who remained, emerging to reassemble their lives. For everyone here, a society once so orderly and prosperous has been fractured...and will never be the same."

I do this again, then ten or twelve more times, because during nearly every take, some clown in a beat-up old Chrysler pulls up at the curb and honks his horn just as I'm about to conclude my performance. "Asshole!" Chris coos. Then the guy drives around the block and all of this happens again.

Out of equipment failure, expulsion from the mosque and the registration queue of foreigners, a useless "secret" interview and the English-speaking woman at the children's carnival who wouldn't talk to us on camera, we are trying to craft a biography of a country in physical and social ruins. On the Desert Network, during a news break in "American Country Countdown," we hear that beginning tomorrow Kuwaiti citizens who have been abroad through all this will be able to return home, free of charge, on special Kuwait Airways charter flights, courtesy of the royal house. As they drop through the oil smoke and circle over Hawalli, the first of these may be able to spot Emad the Palestinian, loading his car and driving away.

The most facile story line we could pursue, with time running out on our visas and our threadbare camaraderie, would be to portray all Kuwaitis as indolent playboys for whom the invasion meant only that they had to spend a whole winter in Switzerland. And who now, upon their return, propose to cleanse their nest with Jabberwocky justice—"sentence first, trial later"—and get back to the business of leisure.

But now, at a youth center in the middle-class district called al-Daiya, we meet a group of Kuwaitis for whom there has been only suffering and grief. The fault lines, it seems, run not only between Kuwaitis and foreigners, but through the Kuwaiti nation itself, dividing those who were on holiday when the Iraqis arrived—or who immediately bolted for the border, including many military officers who abandoned their troops—and those who remained to live the nightmare.

The event we are filming is a bake sale to raise money for the families of Kuwaitis who have not been heard from since the Iraqis took the town. Some were military men, captured in skirmishes. Others were civilians. Some were just kids, like Reem al-Mousa's brother. I suspect these families need the money less than they need to share their sorrows.

Reem al-Mousa is a stocky young woman with wire-rim glasses, a pony tail and a yellow ribbon around her waist and another on her wrist, the American emblem of separation being used here to betoken the same kind of loss. A couple of days after the invasion, Reem's twenty-one-year-old brother made the error of his life, perhaps the last one. He put a poster of the emir in one window of his car and, in another window, a banner that said, The way to Palestine is not through Kuwait.

"That was a mistake, wasn't it?" I ask Reem. She is standing with her mother, who wears a black head-scarf over a long yellow dress.

"Yes," Reem replies. "A big mistake. They took him away, and since that day we don't know anything about him. We have asked and asked, and when we asked the Iraqis about him, they say, 'If you don't stop asking about your brother, we will take the whole family.'"

We're out in the playground, under a basketball hoop. Some smaller children are running and shouting. Women pass by us, carrying trays of honey-soaked sweets. The sun is setting like a Jaffa orange through the smoke from the oil-well fires.

"I try to control myself in front of my mother," Reem al-Mousa says. "I try to be strong so she can be strong. But after nine months, I still don't know anything about my brother. I don't know if he's alive, if he's okay. What would you think about, after nine months?"

"You see, I don't have many brothers. I only have one."

11 MAY
Abdali

Outside the National Bank of Kuwait, fifteen minutes before opening time, there is a queue of about thirty Kuwaiti gentlemen, all in *dishdasha* and *ghuta*, that includes several fidgety young sharks glancing anxiously at gold Rolex watches, older men more full stomached and relaxed, contentedly chatting, and one old-timer who is towing what looks like a hat rack on roller skates that holds an intravenous drip plugged into his spectral right arm. An automated-teller machine next to the bank entrance has been gutted and shot up, but the rest of the building is unblemished. If the Kuwaitis are concentrating on the restoration of their holiest places, the first has been this temple of cash.

We have to change a passel of dollars into the local currency, "k.d. langs," to be able to pay our hotel bills tomorrow. Producer Denike is impatient, as restless as the local Sherman McCoys, as the precious minutes of our final day of shooting slip away, marked not on a Rolex—though Chris, the sound man, wears a silver one—but on Brian's multifunction digital chronograph that is just going peep-peep to mark 9:00 a.m. when the doors to the National Bank swing open. My one-dollar watch from Miami says 8:59.

Inside, the bank is cool, quiet and spotless; we could be in Beverly Hills. More than the frantic overbooking of the International Hotel, or the supermarket at the Sultan Center that could be any Piggly-Wiggly in Tennessee, the National Bank makes me feel that I am seeing at least a small sample of what antebellum Kuwait must have been like. I would like to glide from the cashier's wicket into a whispering Mercedes, but all we have is our filthy little four-wheel-drive.

A week ago at this hour, we were cannonballing south to al-Ahmadi for our rendezvous with Mike Miller and five hundred fires. Now we are heading in the opposite direction, northward from the battered capital toward the Iraqi border, reversing the route of invasion, traveling the Highway of Death.

Since our arrival in Kuwait, Chris has been looking forward to this journey along the motorway on which thousands of escaping Iraqis, driving their own tanks and trucks and stolen vehicles crammed with looted goods, were hunted down by helicopter gunship and annihilated from the air like insects. I don't know what drives his desire—certainly I've not been that eager to see the mechanical carnage, even with the corpses long removed. Maybe he will gain some vicarious revenge for the terror of the first night of bombing in Baghdad. Maybe he just likes junked cars.

The wreckage begins, scattered at first, just north of a cursory police checkpoint at a bend in the road called al-Nutlaa, beyond Kuwait City in the open desert. Here, another highway merges with ours, sweeping down from a freeway cloverleaf. For the next five miles, the destruction is continuous: cars, trucks, buses, troop carriers, pickups, jeeps, wagons, transports, tankers and half-tracks burned, squashed, overturned, blown up and crumpled like foil. When I first saw this scene on CNN, the day after it happened—the reporter, Greg LaMotte, walked among the vehicles, the littered booty, the body parts and severed heads incredulous, stunned—it was the first time the savageness of the war really sank in. Until then, it had all been briefings and videos of smart, surgical bombs. But the Highway of Death was real. I could almost smell it.

Ten weeks later, the pavement itself has been cleared, the wrecks have been bulldozed to the median and shoulder of the four-lane expressway, and soldiers' graffiti sprayed on the rusting hulks have added an air of urban Americana to the scene. The scrawlings say:

IT'S ALL ABOUT FREEDOM
THAT'S RIGHT—COOPER WAS HERE
GRACE AND HARV
DON'T MESS WITH THE U.S.
RUTH AND CEC
FUCK IRAQ

And so on. Regimental numerals are inscribed on nearly everything; there's even the proud paintmanship of a postal squadron from Illinois that got the mail through. And in the midst of this one-sided demolition derby, Maurice gets a wonderful shot of three impassive donkeys in the sand at the side of road, motionless and unconcerned, as if they had been here through all of this madness and saw no reason to budge.

From the crest of a small hill reinforced with a cinder-block bunker, the crew commands a wide shot of the entire scene. It is a panorama of Desert Storm, and the desert: the bomb-blasted, spray-painted junk heap lining the highway; hydro transmission towers stretching toward the horizon, shrinking and shrinking until they vanish in the haze; the endless wasteland; and, rolling down from the border in what must be at least a thousand trucks, the United States Army, pulling out.

At its thickest concentration, the pile of twisted metal at the side of the road contains about fifty vehicles in one lump, jumbled together like boulders at the bottom of a cliff, as if they had been lifted from the earth and dropped from a great height. This must have been the vanguard of the fleeing convoy, the cars and trucks whose liquidation filled the road with wreckage and backed up the rest of the shooting gallery from here to the cloverleaf. The loot they carried has long since been picked over; only shreds of clothing and scraps of wood and metal lie scattered in the sun. I wonder if the men who trashed the oil company golf course were caught in this, or the vandals of the al-Ahmadi kindergarten. Or the ones who knew where Reem al-Mousa's only brother is.

North of the remains of the lead vehicles, the road points straight and clear toward the border, fifty miles away. We are bound for a refugee camp that straddles the frontier, where the last of the unliberated are waiting in the heat and the sand for their personal Gulf War to end. This will be the final act of our troubled, hurried documentary. As a cameraman I worked with a couple of times would say, wishfully, when he botched a scene: "The writing will save it." Not this time.

If ever there was a road on which to put the accelerator to the floor and skyrocket, this is not it. The right-of-way is free of wreckage, but every hundred yards or so, there is a bomb crater in the pavement, some of them mere pinpricks, some of them already filled in by the U.S. Army Corps of Engineers, and some of them car-swallowing monsters that will surely kill us if we fall in.

A quarter-mile or so in front of us, Aboud and the crew are running this giant-slalom course at eighty-five miles an hour. Denike has our boxy little van worked up to seventy-five and is just passing an American hum-vee on the right when, with a little "uh-oh" of a gasp, he sees that we are going to hit a hole at least two feet deep and six across.

There is no time to do anything about it; he doesn't even try to hit the brakes. The front right wheel takes the blow; it drops with a thud; the van lists, takes the second jolt on the rear tire, and keeps going. We exhale and motor on, a lot slower. The Highway of Death has tasted us and spat us out. I guess it has seen enough.

The refugee camp at Abdali is one of the worst patches of squalor I have ever seen. We come upon it suddenly, without warning; only the burned-out buildings of the former Kuwaiti Customs post announce that we are nearing the border. An Egyptian soldier wearing a sky-blue United Nations armband waves us through, and here is Abdali—a fenced-in compound of green and white tents, plastic sheeting and corrugated metal, a thousand or more hovels on a square mile of empty sand. About four thousand people are living here, against their will.

They are Iraqis, fleeing Saddam; non-Kuwaiti Kuwaitis, no longer welcome in the purified emirate; but mostly they are Bedoun, descendents of the traditional herdsmen of the desert, now stateless, in limbo, perhaps doomed.

The camp lies in what is now the official United Nations demilitarized zone, a belt of no-man's land 125 miles long whose breadth includes the first six miles of Iraqi territory north of the border and the first three miles of Kuwait to the south. In principle, no police or military personnel are supposed to enter this truce district, but already the town of Safwan, on the Iraqi side, has been retaken by security forces in civilian clothes, and posters of Saddam Hussein once again proclaim who's boss. As we turn in to the camp gate, we are mere yards from the boundary, but again, as at the mountain crest on the far side of Saddam's unbroken tyranny, neither Brian nor Chris has any desire to revisit Iraq, and by this point, Maurice and I are past caring.

As if to welcome us to this vale of misery, a gale-force wind whips up. Maurice's first images are of veiled women, fighting the sandstorm, laboring with sloshing buckets of truck water to return to their flapping, flying tents. The sand is fine and insidious; you eat it, smell it, feel it as it scours your face. In these conditions, people are living, and this is the side of the border that *won* the war.

It is, incongruously, Children's Day. There have already been footraces in the morning, and now about a hundred scrawny, whining, jostling orphans of the sandstorm are pushing toward one of the larger tents. Periodically, a flap opens and someone hands out a small toy or stuffed animal, donated by American churchgoers. Teenaged boys with cudgels and iron bars keep order, but I see no child struck.

I push my way into the toy tent and find one of the celebrities of Abdali, a bushy-haired woman known as "the Green Card Lady," because, as legions of reporters already have discovered, she once lived in Anaheim, California, and was the assistant manager of a Denny's Restaurant. The Green Card Lady expects to be leaving the camp any day now—her claim to U.S. residence has been verified—and her nightmare of being trapped in Iraq, visiting relatives, when the war began will soon be relieved. Amid the clamor of children, she rummages through cartons of furry bears and elephants and complains that as soon as she hand-stamps the kids who have received a gift they rush to erase the marking and join the boisterous lineup again.

Abdali already has a lengthy history. It began on the Iraqi side of the border as a holding pen for people of many nationalities who were trying to enter Kuwait, which refused to admit them. Most of the Bedoun claimed to have been searching for relatives lost in Iraq. There were Shi'ites from the Basra region, running from their ruinous, failed insurrection. Most of the Iraqi citizens, terrified of punitive raids into the camp by Saddam's death squads, by now have been flown out to safer havens in Saudi Arabia. When the Iraqis departed, the rest were moved down into the Kuwaiti third of the nominal DMZ. This sandy sty, then, is the "new" camp.

It is under the dedicated command of the Red Cross and Red Crescent. In another tent, I meet a heavyset, red-haired nurse named Tobie from Washington, D.C. She is a volunteer, working among these unwanted souls. Her spirit, and that of her colleagues, is magnificent. I couldn't imagine coming here and doing this; my heart's too small.

Every few moments, as we talk about the camp and about home—the Desert Network reports that in our Nation's Capital, today, there has been a very ugly riot in an Hispanic neighborhood—Tobie excuses herself, sprints to an opening in the translucent tent and screams a spectacular assortment of Arabic obscenities at children, and sometimes their mothers, who are trying to sneak a pail of precious water from a tank that the nurses use. After each episode, Tobie comes back over and smiles and says, "It's a little game we play."

As I leave her tent, I am confronted by a small man in a brown suit jacket who is holding up a tiny scrap of paper. The man looks at me imploringly and says, "I am engineer fourteen years. I speak excellent English. Can you help me?"

The paper he holds up is the pitiful stub of a receipt for a registered letter posted in Mississauga, Ontario. The man says, "Is proof I have reply from Canada Immigration. Please, can you help me?"

He leads me to his tent. He says, "My wife, my daughter." A chubby woman and a teenaged girl smile uncertainly at my entrance.

"I am engineer from Basra. I am educated man. Can you help me? I seek refugee status. Saddam kill us if we go back."

I make up a number and tell him, "Eighty-six thousand people are waiting for refugee status. I don't know what I can do." The man bows in gratitude, as if I've helped him in some way, as I skulk off, ashamed. The true number of people who seek our prosperity and liberties equals the sum of all the world's Abdalis. How are we to take them all? How are we to refuse?

The Bedoun—the word means "without"—are not nomadic wanderers, sailing their ships of the desert across the burning sands. In recent decades, most have come in from the empty quarter to settle in urban Kuwait, beyond the mud walls, and the racial walls, of the al-Sabahs' hierarchical society. Many have joined the national army and police force, not as officers, but as lower grades, drivers, janitors. They are pure-blooded Arabs, of course, and their children are Kuwaiti-born, but they still are viewed as aboriginal and outcaste, the house-niggers of the oil state. The Gulf War has destroyed them.

(They never have been very popular. The first European to cross the Arabian peninsula, Capt. G. Forster Sadlier of His Majesty's 47th Regiment, wrote in 1819 of the "procrastination, duplicity, falsity, deception and fraudulence" of the nomadic tribes. These are the identical sins for which the Bedoun now blame the Kuwaiti government.)

I am in the green tent of a Bedoun named Saleh, nineteen years old, handsome, a near-twin to Eddie Murphy. Saleh's father is seated with us, wrapped in a checkered scarf. Saleh is in a white shirt with a cotton kerchief folded atop his head. The tent bucks and billows in the waterless hurricane. Pots and water jugs topple and roll. Between the sand and the wind and the biblical faces, it feels like Judgment Day.

"They talk about racialist countries," Saleh says. "Kuwait is one of the racialist countries. But the United Nations doesn't care about us. Nobody cares about us."

Saleh fishes in the pockets of his shirt and produces a neatly folded letter from one of his high-school teachers. The letter says that he has been "excellent in studies and conduct." But he was denied admission to Kuwait University, which is restricted to citizens only. Palestinians, Pakistanis, Egyptians—and Bedoun—need not apply. The young scholar is crushed, bewildered. He says, "For this, I cry." He does not want to come to Canada. He only wants to go to Kuwait City, down the pockmarked freeway.

The Kuwaiti authorities suspect that many of the Bedoun at al-Abdali are treacherous gypsies who shredded their Iraqi or Palestinian identity papers in order to try to sneak into Kuwait. This may be true of some; I have no way of knowing. It cannot be true of Saleh, the high-school graduate, whose scholastic average, he proudly tells me, was a rock-solid eighty-four percent. But they will not let him go home.

"I am very disappointed and let down," he says, as the tent fairly lifts off like a hot-air balloon in the demonic wind. "I look at our situation here, I cannot believe it."

"I spoke to an American soldier. I said, 'You didn't liberate Kuwait.'" He pronounces the word with a long *I*—lie-berate.

"The soldier said, 'Yes, we liberated Kuwait from Iraqi occupation.'"

"And I said, 'Yes. But you did not liberate Kuwait from itself.'"

Some of the men at Abdali are in knitted white skullcaps. Some wear thick, knotted turbans; some are bareheaded, or wrapped in red-checkered *kufiyahs*. As we leave the Bedoun tent, the men cluster around me, all talking at once, pleading, holding up passports, military ID cards, old photographs. I think of the scene on the highway near Paveh, Iran: I say, "I am not the Canadian government...."

I stand just outside the gate to try a stand-up. The fence is a-flutter with hundreds of plastic grocery and garbage bags, the festive bunting of a derelict place. Hundreds of children see us and run to the barrier, poke their slender hands through the wire mesh, caterwaul, giggle, shout "Hallo! Hallo!"

The shoot is ending as it began, in a tent city of canvas and charity and despair. When I finish the stand-up and we are stowing the gear for the final time, I ask Maurice, who has seen so much of the world's misery, how he keeps it inside him.

"Usually, I'm okay," the cameraman says. "Like, today—I just close my mind and try to get the shots. But then, there was this one kid. Did you see him? The others were all running and shouting but he just stood there, so small. He just stood there waving at me. He really got to me. So gentle. So gentle...."

12 MAY
Kuwait City–Dubai

The final morning dawns bright and Caribbean, cloudless, sparkling and blue. The smoke that so menacingly darkened our first day in Kuwait City has never returned. If it was intended, at the time, as a cryptic warning from Saddam Hussein to a belated arrival in the combat zone—"Look on my works, ye Mighty, and despair!"—it has been futile. There is no desperation in me. Not today.

I am down in the lobby by five-thirty, paying my bill—seven hundred crisp new "langs" counted, recounted, counted again by the half-awake auditor—then I make a great pantomime of handing over the invisible key to my nonexistent lock to the door that never got fixed. No one else has come down yet. I take my possessions—suitcase, knapsack, leather jacket—to the sidewalk and sit in the benevolent sun. Nobody waits for the Abels.

At ten after six, Aboud slides up in the Audi, and behind him is a rattling blue cargo truck, piloted by a wafer-thin Indian motorman, that will convey our cases of gear to the airport, or what's left of it. Soon enough, Baggages Meester emerges from the marble lobby with the first trolley of equipment of the last lap of the shoot. Within a few minutes, we are ready.

In the Audi, with the shimmering Persian Gulf on our left and the shattered seaside palaces of the royals to our right, Maurice turns to me in the back seat and says, "God, Allen, I love to travel," and, even after all of this, I think he means it.

The last night in Kuwait had been rather tame. Maurice and Chris and I decided to go downtown to the Sultan Center and poke around. Brian, the knots in his legs increasingly painful, stayed at the hotel, packing. He sent Aboud to find someone to wash down the oil-splattered van with a bath of gasoline.

We walked out of the International and right into a fight. Rochester, the lead-footed cabbie in the dirty *dishdasha*, grabbed us as soon as we stepped out of the door. (I think he'd been there since our city tour, nine days earlier, "Waiting," one might say, "for Chabot.") But there was another driver whose car was ahead of Rochester's in the rank. They snarled and spat but Baggages Meester broke it up and we went with our man Roch. At unusually reasonable speeds—"slowly, slowly," he said to me, by way of greeting—he dropped us off in the shopping district where we had filmed the "youth gang." Then he announced that he was going home for an hour and would come back to pick us up.

"Go home, see wife," Rochester said.

"Rochester," said Chris Davies. "How many children?"

"Seven," the hackie boasted.

"Go home, see wife, make number eight, you sly devil," the sound man chimed.

"Go home, see wife, sleep," Rochester demurred.

We ate some dinner at an Indian-style fast-food joint called Chicken Tikka (motto: I Like It Spicy!) and then, in a small stationery store, I bought a book of political cartoons with portraits of Saddam Hussein and The Great Dictator on the cover and the title, *Hitler Again.*

The cartoons, drawn by a Kuwaiti named Ibrahim Ismail, were black-and-white grotesqueries with wonderfully butchered English captions: Saddam as a plucked chicken, hung from the gallows ("Died Like A Hean"); Saddam with the head of a pit-bull terrier ("Dogs Bonlking"); Saddam in military uniform with death's-heads on his epaulets, his neck in a noose ("Lived as a Jeark and Died Irrilegose"), and my personal favorite, a contortionist Saddam, completely nude, with his mouth on his own genitals, entitled, beyond comprehension, "The Unbsbced."

I thought of Ahmed at the National Museum: "All I can do is to hate them." And the Christians at the refugee camp in the majestic Sirvan Valley in Iran, afraid to go on camera: "Saddam will see." I had danced around the realm of this universal supervillain, and once, up on the ridge with the CNN trailer, I had put my toe across the line. Now, finally, here he was again: Saddam stripped to his underwear, his arms and legs revealed to be hiding dozens of stolen watches: "The Iraqi Soldier Uniform." Saddam in hell, with long, devil's fingernails, bats circling overhead, a scorpion on his chest, playing a harp. "Death Semphony."

At the hotel, I got everything in order, laid out my traveling clothes, and gaffer-taped the hole in the door. I decided against the Iraqi helmets and left them in the van. Long ago, on a dare, I had swiped part of a skull from the Catacombs in Paris when no one else on the tour was looking. After a few days, I felt it staring at me and heaved it into Lake Geneva. Twenty years later, I didn't care one way or the other about the metal army helmets. It's the specters of their owners I disown.

Aboud's last act is to deliver us to the wrong terminal. I see his mistake coming as we exit from a soaring freeway cloverleaf onto an access road that leads in exactly the opposite direction from the only part of the sprawling airport that has not been blown up and burned. But it is too late, and as I whimper and moan my certitude that we are going to miss the plane and have to stay here another six weeks, the Lebanese wheels smartly, careers around the parking-lot loop in faithful disobedience to the one-way signs, zips past the charred hull of the parking-fee collection booth—"Receipt, please!" I call out, as we pass, from habit—and reenters the airport access road to take us to the proper gate, three miles away.

By now, I am fairly disassembled with panic, for it is nearly seven-thirty and not once but twice last night, Kuwait Airways called Brian Denike in his hotel room to advise him that the flight to "Do Buy" has been moved up from nine-thirty to half past eight. By now, I am certain, our seats have been allotted to some second cousin of one of the emir's myriad mothers-in-law, and so it is with considerable dispatch that I bolt from the Audi, whip my backpack through a security screening, forget it on the conveyor, run back for it, gallop to the check-in counter and learn that the nine-thirty flight, rescheduled for half past eight, will now leave at ten, if Allah wills.

When the gear has been tagged and accepted and we have our boarding passes, we make our goodbyes to Aboud, quite warmly, and move toward the immigration queue. Above us, the big electronic Departures board remains frozen at the preinvasion midnight, a mirror of Kuwait itself, with some lines secure and operational—DUBAI, BAHRAIN and others screaming in agony, GHEF6WU and RJKOWC.

Otherwise, the terminal is unremarkable, with a small drinks counter serving orange juice and cakes and a large, clean waiting area holding our fellow passengers—mostly Arabs, with a sprinkling of Europeans—booked on the sixty-minute hop down the gulf to the Croesean, unscarred United Arab Emirates. We are very much looking forward not only to an orgy of duty-free bargains but also to a celebratory dinner at some posh waterside restaurant. (There is a tradition at "The Journal" that the reporter pay for this "wrap-up, slap-up" grand finale to a grueling shoot, but I have never been a stickler for tradition.)

So it is a bit of a letdown, to say the least, when, after we clear Kuwaiti Immigration and have our passports stamped, a smiling, heavy-set man with three gold stripes on his blue epaulets comes over to inform us that our flight to paradise has been canceled.

Not to worry—a 747 is being readied to take everyone in the terminal to Dubai, and it should be ready within an hour, or three. We settle in to wait. Maurice stretches out across four chairs and soon begins to entertain us with *Eine kleine Nachtmusik*, the sore-legged Denike attempts to set a world record for most cigarettes smoked in one hour, and I painstakingly unwrap my last granola bar—the chocolate has melted, congealed, melted again and turned orange—and eat it, grain by grain, kernel by kernel, having had no breakfast, while saving my very last Fruit Roll-Up in the event, which appears likely, that there will not be any lunch.

While we are thusly engaged in the art of doing nothing, a skill at which we gained considerable experience in Iran, what should come through the security checkpoint but Mike Miller's mustache, followed by Miller himself and a couple of his crewmen from the Canadian fire fighting brigade, Safety Boss. After six weeks in-country, Miller is going home to Calgary for a rest. He also is flying via Dubai today, but not on our (perhaps nonexistent) flight with Kuwait Airways. The management company that is coordinating the assault on the flaming wellheads is running a daily round-trip on a chartered 727 to the Emirates, ferrying men and supplies. We chat awhile, and then, while we remain immobile and defeated, he is gone, triumphantly, on the Larry Flack Shuttle.

Eventually, four hours and change from the time Aboud dove off the cloverleaf and reared up to the wrong station, we are called to board the substitute jumbo to begin the long trip home. First Class, which we booked, expressly violating CBC policy, to avoid the huge lineup at Kuwait Airlines downtown, is sumptuous, with legroom sufficient for Larry Bird and seats as wide as beds. Orange juice is served—these are the last dry instants—and the engines roar and it looks as though God is going to bring me home safe to Linda, after all.

We are flying southward, along the gulf coast, when down to the right I see the first of the fires beyond gray al-Ahmadi town. Now there are dozens—I spot Old Smokey, and the double-barreled Mustache—and then the smoke is on us, and darkness swallows the plane. For a minute or two, we buck and haw through war's frightful shadows, then we break through the night and burst back into sunlight again. The smoke sags below us, its plume still thick and all obscuring for at least a hundred miles.

I am in row 4 of the mammoth plane, entranced at the vista below. We have broken out of the path of the ghastly smoke, and now to the west I see Bahrain and, beyond it, again the Martian red of Saudi Arabia. Next to me is a young bearded Arab in full regalia, fidgeting, kicking off his sandals, wiggling his toes, fingering his worry beads, leafing through a binder of glossy prospectuses for some financial-services firm. After about half an hour of flying, the young man faces me and says something that I do not understand.

"I'm sorry, I don't speak Arabic," I say, turning from the window.

"Oh," my seatmate responds. "I thought you were Egyptian."

In Dubai, Wilfred Thesiger found, in 1948, "life moved in time with the past. These people still valued leisure and courtesy and conversation. They did not live their lives at second hand, dependent on cinemas and wireless."

Dubai, in those last prepetroleum hours, was a place where "naked children romped in the shallows...the *suqs* were crowded with many races—pallid Arab townsmen, armed Bedu, quick-eyed and imperious; Negro slaves; Baluchis, Persians and Indians." But now we were circling low over a turquoise, Tahitian bay and below us were lavish villas, swimming pools, the first all-grass golf course in the Middle East. Just before touchdown, in someone's fenced-in square of desert beyond the city limits, I spot a brace of camels, standing stock-still, with no load to carry and nowhere to go, as if expelled from the jet-age Ark.

The first breath of Dubaian air, as we walk from the plane to the terminal, is a jarring reminder of what we must have been inhaling in Kuwait even on the clearest mornings. Here, it is clean, moist, almost sugary. Consciously, I draw a few deep drafts before the automatic doors open and I go inside, to the air conditioning.

To the left, as we enter, in a lobby adjacent to the Immigration booths, is the Transit Desk where, I was told on the phone when I made our onward air reservations, we could exchange our passports for a day pass into the city. I collect the documents from my companions—we are as eager as schoolboys—and approach the clerk, who is a dark, round-faced man, South Indian.

"Ah, you are French," he says, before I even hand over the passports.

"No," I say, pointing to the hirsute Maurice, who is sitting on a low, padded bench with Lucille on his knee. "He is French."

"But I am sure you are French," the Dravidian insists.

"I am Egyptian," I say, to end this game.

He takes the passports, asks what flight we are connecting to, verifies our reservation in his computer, and then, with a delighted grin, informs me that we cannot leave the airport transit lounge under any circumstances.

"You must have a visa," he explains.

"But they said you could issue a visa here, just for the afternoon and evening." (Our onward flight leaves at midnight.)

"Visas are not issuing here," the Indian concludes.

I am writing this in room number 1 of the minihotel in the transit area of Dubai International Airport. The others are somewhere in the duty-free shopping mall, looking at luggage and CD players and gold jewelry for their ladies. Room number 1 is a pigeon-hole, a near-twin of the cubicle where I took a few hours' rest at the airport in Vienna, en route to Asia, twenty-seven days ago. But on the wall above me is a photograph of a small boy with two toothy camels, an echo of the vanished ways of Arabia, when life moved in time with the past.

We have been granted a free dinner of steak and *frites* and I have had a short nap and a shower, in a stall whose outflow floods the tiny bathroom and cascades out into the miniature bedchamber with its small dresser and seven lamps. Flight time is still five hours away.

I leave this confinement and wander out into the transit lounge, crowded with many races, the *suq* of a technological century. The television monitors reduce the maelstrom of Asia to a few flickering white-on-black lines: Bombay, Karachi, Colombo, Hong Kong, all the panicked station-stops of my brilliant correspondent's career. The lounge, deserted when we arrived in early afternoon, is teeming now, a caravanserai where family groups encamp—dark-jacketed men, robed and veiled women, mewling babes—as if they were as homeless as Kurds, which, for a moment, until their plane comes, I suppose they are.

Now a man comes up and tells me that I must accompany him to the baggage area to verify that all of our equipment and personal bags are correctly tagged. Another passenger also is to be led downstairs to perform the same double-check. I watch the agent rouse him from his sleep on the floor of the lounge. The three of us, saying nothing, take the escalator to the lower level.

All of our gear is in order—the tripods, lighting kits, spare recorder, suitcases, battery bags, food hamper (now empty), and the shiny metal box that holds our tapes of the fires and the emir's thoroughbreds, the Bedoun refugees and the families of the unaccounted prisoners of war—all of Maurice's artistry, encoded as dancing magnetic impulses on the reels of thin brown plastic.

The other traveler is a small, walnut-skinned man whose baggage, as he points it out among the jetsam of the cavernous hall, is a tightly roped cardboard box. The agent has taken his ticket, and mine, and laid them on a countertop. When neither is looking, I pick up the other man's ticket and look inside. It says Dubai to Dhaka to Chittagong.

When the tagging procedure is finished and we make our way back upstairs, I smile and nod to the other voyager.

"Bangladesh?" I say, and he nods, but my smile is not returned.

Oh, God, the cyclone, I remember. The latest report has the number of deaths at three hundred thousand. My friend is returning to toll the knell of family, enemies, friends.

For a moment, we stand there, eyes locked, uncomprehending. A flight is called, people scramble madly to line up, their current breaks around us, as around boulders in a stream. I don't know what to say.

Suddenly I see Brian, waving at me. He is carrying a brand-new briefcase that he bought in the duty-free store. He holds up his right hand and twists it. He wants the key to room number 1. I reach in my pocket and toss it to my boss.

When I turn around, the man from Bangladesh is gone.